Lecture Notes in Computer Science 11250

Commenced Publication in 1973
Founding and Former Series Editors:
Gerhard Goos, Juris Hartmanis, and Jan van Leeuwen

More information about this series at http://www.springer.com/series/8637

Abdelkader Hameurlain · Roland Wagner
Sven Hartmann · Hui Ma (Eds.)

Transactions on Large-Scale Data- and Knowledge-Centered Systems XXXVIII

Special Issue on Database- and Expert-Systems Applications

 Springer

Editors-in-Chief
Abdelkader Hameurlain
IRIT, Paul Sabatier University
Toulouse, France

Roland Wagner
FAW, University of Linz
Linz, Austria

Guest Editors
Sven Hartmann
Clausthal University of Technology
Clausthal-Zellerfeld, Germany

Hui Ma
Victoria University of Wellington
Wellington, New Zealand

ISSN 0302-9743   ISSN 1611-3349   (electronic)
Lecture Notes in Computer Science
ISSN 1869-1994   ISSN 2510-4942   (electronic)
Transactions on Large-Scale Data- and Knowledge-Centered Systems
ISBN 978-3-662-58383-8   ISBN 978-3-662-58384-5   (eBook)
https://doi.org/10.1007/978-3-662-58384-5

Library of Congress Control Number: 2018961378

This Springer imprint is published by the registered company Springer-Verlag GmbH, DE
part of Springer Nature
The registered company address is: Heidelberger Platz 3, 14197 Berlin, Germany

Preface

The 27th International Conference on Database and Expert Systems Applications (DEXA 2016), with proceedings published in volumes 9827 and 9828 of Springer's *Lecture Notes in Computer Science* (LNCS), showcased state-of-the-art research activities in the intersection of data management, knowledge engineering, and artificial intelligence. The conference and its associated workshops provided a premier forum for scientists, developers, and users to present and discuss original research results, exchange new ideas, share industry experiences, and explore future directions.

As is the tradition of the conference series, the authors of selected papers of the DEXA 2016 conference were invited to submit original, revised, and substantially extended versions of their conference papers to a special issue of the Springer journal *Transactions on Large-Scale Data- and Knowledge-Centered Systems* (TLDKS). Invitations were given to only the very best of the 68 papers in the conference proceedings. Following the invitation, eight articles were submitted, each of which was carefully reviewed by three international experts in two reviewing rounds. In the end, six of the eight articles were accepted for inclusion in this special issue. We commend these articles to you and hope you find them useful.

The article "Bound-and-Filter Framework for Aggregate Reverse Rank Queries," authored by Yuyang Dong, Hanxiong Chen, Kazutaka Furuse, and Hiroyuki Kitagawa, introduces a new class of preference queries and presents efficient algorithms for computing their answers. Preference queries are an important technique for query personalization in databases. Top-k preference queries ask for a ranked list of the best k answers to a query. Usually, preferences are defined based on a consumer-view rank model. When changing the perspective and assuming a manufacturer-view model, one can ask for the top-k consumers who assign a product the highest ranking. Studying this question may help manufacturers to discover target consumers for their products. While previous research has addressed this question for single products only, this article investigates this question for sets of products (so-called product bundles). Different aggregation functions are considered to define aggregate reverse rank-k queries. The proposed method first computes suitable bounds for the query products, and then prunes them using R-trees. Experiments demonstrate the scalability of the approach and compare two implementation options. The conference version of this article received the Norman Revell Best Paper Award of DEXA 2016.

The article "Syntactic Anonymization of Shared Datasets in Resource Constrained Environments," authored by Anne V. D. M. Kayem, C. T. Vester, and Christoph Meinel, is motivated by the interest in privacy-preserving data publishing schemes that are tailored toward computationally constrained settings. A multi-objective approach to data anonymization is presented that extends the common k-anonymization and ℓ-diversity schemes to enable automatic classification and anonymization of data. In order to reduce information loss and to achieve a good balance between privacy and data utility, sensitive attributes are weighted in terms of the severity of privacy disclosure. To provide additional protection against skewness and similarity attacks, the approach is further extended to satisfy t-closeness. Common t-closeness schemes, however, are known to be computationally expensive. In an effort to address the resource constraints, a novel scheme based on t-clustering is proposed where classification is used to minimize the risk of privacy disclosure of records containing sensitive attributes with high-severity weight. Extensive experiments with real-world data demonstrate that the proposed scheme is promising.

The article "Toward Faster Similarity Search by Dynamic Reordering of Streamed Queries," authored by Filip Nalepa, Michal Batko, and Pavel Zezula, proposes a new method for similarity search against a large database of complex objects. These objects may, for example, be digital images that are represented as high-dimensional data vectors. The task is, for each query object in an incoming query stream, to retrieve the top-k most similar objects from the database. The proposed solution combines a caching mechanism with a smart reordering scheme that dynamically modifies the order in which the query objects from the stream are processed. To efficiently compute a query order that maximizes the overall throughput, a query graph is constructed and maintained as an auxiliary data structure. The proposed method has been implemented and experimentally tested with positive outcomes. A particular strength of the approach is that the increase of the throughput does not come at the expense of a precision loss of the similarity search. Furthermore, the article investigates the trade-off between maximizing the throughput and minimizing the overall waiting time.

The article "*SjClust*: A Framework for Incorporating Clustering into Set Similarity Join Algorithms," authored by Leonardo Andrade Ribeiro, Alfredo Cuzzocrea, Karen Aline Alves Bezerra, and Ben Hur Bahia do Nascimento, is motivated by the quest for computational methods for entity resolution and its applications in data cleaning and data integration. Similarity join is a popular operator that aims to determine all sufficiently similar pairs between two collections of records representing real-world entities. Similar records can then be grouped together to derive better representations of real-world entities. While previous approaches in the literature use similarity join and clustering as two separate steps in data processing, this paper presents a new method that combines similarity join and clustering into a single step. A particular advantage of the proposed approach is its flexibility as it can incorporate different clustering techniques and merging strategies. The new method is implemented, and its accuracy and efficiency are empirically verified with benchmark data sets that have been used in the literature to evaluate duplicate identification algorithms.

The article "A Query Processing Framework for Large-Scale Scientific Data Analysis," authored by Leonidas Fegaras, aims to provide effective high-level support for array-based computations in big data analytics. The idea is to model basic matrix operations like matrix multiplication or matrix transposition as generic algebraic operators, so that programmers can take advantage of an SQL-like declarative query language. The article presents an optimization scheme that translates the generic operators into efficient distributed algorithms. In particular, inter-operator optimizations are performed, for example, to efficiently fuse matrix multiplications and transpositions. The approach uses group-by-join operations and the MRQL algebra, which is part of Apache MRQL, an emerging query processing and optimization system for large-scale, distributed data analysis. It is implemented and tested using state-of-the-art big data platforms (Hadoop Map-Reduce, Apache Flink, Apache Spark). Experiments are conducted to evaluate the performance even for more complex array-based computations such as matrix factorization.

The article "Discovering Periodic-Correlated Patterns in Temporal Databases," authored by J. N. Venkatesh, R. Uday Kiran, P. Krishna Reddy, and Masaru Kitsuregawa, introduces a new measure for the interestingness of a periodic-frequent pattern in a transactional database, and proposes a pattern-growth algorithm for detecting interesting patterns. The research is motivated by the rare item problem in pattern mining: When analyzing a temporal transactional database, one is usually interested in patterns that have sufficiently high support and sufficiently low periodicity. Even for experienced users it is challenging to define appropriate thresholds for these two dimensions. If the chosen thresholds are too strict then one will miss relevant periodic-frequent patterns that correspond to rare items. Relaxing the thresholds, however, may produce far too many patterns due a combinatorial explosion. The article addresses this problem by defining and exploring the notion of periodic-correlated patterns. An extensive experimental evaluation with synthetic and real-world databases demonstrates that the new algorithm outperforms existing baseline approaches.

Major credit for the quality of this special issue goes to the authors, who carefully revised and significantly extended their contributions. We are grateful to all reviewers for their invaluable work in assessing the submissions and ensuring the high quality of this collection of articles. We wish to express our deep appreciation to Gabriela Wagner, whose excellent support and editorial assistance made this special issue possible.

October 2018   Sven Hartmann
                                                                          Hui Ma

Organization

Editorial Board

Reza Akbarinia	Inria, France
Bernd Amann	LIP6 – UPMC, France
Dagmar Auer	FAW, Austria
Djamal Benslimane	Lyon 1 University, France
Stéphane Bressan	National University of Singapore, Singapore
Mirel Cosulschi	University of Craiova, Romania
Tran Khanh Dang	Ho Chi Minh City University of Technology, Vietnam
Dirk Draheim	Tallin University of Technology, Estonia
Johann Eder	Alpen Adria University Klagenfurt, Austria
Anastasios Gounaris	Aristotle University of Thessaloniki, Greece
Theo Härder	Technical University of Kaiserslautern, Germany
Sergio Ilarri	University of Zaragoza, Spain
Petar Jovanovic	Universitat Politècnica de Catalunya, BarcelonaTech, Spain
Dieter Kranzlmüller	Ludwig-Maximilians-Universität München, Germany
Philippe Lamarre	INSA Lyon, France
Lenka Lhotská	Czech Technical University in Prague, Czech Republic
Liu Lian	University of Kentucky, USA
Vladimir Marik	Czech Technical University in Prague, Czech Republic
Jorge Martinez Gil	Software Competence Center Hagenberg, Austria
Franck Morvan	Paul Sabatier University, Toulouse, France
Kjetil Nørvåg	Norwegian University of Science and Technology, Norway
Themis Palpanas	Paris Descartes University, France
Torben Bach Pedersen	Aalborg University, Denmark
Günther Pernul	University of Regensburg, Germany
Soror Sahri	Descartes Paris University, France
A Min Tjoa	Vienna University of Technology, Austria
Shaoyi Yin	Paul Sabatier University, Toulouse, France

Reviewers

Ladjel Bellatreche	ENSMA, France
Nadia Bennani	INSA Lyon, France
Barbara Catania	University of Genoa, Italy
Zhi-Hong Deng	Peking University, China
Yves Denneulin	University of Grenoble Alpes, France
Vincenzo Deufemia	University of Salerno, Italy
Cedric du Mouza	CNAM, France
Michal Huptych	Czech Technical University in Prague, Czech Republic

Carsten Kleiner	University of Applied Sciences and Arts Hannover, Germany
Hong-Cheu Liu	University of South Australia, Australia
Ismael Navas-Delgado	University of Malaga, Spain
Nazha Selmaoui	University of New Caledonia, New Caledonia
Lubomir Stanchev	California Polytechnic State University, USA
Dietrich Steinmetz	Clausthal University of Technology, Germany

Contents

Bound-and-Filter Framework
for Aggregate Reverse Rank Queries

Yuyang Dong$^{(\boxtimes)}$, Hanxiong Chen, Kazutaka Furuse, and Hiroyuki Kitagawa

Department of Computer Science, University of Tsukuba, Ibaraki, Japan
tou@dblab.is.tsukuba.ac.jp,{chx,furuse,kitagawa}@cs.tsukuba.ac.jp

Abstract. Finding top-rank products based on a given user's preference is a user-view rank model that helps users to find their desired products. Recently, another query processing problem named reverse rank query has attracted significant research interest. The reverse rank query is a manufacturer-view model and can find users based on a given product. It can help to target potential users or find the placement for a specific product in marketing analysis.

Unfortunately, previous reverse rank queries only consider one product, and they cannot identify the users for product bundling, which is known as a common sales strategy. To address the limitation, we propose a new query named *aggregate reverse rank query* to find matching users for a set of products. Three different aggregate rank functions (SUM, MIN, MAX) are proposed to evaluate a given product bundling in a variety of ways and target different users. To resolve these queries more efficiently, we propose a novel and sophisticated bound-and-filter framework. In the bound phase, two points are found to bound the query set for excluding candidates outside the bounds. In the filter phase, two tree-based methods are implemented with the bounds; they are the tree pruning method (TPM) and the double-tree method (DTM). The theoretical analysis and experimental results demonstrate the efficacy of the proposed methods.

Keywords: Similarity search · Aggregate reverse rank queries
Bound-and-filter · Tree-based method

1 Introduction

Suppose that there are two types of datasets: user dataset and product dataset. The top-k query and reverse k-rank query are two different kinds of view-models. The top-k query is a user view-model that helps users by obtaining the best k products matching a user's preference. On the other hand, the reverse k-rank query [23] supports manufacturers by discovering potential users by retrieving the most appropriate user preferences. Therefore, it is a manufacturer view-model, and can be used as a tool for analysis and estimating product marketing.

A. Hameurlain et al. (Eds.): TLDKS XXXVIII, LNCS 11250, pp. 1–26, 2018.
https://doi.org/10.1007/978-3-662-58384-5_1

Example 1. *Figure 1 shows an example of a reverse 1-rank query. Five products, cell phones p_1 to p_5, are scored on two attributes: "smart" and "ratings" in a table (Fig. 1(b)). The preferences of two users Tom and Jerry are presented in another table (Fig. 1(a)) and consist of the weights for all attributes. The score of a cell phone based on user preference is computed with the inner product of the cell phone attributes vector and the user preference vector. Without loss of generality, we assumed that minimum values are preferable. The reverse k-rank query is to find the top-k users with the highest ranking value for a given product. The results of the reverse 1-rank query are given in the last row of Fig. 1(b). For example, Tom believes that p_1 is the third-best phone (Fig. 1(a)), while Jerry thinks that p_1 is the fifth-best. To manufacturers, Tom is more likely to buy p_1 than Jerry; hence, the reverse 1-rank query returns Tom as the result.*

(a) User preferences and Ranks

user	w[smart]	w[rating]	Ranks
Tom	0.8	0.2	p3,p2,p1,p4,p5
Jerry	0.3	0.7	p2,p5,p3,p4,p1

(b) Cell phone ranks and R-1Rank

	p[smart]	p[rating]	Score on Tom	Score on Jerry	Rank in Tom	Rank in Jerry	R-1Rank
p1	6	7	6.2	6.7	3rd	5th	Tom
p2	2	3	2.2	2.7	2nd	1st	Jerry
p3	1	6	2.0	4.5	1st	3rd	Tom
p4	7	5	6.6	5.6	4th	4th	Tom
p5	8	2	6.8	3.8	5th	2nd	Jerry

Fig. 1. An example of reverse 1-rank queries.

1.1 Motivation

Besides the case of the single-product selling in Fig. 1, manufacturers also use "product bundling"[1] for many marketing purposes. Product bundling offers several products for sale as one combined product. It is a common feature in many imperfectly competitive product markets. For example, Microsoft Co., Ltd. includes a word processor, spreadsheet, presentation program, and other useful software into a single Office Suite. The cable television industry often

---

[1] https://en.wikipedia.org/wiki/Product_bundling.

bundles various channels into a single tier to expand the channel market. Manufacturers of video games are also willing to group a popular game with other games of the same theme in the hope of obtaining more benefits by selling them together.

Group IQI = 2	sum Rank in Tom	sum Rank in Jerry	AR-1 Rank
p1,p2	5 (3 + 2)	6 (5 + 1)	Tom
p2,p3	3 (2 + 1)	4 (1 + 3)	Tom
p4,p5	9 (4 + 5)	6 (4 + 2)	Jerry

Fig. 2. An example of aggregate reverse 1-rank queries.

Because product bundling is a common business approach, helping manufacturers target users for their bundled products becomes an important issue. Unfortunately, the previous work on reverse k-rank query and other kinds of reverse rank queries [14,15] were all designed for just one product. To address this limitation, we propose a new query definition named *aggregate reverse rank query (AR-k query)* that finds k users with the smallest aggregate rank values. In our previous work, we [5] evaluated the aggregate rank by only summing up each rank (SUM function). In this work, we extend two more MAX and MIN aggregate functions that can target the other kinds of users (Details are provided in Sect. 3).

Example 2. *Figure 2 shows an example of an AR-1 query with the SUM function. Assume that there are three bundled products: $\{p_1, p_2\}$, $\{p_2, p_3\}$, and $\{p_4, p_5\}$. The aggregate rank of $\{p_1, p_2\}$ is 5 according to Tom's preferences and 6 according to Jerry's. Thus, the AR-1 query returns Tom as the result because Tom prefers this bundle the most.*

Contribution. This paper makes the following contributions:

- To the best of our knowledge, we are the first to address the "one product" limitation of the reverse rank query. We propose a new AR-k query that returns k user preferences that best match a set of products.
- We propose a bound-and-filter framework. In the bounding phase, we preprocess preferences to determine possible upper and lower bounds. In the filtering phase, we develop and implement two methods: the tree-pruning method (TPM) and the double-tree method (DTM). We also propose a method to reduce unnecessary query points.
- Along with the theoretical analysis, we also perform experiments on both real and synthetic data. The experimental results validate the efficiency of the proposed methods.

The rest of this paper is organized as follows: Sect. 2 summarizes related work. Section 3 states the definitions. In Sect. 4, we present the method of bounding the query set. Sections 5 and 6 propose two solutions (TPM and DTM) of AR-k. Section 7 presents a method to reduce unnecessary query points for the MAX and MIN functions. Section 8 discusses the cost of the proposed bound-and-filter framework. Experimental results are shown in Sect. 9 and Sect. 10 concludes the paper.

2   Related Work

Ranking is an important property used for evaluating the position of a product. Many variants of rank-aware queries have been widely researched.

Ranking Query (top-k query). The most basic approach is the top-k query. When given a user preference, the top-k query returns k products with minimal ranking scores found by a score function. One possible approach to the top-k problem is the onion technique [2]. This algorithm precomputes and stores convex hulls of data points in layers like an onion. [6] is an important investigation that describes and classifies top-k query processing techniques in relational databases.

Reverse Rank Query (RRQ). Reverse top-k queries [14,15] have been proposed to evaluate the impact of a potential product on the market based on the preferences of users who consider it as a top-k product. For an efficient reverse top-k process, Vlachou et al. [18] proposed a branch-and-bound algorithm (BBR) using boundary-based registration and a tree base. Vlachou et al. [16,17] reported various applications of reverse top-k queries. To answer the reverse query for some less-popular objects, [23] proposed the reverse k-rank query to find the top-k user preferences with the highest rank for a given object among all users. We proposed AR-k in our previous work [5], in which we concentrated on the aggregate function SUM. This paper extends the work to efficient processing for aggregate functions MAX and MIN.

Other Reverse Queries. Other related research on reverse queries is listed below. Given a data point, queries are performed to find result sets containing this data point. In contrast to the nearest-neighbor search, Korn and Muthukrishnan [7] proposed the reverse nearest-neighbor (RNN) query. Yao et al. [22] proposed the reverse furthest neighbor (RFN) query to find points where the query point is deemed as the furthest neighbor. Wang et al. [19] extended the RFN to RkFN queries for an arbitrary value of k and proposed an efficient filter in the search space. Considering the reverse k-nearest neighbor (RKNN), Yang et al. [20] analyzed and compared notable algorithms from [3,11–13,21]. RKNN differs from RRQ because it evaluates the relative L_p distance between two points in one Euclidean space. However, RRQ focuses on the absolute ranking among all objects, and scores are found via the inner product function. In addition, RKNN treats the user preference and the product as the same kind of point in the same space, whereas RRQ has two datasets of different data spaces. The reverse skyline query uses the advantages of products to find potential users based on the dominance of competitors' products [4,8]. The preference of each user is described as a data point representing the desirable product; however, the preference is described as a weight vector in RRQ. In [9,10], a group nearest neighbor query that finds the point having the smallest aggregate L_p distance for multiple query points.

Collaborative Filtering. Our research is related to the collaborative filtering methods of recommendation systems [1]. Nevertheless, they are two different strategies. Collaborative filtering only considers the similarity among users, and recommends the product bought by a user to other similar users. However, our research is on content-based recommendation that considers the similarity between users and products.

3   Aggregate Reverse Rank Query

3.1   Preliminary Definitions

The assumption of the product data, preference data, and the score function are the same as in the related research [5,14,18,23]. Let there be a product dataset P and a preference dataset W. P and W in a d-dimensional Euclidean space. Each product in the product dataset $p \in P$ is a d-dimensional vector that contains d nonnegative values. p is represented as a point $p = (p[1],\ p[2],\ \dots,\ p[d])$ where $p[i]$ is the attribute value of p in the ith dimension. The preference $w \in W$ is also a d-dimensional weighting vector, and $w[i]$ is a nonnegative weight that evaluates the ith attribute of products, where $\sum_{i=1}^{d} w[i] = 1$. The score of a product p based on a preference w is defined as the inner product of p and w expressed by $f(w,p) = \sum_{i=1}^{d} w[i] \cdot p[i]$. Given q as the query product, which is in the same space of P, but not necessarily an element of P, the reverse k-rank query [23] is defined as follows:

Definition 1 (rank(w,q)). *Given a point set P, weighting vector w, and query q, the rank of q by w is $rank(w,q) = |A|$, where $A \subseteq P$ and $\forall p_i \in A$, $f(w,p_i) < f(w,q) \wedge \forall p_j \in (P - A)$, $f(w,p_j) \geq f(w,q)$.*

Definition 2 (reverse k-rank query). *Given a point set P, weighting vector set W, positive integer k, and query q, the reverse k-rank query returns S, $S \subseteq W$, $|S| = k$, such that $\forall w_i \in S, \forall w_j \in (W - S)$, $rank(w_i, q) \leq rank(w_j, q)$ holds.*

3.2   The Proposed Aggregate Reverse Rank Query

As the above statement indicates, it is desirable for sellers to find potential users of their product bundles by using the reverse rank technique. Such queries can be dealt by extending the reverse rank query for more than one query point. We propose the *aggregate reverse rank query* [5], which is formally defined as follows.

Definition 3 (*aggregate reverse rank query, AR-k*). *Given a point set P, weighting vector set W, positive integer k, and a set of query points Q, the AR-k query returns the set S, $S \subseteq W$, $|S| = k$, such that $\forall w_i \in S, \forall w_j \in (W - S)$, $ARank(w_i, Q) \le ARank(w_j, Q)$ holds. If multiple w's have an equal $ARank(.)$ value around boundary (k-th rank) of S, S contains a part of them randomly for the result.*

$ARank(w, Q)$ is the function used to evaluate the ranking of the query product set Q, which is the bundled product for which we want to find the target users.

- **SUM** : $ARank_S(w, Q) = \sum_{q_i \in Q} rank(w, q_i)$

- **MAX** : $ARank_M(w, Q) = \operatorname*{Max}_{q_i \in Q}(rank(w, q_i))$

- **MIN** : $ARank_m(w, Q) = \operatorname*{Min}_{q_i \in Q}(rank(w, q_i))$ (1)

Notice that in our previous work [5], we only define the SUM function. In this paper, we propose two more aggregate functions MAX and MIN to ensure that AR-*k* can deal with other situations in real applications. Specifically, suppose that there is a set of products offered by a manufacturer, and we want to help find the most likely potential users.

Then, the above three evaluating functions correspond to the following requests:

- **SUM:** Find users who more strongly believe than other users that this product set is better.
- **MAX/MIN:** Find users who more strongly believe than other users that the worst/best product in this set is better.

Example 3. *Figure 3 shows the geometric image of rank in a 2-dimensional data space of P. One product data $p \in P$ is represented as a point and a user preference w is represented as a vector. The score of inner product $f(w, p)$ is equal to the distance from o to the projection of p on w. The line that crosses the point p and is perpendicular to w is a borderline of the score $f(w, p)$. Obviously, the rank of q on w is the number of points under this borderline. For example, p_2 and p_3 are under the perpendicular line passing through q_2; hence, $f(w, p_2) < f(w, q_2)$ and $f(w, p_3) < f(w, q_2)$. By Definition 2, $rank(w, q_2) = 2$. For the aggregate rank of $Q = \{q_1, q_2, q_3\}$: $ARank_S(w, Q) = rank(w, q_1) + rank(w, q_2) + rank(w, q_3) = 3 + 2 + 5 = 10$; $ARank_M(w, Q) = rank(w, q_3) = 5$; $ARank_m(w, Q) = rank(w, q_2) = 2$.*

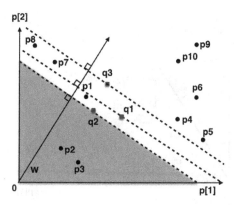

Fig. 3. Geometric view of rank in 2-dimensional data, $ARank_S(w,Q) = 3+2+5 = 10$, $ARank_M(w,Q) = 5$, $ARank_m(w,Q) = 2$

4 Bounding Phase

The naive solution to the $AR\text{-}k$ query is to sum up the ranks for $q \in Q$ one by one against each $w \in W$ and $p \in P$. This is inefficient, especially when Q is large. In this section, we introduce the bounding phase of our bound-and-filter framework, in which a sophisticated method determines two points $Q.up$ and $Q.low$ that bound Q. Our proposal is to bound the query point set Q with respect to W to avoid checking each $q \in Q$.

An intuitive method for bounding Q is to bound with the left-low corner and right-up corner points of Q's minimum bounding rectangle (MBR), denoted as $MBR(Q).low$ and $MBR(Q).up$. In the general case, $MBR(Q).low$ is dominated by any $q \in Q$ in all d dimensions, because the attribute values of $MBR(Q).low$ is always smaller than or equal to that of q. Moreover, all values are nonnegative so that the score function $f(w,q)$ is monotonically increasing; thus, it is obvious that for an arbitrary w, the score of $MBR(Q).low$ is smaller than or equal to that of $q \in Q$:

$$f(w, MBR(Q).low) \le f(w,q), \ where \ q \in Q, w \in W. \tag{2}$$

On the other hand, $MBR(Q).up$ is the upper bound of Q in a similar way.

Example 4. *Figure 4 shows the search space and filter space of data P with $MBR(Q)$. For computing the $ARank(Q,u)$, the "search space" is the space in which we need to compute the scores of the inside data. "Filter space" means that we do not need to compute the data inside and just need to filter them since they have a clear relationship with Q. The search space is the middle part between the two perpendicular lines w.r.t $MBR(Q).low$ and $MBR(Q).up$. Apparently, a tighter bound (higher $MBR(Q).low$ and/or lower $MBR(Q).up$) can make this middle space smaller and filter more data in processing.*

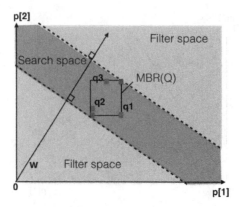

Fig. 4. A 2-dimensional example of search space (gray) and filtering space (blue) with basic MBR(Q) bounding. (Color figure online)

Motivated by the above observation, we propose a tighter bounding strategy. To bound Q for an arbitrary $w \in W$, we first find out the top-weighting vector in each dimension, denoted as $w_t^{(i)}, i = 1, 2, 3, .., d$. $w_t^{(i)}$ is the closest vector (the smallest angle) to the orthonormal basis vector of the ith dimension, as defined in the following.

Definition 4 *(top-weighting vector). Given a set of weighting vectors W, let e_i be the orthonormal basis vector for dimension i such that $e_i[i] = 1$ and $e_i[j] = 0, i \neq j$ and let $cos(a, b) = a \cdot b/(|a||b|)$ be the cosine similarity between vectors a and b. The top-weighting vector for dimension i is defined by $w_t^{(i)}$ where $w_t^{(i)} \in W$ and $\forall w \in W, cos(w_t^{(i)}, e_i) \geq cos(w, e_i)$.*

A subset of W, denoted by $W_t = \{w_t^{(i)}\}_1^d$, is the set of *top-weighting vectors* for all dimensions. Because W_t contains the border of the weighting vector in all dimensions, we can use it to find the upper bound and lower bound points set of Q.

Definition 5 *(upper and lower bound query sets Q_u and Q_l). Let Q be a set of d-dimensional queries.*

$Q_u = \{q_i | q_i \in Q \wedge \forall q_j \in Q, \exists w_t^{(i)} \in W_t, f(w_t^{(i)}, q_i) \geq f(w_t^{(i)}, q_j)\}$ *and*
$Q_l = \{q_i | q_i \in Q \wedge \forall q_j \in Q, \exists w_t^{(i)} \in W_t, f(w_t^{(i)}, q_i) \leq f(w_t^{(i)}, q_j)\}$.

By definition, for each $w_t^{(i)}$, we can find a $q_i \in Q_u$ (Q_l) such that q_i's score with respect to $w_t^{(i)}$ is the largest (smallest) among Q. Different $w_t^{(i)}$ may apply to the same q_i. Generally, it is easy to find the MBR of a point set Q_u, and its upper-right and lower-left corners are the two bounding points required.

$$Q.up = MBR(Q_u).up \tag{3}$$
$$Q.low = MBR(Q_l).low \tag{4}$$

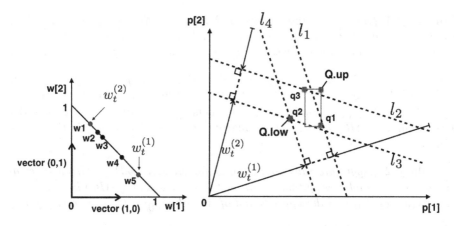

Fig. 5. A 2-dimensional example. $w_t^{(1)} = w_5$, $w_t^{(2)} = w_1$, and $Q_u = \{q_1, q_3\}$, $Q_l = \{q_2\}$, $Q.low = MBR(Q_l).low = q_2$, $Q.up = MBR(Q_u).up$

Example 5. *Figure 5 shows the example of Q.low and Q.up where $Q = \{q_1, q_2, q_3\}$. $w_t^{(1)} = w_5$ and $w_t^{(2)} = w_1$ are the top-weighting vectors in dimensions 1 and 2, respectively. Each $w_t^{(i)}$ is also a normal vector of the hyperplanes $H(w_t^{(i)})$. For Q.up, in 2-dimensional space, the hyperplanes $H(w_t^{(1)})$ are the dashed lines l_1, which are perpendicular to $w_t^{(1)}$. By sweeping l_1 parallelly from far infinity toward the original point $(0, 0)$, q_1 is the first point that is touched. Hence, q_1's score with respect to w is equal to $max_{q \in Q} f(w_t^{(1)}, q)$, and q_1 is included in Q_u. In the same manner, l_2 touches q_3 first; hence, $q_3 \in Q_u$. $Q.up = MBR(Q_u).up$ upper-bounds the scores for Q_u. Similarly, sweeping the perpendicular dashed lines l_3 and l_4 from $(0, 0)$ toward infinity, both touch q_2; hence $Q_l = \{q_2\}$ and $Q.low = q_2$. We show here that Q.up and Q.low bound the query set Q for the AR-k query.*

Theorem 1 *(Correctness of Q.up and Q.low). Given a set of d-dimensional query points Q, a set of weighting vectors W, and the bounds of Q: Q.up and Q.low. For each $w \in W$ and each $q \in Q$, $f(w, Q.low) \leq f(w, q) \leq f(w, Q.up)$ always holds.*

Proof. By contradiction. For $Q.up$, assume that $\exists q \in Q, q \notin Q_u$ holds so that $f(w, q) \geq f(w, Q.up)$. Therefore, $\exists q[i] > Q.up[i], i \in [1, d]$; therefore, there must exist a $w_t^{(j)} \in W_t, j \in [1, d]$, where W_t is a set of top-weighting vectors that makes $f(w_t^{(j)}, q)$ the maximum value, and q should be in Q_u. This leads to the contradiction (The geometric view is that there exists a hyperplane $H(w_t^{(j)})$ that first touches q rather than others.). A similar contradiction occurs with $Q.low$.

We can use the rank of $Q.low$ to infer the bounds of the aggregate rank of Q for the three aggregate rank functions SUM, MIN, and MAX in Eq. (1).

Corollary 1 *(Aggregate rank bounds of Q for w, SUM): Given a set of query points Q and a weighting vector w, the lower bound of $ARank_S(w,Q)$ is $|Q| \times rank(w, Q.low)$, and the upper bound of $ARank_S(w,Q)$ is $|Q| \times rank(w, Q.up)$.*

Proof. $\forall q_i \in Q$, $\forall w \in W$, it holds that $f(w, q_i) \geq f(w, Q.low)$; hence, $rank(w, q_i) \geq rank(w, Q.low)$. By definition, $ARank_S(w, Q) = \sum rank(w, q_i) \geq |Q| \times rank(w, Q.low)$; hence, $|Q| \times rank(w, Q.low)$ is the lower bound of $ARank_S(w, Q)$. Similarly, $|Q| \times rank(w, Q.up)$ is the upper bound.

Corollary 2 *(Aggregate rank bounds of Q for w, MAX/MIN): Given a set of query points Q and a weighting vector w, the lower bound of $ARank_{M(m)}(w,Q)$ is $rank(w, Q.low)$, and the upper bound of $ARank_{M(m)}(w,Q)$ is $rank(w, Q.up)$.*

We only prove the MIN function case since the MAX function case is similar.

Proof. $\forall q_i \in Q$, $\forall w \in W$, it holds that $Min(f(w, q_i)) \geq f(w, Q.low)$; hence, $Min(rank(w, q_i)) \geq rank(w, Q.low)$. By Eq. 1, $ARank_m(w, Q) = Min(rank(w, q_i)) \geq rank(w, Q.low)$. Similarly, $rank(w, Q.up)$ is the upper bound of $ARank_m(w, Q)$.

5   Tree-Pruning Method (TPM)

Instead of comparing the product data $p \in P$ one by one with the query bounds, we use the index to compare similar data simultaneously, thus making the process efficient. *Tree-Pruning Method (TPM)* indexes the dataset P in an R-tree to group similar points, and compares the bounds of MBRs (the R-tree entries, also denoted by e) with $Q.up$ and $Q.low$ to reduce computing costs.

Example 6. *First, we introduce how TPM filters P with Q.low and Q.up. Figure 6 shows the geometric view for an example of 2-dimensional data. The two dashed lines across the bounds Q.low and Q.up respectively, and are perpendicular to the weighting vector w_i, and form the boundary values of the score. The space is partitioned into three parts, which are marked as BelowQ, InQ, and AboveQ in Fig. 6. For example, e_2 is in BelowQ and e_5 is in AboveQ. MBRs in BelowQ or AboveQ can be filtered by checking the upper and lower boundaries; otherwise, it needs further refinement.*

Formally, the pruning rules are as follows. Notice that the filtering methodology of partitioned spaces can also apply to the multiple dimensional spaces.

- *Rule 1*(MBR e in *BelowQ*). If $f(w, e.up) < f(w, Q.low)$, then count the number of points in e because $\forall p \in e, \forall q \in Q, f(w, q) > f(w, p)$ holds.
- *Rule 2*(MBR e in *AboveQ*). If $f(w, e.low) > f(w, Q.up)$, then discard e because $\forall p \in e, \forall q \in Q, f(w, q) < f(w, p)$ holds.
- *Rule 3*(MBR e overlaps *InQ*). If $f(w, e.low) > f(w, Q.low)$ and $f(w, e.up) < f(w, Q.up)$, then add e to the candidate list for further examination.

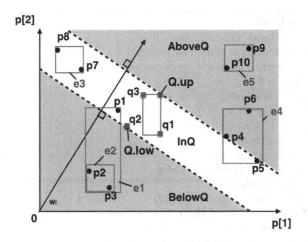

Fig. 6. The sub-spaces of BelowQ, InQ, and AboveQ based on $Q.low$ and $Q.up$ with a single w_i in the 2-dimensional space of dataset P.

5.1   ARank-P algorithm

Given P, w, Q, $Q.up$, $Q.low$, and a positive integer $minRank$, the ARank-P algorithm checks whether the aggregate rank of Q is smaller than the given $minRank$. It also returns the value of the aggregate rank when $ARank(w, Q) < minRank$. Algorithm 1 shows that the ARank-P function uses the R-tree to prune similar points in a node of the R-tree. In this algorithm, the counter rnk is used to count the aggregate rank of Q (Line 1). Then, the algorithm recursively checks the MBRs in the R-tree of P from the root (Line 2). If e_i is contained in $BelowQ$, the counter rnk is increased by the return value from the counting function in Eq. 5, which is based on Corollaries 1 and 2.

$$Counting(e, Q) = \begin{cases} e.size \times |Q|, & \textbf{SUM} \\ e.size, & \textbf{MAX or MIN} \end{cases} \quad (5)$$

When rnk becomes larger than $minRank$, the algorithm returns -1 to terminate (Lines 9–10). If e_i overlaps the space of InQ, then it is added into the candidate set $Cand$ for refinement, and either it is an internal node (Lines 11–12) or data point (Lines 14–15). Otherwise, e_i is added to the queue (Line 17). After the traversal of RtreeP, refinement is performed where the $Cand$ set is compared with each $q \in Q$ and rnk is updated (Line 18). Note that $Cand$ contains both the MBR and data point p in InQ. The refinement also considers the upper and lower bounds of the MBR to filter each q. As the results, rnk is returned as the aggregate rank if $rnk < minRank$, or -1 is returned that indicates that the current w is not a result.

Algorithm 1. ARank-P

Input: $P, w, Q, minRank, Q.up, Q.low$
Output: return rnk when w should be included
                      return -1 when w should be discarded
1: $rnk \Leftarrow 0, Cand \Leftarrow \emptyset$
2: Initialize $heapP$ as an empty queue structure.
3: $heapP.enqueue(RtreeP.Root())$
4: **while** $heapP.isNotEmpty()$ **do**
5:     $e_p \Leftarrow heapP.dequeue()$
6:     **for** each child $e_i \in e_p$ **do**
7:         **if** $f(w, e_i.low) < f(w, Q.up)$ **then**
8:             **if** e_i in $BelowQ$ **then**
9:                 $rnk \Leftarrow rnk + Counting(e_i, Q)$ //Rule 1
10:                 **if** $rnk \geq minRank$ **then**
11:                     **return** -1
12:             **else if** e_i in InQ **then**
13:                 $Cand \Leftarrow Cand \cup e_i$ //Rule 3
14:             **else**
15:                 **if** e_i is a data point **then**
16:                     $Cand \Leftarrow Cand \cup e_i$
17:                 **else**
18:                     $heapP.enqueue(e_i)$
19: Refine $Cand$ by processing the MBRs and points in $Cand$ with each $q \in Q$.
20: **if** $rnk \leq minRank$ **then**
21:     **return** rnk
22: **else**
23:     **return** -1

5.2   Tree-Pruning Method (TPM)

Let us consider the proposed TPM in Algorithm 2. Initially, the first k weighting vectors are stored into $heap$ as well as their aggregate ranks with Q (Line 1). The last rank of $heap$ stores the kth best ranked w, indicating that a worse ranked weight vector cannot be the answer. Then, for the remaining weighting vectors,

---

Algorithm 2. Tree-Pruning Method (**TPM**)

Input: $P, W, Q, Q.up, Q.low$
Output: result set $heap$
1: initialize $heap$ with the first k weighting vectors and aggregate ranks of Q
2: $minRank \Leftarrow heap$'s last rank.
3: **for** each $w \in W - \{$first k element in $W\}$ **do**
4:     $rnk \Leftarrow$ ARank-P$(P, w, Q, minRank, Q.up, Q.low)$
5:     **if** $rnk \neq -1$ **then**
6:         $heap.insert(w, rnk)$
7:         $minRank \Leftarrow$ last rank of $heap$.
8: **return** $heap$

---

the ARank-P Algorithm is called to check the aggregate rank of the query set Q (Line 4). If the current w can make the rank of Q better than the last rank in *heap*, this w is inserted into *heap* with its rank. To ensure that the size of the result is k, *heap* updates itself by removing the last element and inserting the new w and aggregate rank while keeping the sorted order of rank (Line 6) *minRank* also updated with the current last rank in *heap* (Line 7). Eventually, the algorithm returns *heap* as the result of the *AR-k* query.

6   Double-Tree Method (DTM)

TPM is limited in that it evaluates each w one by one, and its efficiency declines when the W set becomes large. This limitation inspired us to remove redundant computing by grouping similar w. We propose the *double-tree method (DTM)* that indexes the W set in an R-tree as well. The R-trees for P and W are denoted as *RtreeP* and *RtreeW*, respectively.

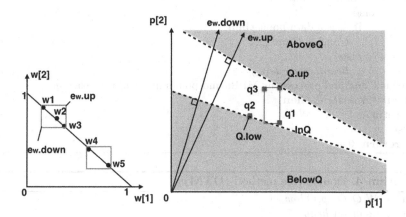

Fig. 7. The sub-spaces of BelowQ, InQ, and AboveQ based on *Q.low* and *Q.up* with an MBR e_w in the 2-dimensional space of dataset P.

Example 7. *Figure 7 shows the three parts of BelowQ, InQ, and AboveQ, which are separated by the bounds of the MBR e_w in RtreeW and Q.up (Q.low). Based on the MBR features in RtreeP and RtreeW, we can obtain the score bounds of a single data point on the MBR e_w of RtreeW.*

Lemma 3 (*Score bound of p*): *Given an MBR with the weighting vector e_w in RtreeW and $p \in P$, the score $f(w,p)$ is lower-bounded by $f(e_w.low,p)$ and upper-bounded by $f(e_w.up,p)$.*

Proof. For $w \in e_w$, $\forall i, w[i] \geq e_w.low[i]$ holds, hence $\sum_{i=1}^{d} e_w.low[i] \cdot p[i] \leq \sum_{i=1}^{d} w[i] \cdot p[i]$, that is $f(w,p) \geq f(e_w.low,p)$. Similarly, $f(w,p) \leq f(e_w.up,p)$.

Algorithm 3. ARank-WP

Input: $P, e_w, Q, minRank, Q.up, Q.low$
Output: return rnk when all $w \in e_w$ should be included
    return -1 when all $w \in e_w$ should be discarded
    return -1 when it is uncertain

1: $rnk \Leftarrow 0, Cand \Leftarrow \emptyset$
2: Initialize $heapP$ as an empty queue structure.
3: $heapP.enqueue(RtreeP.root())$
4: **while** $heapP.isNotEmpty()$ **do**
5:    $e_p \Leftarrow heapP.dequeue()$
6:    **for** each child $e_i \in e_p$ **do**
7:       **if** $f(e_w.low, e_i.low) < f(e_w.up, Q.up)$ **then**
8:          **if** e_i in $BelowQ$ **then**
9:             $rnk \Leftarrow rnk + Counting(e_i, Q)$
10:            **if** $rnk \geq minRank$ **then**
11:               **return** -1
12:         **else if** e_i in InQ **then**
13:            $Cand \Leftarrow Cand \cup e_i$
14:         **else**
15:            **if** e_i is a data point **then**
16:               $Cand \Leftarrow Cand \cup e_i$
17:            **else**
18:               $heapP.enqueue(e_i)$
19: Refine $Cand$ and process the MBRs and points in $Cand$ with each q.
20: **if** $rnk \leq minRank$ **then**
21:    **return** 1
22: **else**
23:    **return** 0

Algorithm 4. Double-tree method (DTM)

Input: $P, W, Q, Q.up, Q.low$
Output: result set $heap$

1: initialize $heap$ with the first k weighting vectors and the aggregate ranks of Q
2: $minRank \Leftarrow heap$'s last rank.
3: $heapW.enqueue(RtreeW.root())$
4: **while** $heapW.isNotEmpty()$ **do**
5:    $e_w \Leftarrow heapW.dequeue()$
6:    **if** e_w is a single weighting vector **then**
7:       call the function ARank-P and update $minRank$.
8:    **else**
9:       $flag \Leftarrow ARank\text{-}WP(P, e_w, Q, minRank, Q.up, Q.low)$
10:      **if** $flag = 0$ **then**
11:         $heapW.enqueue(\text{all children} \in e_w)$
12:      **else**
13:         **if** $flag = 1$ **then**
14:            **for** each $w \in e_w$ **do**
15:               call the function ARank-P and update $minRank$.
16: **return** $heap$

The score bounds of the MBR e_p of *RtreeP* based on e_w of *RtreeW* can also be inferred from the following lemma.

Lemma 4 (*Score bound of MBR*): *Given the MBR e_w of RtreeW and the MBR e_p of RtreeP, the score of every $p \in e_p$ is lower-bounded by $f(e_w.low, e_p.low)$ and upper-bounded by $f(e_w.up, e_p.up)$.*

Proof. For $p \in e_p$, $\forall i, e_p.low[i] \le p[i]$ holds based on the proof in Lemma 2; hence, $\sum_{i=1}^{d} e_w.low[i] \cdot e_p.low[i] \le \sum_{i=1}^{d} e_w[i].low \cdot p[i] \le \sum_{i=1}^{d} w[i] \cdot p[i]$. Hence, $f(w, p) \ge f(e_w.low, e_p.low)$. Similarly, $f(w, p) \le f(e_w.up, e_p.up)$ holds.

By the above Lemmas, we can construct the bounds of the aggregate rank for Q on MBR e_w. Corollaries 1 and 2 lead to the following conclusion almost straightly.

Theorem 2 (*Aggregate rank bounds of Q for e_w*): *Given the set of query points Q and the MBR of the weighting vector e_w. For the SUM function, the lower bound of rank for every $w \in e_w$ is $|Q| \times rank(e_w.low, Q.low)$, and the upper bound of $ARank(w, Q)$ is $|Q| \times rank(e_w.up, Q.up)$. For the MAX/MIN function, the lower bound of rank for every $w \in e_w$ is $rank(e_w.low, Q.low)$, and the upper bound is $rank(e_w.up, Q.up)$.*

The ARank-P algorithm computes the rank of Q with respect to a single w. Instead, ARank-WP in the algorithm checks a node of the R-tree that contains multiple similar w's. Algorithm 3 helps check these $w \in e_w$ with Q and *minRank*. The algorithm returns 1 if all $w \in e_w$ make the Q rank in *minRank* and returns -1 if none of $w \in e_w$ makes the Q rank better than *minRank*. Otherwise, the algorithm returns 0, indicating that e_w cannot be filtered and its children entries need to be checked.

Unlike the TPM algorithm in Algorithm 2, DTM indexes both P and W in two R-trees. Hence, it enables the pruning of both the weighting vectors and points. Algorithm 4 shows the detail of DTM. Different from TPM, DTM checks the nodes in *RtreeW*, and calls Algorithm 3 to check the aggregate rank of Q on a node e_w (Line 9). If $flag$ (the returned value from ARank-WP) is 0, all children MBRs are added to *heapW* for further check (Lines 10–11). If $flag$ is 1, this means that every w in e_w makes Q rank better than *minRank*. Thus, Algorithm 1 computes the rank of each w in e_w and *heap*, which keeps the best k answers so far, and *minRank* are updated (Lines 14–15). When the leaf node of a single w is being checked, Algorithm 1 is called exactly as in TPM (Lines 6–7). When the algorithm terminates, *heap* is returned as the result of the aggregate reverse rank query.

7   Query Reducing For MAX/MIN *AR-k*

The MAX and MIN functions in the *AR-k* query enable to analyze the potential users who are interested only in the worst or best product in a product bundle. Different from the SUM function that requires summing up the ranks for all $q \in Q$, it is sufficient to only check the necessary q's instead of the whole Q.

This means that we can make the proposed bound-and-filter framework more efficient. In this section, we introduce a method of reducing Q for the MAX and MIN functions.

It is natural to believe that such necessary query points are those located in the up-right and low-left parts of Q for MAX and MIN functions, respectively. Defined in the following, the *left corner MBR* and the *right corner MBR* try to remove unnecessary query points of Q.

Definition 6 *(Left-corners and right-corners, CM). Let Q be a point set. The left-corners of Q is a subset of Q and is denoted as $CM(Q).l$. $CM(Q).l$ contains the points in the MBR formed by $\{h^{(i)}\}_{i=1}^{d}$, where $h^{(i)} \in Q$ satisfies: (1) $h^{(i)}[i] = MBR(Q).low[i]$, and (2) $h^{(i)}$ is the nearest point to $MBR(Q).low$ among all points p satisfying $h^{(i)}[i] = MBR(Q).low[i]$. The right-corners of Q, denoted as $CM(Q).r$ is defined in a similar manner.*

Example 8. *Figure 8a gives an example of left-corners and right-corners in 2-dimensional data. There are q_1 to q_7 in a query points set Q. q_4 is the nearest point to $MBR(Q).low$ and is on the left vertical edge of $MBR(Q)$. On the down horizontal edge, q_2 is the nearest point to $MBR(Q).low$. Therefore, $CM(Q).l = \{q_1, q_2, q_3, q_4\}$ is formed by $\{q_2, q_4\}$. In the same way, $CM(Q).r = \{q_5, q_6\}$ is formed by $\{q_5, q_6\}$.*

Obviously, the points in $CM(Q).l$ have smaller values in all dimensions than the other points of Q. Therefore, given an arbitrary w:

$$\underset{q \in Q}{\text{Min}} \ rank(w, q) = \underset{q \in CM(Q).l}{\text{Min}} \ rank(w, q). \tag{6}$$

In other words, the $q \in Q$ that minimizes $rank(w, q)$ is always found from $CM(Q).l$. Similarly, the $q \in Q$ that maximizes $rank(w, q)$ is always found from $CM(Q).r$.

Lemma 5 *(Reduce Q to $CM(Q)$): Given a set of query points Q, $ARank_m(w, Q) = ARank_m(w, CM(Q).l)$ and $ARank_M(w, Q) = ARank_M(w, CM(Q).l)$.*

Another way to reduce Q for MAX and MIN functions is to build the convex hull of Q. The convex hull is the smallest convex set that contains all $q \in Q$, and we denote the vertices set of the convex hull of Q by $CH(Q)$.

Example 9. *Figure 8b shows the convex hull of the given Q in the same example, where $CH(Q) = \{q_2, q_4, q_5, q_6, q_7\}$. Viewing a point as a vector, when $q \in Q$ are projected to an arbitrary vector w, both the shortest and the longest length of projection are from $CH(Q)$, because the vertices of the convex hull are the boundary points. Recall that the inner product $f(w, q)$ is equal to the length of q's projection on w, and $CH(Q)$ contains such q's that minimize and maximize $rank(w, q)$.*

Lemma 6 *(Reduce Q to $CH(Q)$): Given a set of query points Q, $ARank_m(w, Q) = ARank_m(w, CH(Q))$ and $ARank_M(w, Q) = ARank_M(w, CH(Q))$.*

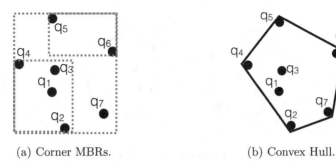

(a) Corner MBRs.   (b) Convex Hull.

Fig. 8. Two ways to reduce Q.

Taking the advantages of both $CM(Q)$ and $CH(Q)$, we can only check the query points at their intersection. Lemmas 5 and 6 help to conclude the following Theorem.

Theorem 3 *(Correctness of query reducing). Given a set of query points Q, let $Q_m = CM(Q).l \cap CH(Q)$ and $Q_M = CM(Q).r \cap CH(Q)$. Then $ARank_m(w, Q) = ARank_m(w, Q_m)$ and $ARank_M(w, Q) = ARank_M(w, Q_M)$.*

Algorithm 5. Reduce Q

Input: Q
Output: reduced set Q_R
 1: $CH(Q) \Leftarrow ConvexHull(Q).getVertex()$
 2: **if** MIN function **then**
 3:    $CM(Q) \Leftarrow get\ CM(Q).l$
 4: **if** MAX function **then**
 5:    $CM(Q) \Leftarrow get\ CM(Q).r$
 6: $Q_R \Leftarrow CM \cap CH(Q)$
 7: **return** Q_R

The above theorem guarantees that for MAX/MIN $AR\text{-}k$ queries, we only need to process the reduced Q_M/Q_m instead of the original Q. Figure 9 shows an example of reducing Q. $CH(Q) = \{q_2, q_4, q_5, q_6, q_7\}$, $CM(Q).l = \{q_1, q_2, q_3, q_4\}$ and $CM(Q).r = \{q_5, q_6\}$. By Theorem 3, the reduced query set for the MAX function is $Q_M = CH(Q) \cap CM.l = \{q_2, q_4\}$, and the reduced query set for the MIN function is $Q_m = CH(Q) \cap CM.r = \{q_5, q_6\}$.

Algorithm 5 gives a pseudocode of reducing Q for the MAX and MIN functions. Q_R is the reduced set (Q_M or Q_m) and is a subset of Q. Based on the reducing method, we propose a CHDTM algorithm that calls Algorithm 5 before bounding and DTM, shown in Algorithm 6.

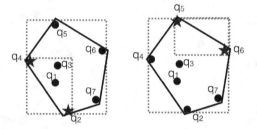

Fig. 9. Query points in convex hull vertices and corner MBRs. Necessary queries for MAX function: $\{q_2, q_4\}$, for MIN function: $\{q_5, q_6\}$.

Algorithm 6. CHDTM

Input: P, W, Q
Output: result set for AR-k
 1: $Q_R \Leftarrow$ reduce Q with Algorithm 5
 2: $\{Q.up, Q.low\} \Leftarrow$ bound Q
 3: $Result \Leftarrow$ run $DTM(P, W, Q_f, Q.up, Q.low)$
 4: **return** $Result$

---

8   Cost Estimation

We make a rough analysis on the complexity of the methods here.

8.1   Computational Cost of Bounding Q

For the cost of bounding Q described in Sect. 4, because the set of *top-weighting vectors* W_t can be found before the query set Q is issued, it can be considered as an ignorable cost in terms of query processing. Having W_t, the time cost of finding $Q.low$ and $Q.up$ is reduced from $O(|Q| \times |W|)$ to only $O(|Q| \times d)$, where d is the dimensionality of data. Considering that $|Q| \times d$ is much smaller than the size of the dataset P and W, the overhead of obtaining $Q.low$ and $Q.up$ is negligible.

8.2   Computational Cost of Reducing Q in MAX/MIN Function

For reducing Q for AR-k processing with Max and Min functions, Sect. 7 explained that the final filtering result is the intersection set between $CM(Q)$ and $CH(Q)$. The cost of obtaining either of $CM(Q).l$ or $CM(Q).r$ is $O(|Q|)$, and the worst case of building a convex hull for a given set of points Q costs $O(|Q|^2)$. Therefore, the total cost of this phase is $O(|Q| + |Q|^2) = O(|Q|^2)$. With the same reason that the query set Q is very small, the cost of filtering Q in MAX/MIN function is also negligible.

8.3   Summary of Bound-and-Filter Framework

Based on above conclusions, the cost of the proposed bound-and-filter framework is dominated by the tree-based method in the filtering phase. Table 1 summarizes the comparison of space and time complexities for Naive and the proposed TPM and DTM. NA has the highest cost in terms of time complexity because $O(|P| \cdot |W|)$. However, it requires no extra index and only needs $O(k)$ space complexity. The proposed TPM and DTM algorithms need space to store the R-tree but have lower computation costs.

Table 1. Time complexity and space complexity for algorithms NA, TPM, and DTM.

Algorithm	Index	CPU cost	I/O cost	Storage cost
Naive	None	$O(|W| \cdot |P|)$	$|P| + |W|$	$O(k)$
TPM	RtreeP	$O(|W| \cdot \log |P|)$	$\log |P| + |W|$	$O(\log |P|)$
DTM	RtreeP, RtreeW	$O(\log |W| \cdot \log |P|)$	$\log |W| + \log |P|$	$O(\log |P| + \log |W|)$

9   Experiment

We present the experimental evaluation of the NAIVE, TPM, and DTM algorithms for $AR\text{-}k$ with SUM, MIN, and MAX functions. All algorithms were implemented in C++, and the experiments were run on a Mac with 2.6 GHz Intel Core i7 and 16 GB RAM. The page size was 4K.

9.1   Experimental Settings

Dataset. Both synthetic and real data were employed for the dataset P. The synthetic datasets were uniform (UN), clustered (CL), and anti-correlated (AC) with an attribute value range of $[0, 1)$. We used the same method as in related work [14,18,23] to generate synthetic datasets:

- UN: All attribute values are generated independently and following a uniform distribution.
- CL: The cluster centroids are selected randomly and follow a uniform distribution. Then, each attribute is generated with the normal distribution.
- AC: Select a plane perpendicular to the diagonal of the data space. Then each attribute is generated in this plane and follows a uniform distribution.

We also performed comparison experiments on two real datasets: HOUSE and NBA[2]. HOUSE contains 201,760 6-dimensional tuples and represents the annual payments of American families (gas, electricity, water, heating, insurance, and property tax) in 2013. NBA is a 20,960-tuple dataset of box scores of players in the NBA from 1949 to 2009. We extracted the NBA statistics for points,

---

[2] NBA: http://www.databasebasketball.com/; HOUSE: https://usa.ipums.org/usa/.

rebounds, assists, blocks, and steals to form a 5-d vector that represents a player. The UN and CL datasets for W were generated in the same manner as the datasets of P. We generated Q by using clustered data.

Performance Evaluation. In all experiments, we used three measurements to evaluate the performance of all algorithms: (a) The CPU cost that is the executing time of queries. (b) The I/O cost that is estimated by the node accessed in the R-tree. (c) The number of pairwise computations between P and W. We report the above measurements with the average values over 100 times.

9.2   Experimental Results

UN Data on Varying d. Figure 10 shows the experimental results for the synthetic datasets UN with varying dimensions d (2–5), where the *ARank* function is SUM. Both datasets P and W contained 100K tuples. Q had five query points, and the target is to find the five best preferences ($k = 5$) for this Q. According to the CPU cost comparison results shown in Fig. 10a, it is easy to know that TPM and DTM were at least ten times faster than NAIVE. DTM performed the best because it avoids checking each p and w, and the performance is also stable for various dimensional cases. Figure 10b and c show that DTM had less I/O cost and less pairwise computations than TPM. This is because TPM can only prune P but DTM can prune both P and W with its double R-trees.

The comparison results with regard to the MAX and MIN functions are shown in Figs. 11 and 12. As stated in Sect. 7, CHDTM optimized DTM by reducing unnecessary $q \in Q$ on the MAX/MIN function. The experimental results also confirm that CHDTM was better than DTM in terms of CPU cost, I/O cost, and pairwise computations on UN data.

CL and AC Data on Varying d. We also tested other synthetic data CL and AC and the comparison results of $AR - k$ query with the SUM function are shown in Figs. 13 and 14. According to these results, DTM also has better performance than other algorithms on both CL data and AC data. Tree-based methods (TPM, DTM) require less querying time for CL data than other data distributions because it is easier to index clustered data with the R-tree. This also makes the proposed method have less I/O cost and pairwise computations.

UN Data on Varying $|Q|$. For the varying $|Q|$ in Fig. 15, because the number of products in a product bundle is not large, we test the Q from 5 to 25. The CPU time of TPM and DTM had only a slight increase because they bounded Q in advance. However, the efficiency of the Naive decreased with increasing $|Q|$ since it had to calculate every $q \in Q$ for assembling ARank.

CL Data on Varying k. From the results provided in Fig. 16, we can see that all algorithms are insensitive to k. This is because of the following two reasons: (a) k is far smaller than the cardinality of W and P. (b) In our proposed bound-and-filter framework, a k-element buffer in ascending order is kept to store the top-k $w's$ and their ranking while processing, and the comparing only happens with the last element ($minRank$) rather than all k candidates in the buffer.

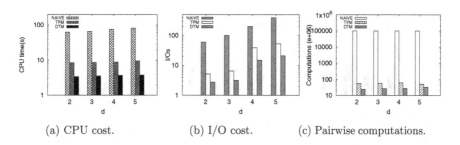

(a) CPU cost.   (b) I/O cost.   (c) Pairwise computations.

Fig. 10. Comparison results of varying d on UN data with AR-k query (SUM function), $|P| = |W| = 100$K, all with $|Q| = 5$, $k = 10$.

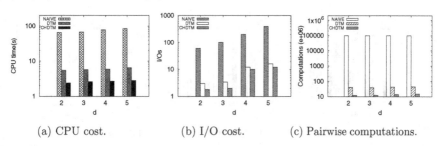

(a) CPU cost.   (b) I/O cost.   (c) Pairwise computations.

Fig. 11. Comparison results of varying d on UN data with AR-k query (MAX function), $|P| = |W| = 100$K, all with $|Q| = 5$, $k = 10$.

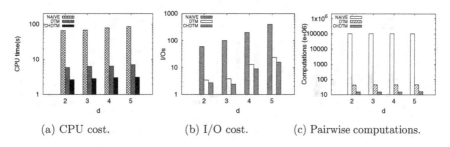

(a) CPU cost.   (b) I/O cost.   (c) Pairwise computations.

Fig. 12. Comparison results of varying d on UN data with AR-k query (MIN function), $|P| = |W| = 100$K, all with $|Q| = 5$, $k = 10$.

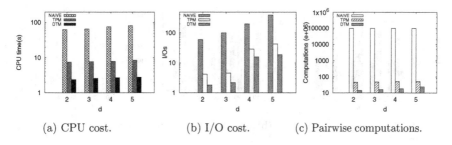

(a) CPU cost.   (b) I/O cost.   (c) Pairwise computations.

Fig. 13. Comparison results of varying d on CL data with AR-k query (SUM function), $|P| = |W| = 100$K, all with $|Q| = 5$, $k = 10$.

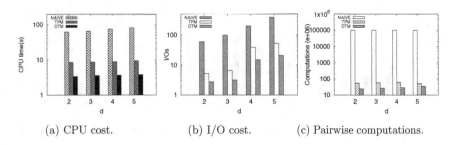

(a) CPU cost.   (b) I/O cost.   (c) Pairwise computations.

Fig. 14. Comparison results of varying d on AC data with AR-k query (SUM function), $|P| = |W| = 100K$, all with $|Q| = 5$, $k = 10$.

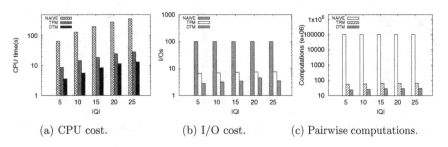

(a) CPU cost.   (b) I/O cost.   (c) Pairwise computations.

Fig. 15. Comparison results of varying $|Q|$ on UN data with AR-k query (SUM function), $|P| = |W| = 100K$, all with $d = 3$, $k = 10$.

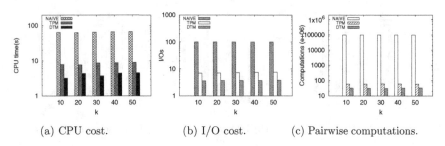

(a) CPU cost.   (b) I/O cost.   (c) Pairwise computations.

Fig. 16. Comparison results of varying k on CL data with AR-k query (SUM function), $|P| = |W| = 100K$, all with $|Q| = 5$, $d = 3$.

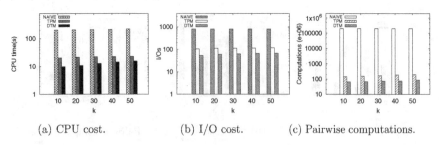

(a) CPU cost.   (b) I/O cost.   (c) Pairwise computations.

Fig. 17. Comparison results of varying k on HOUSE data with AR-k query (SUM function), W: UN data, $|W| = 100K$, all with $|Q| = 5$.

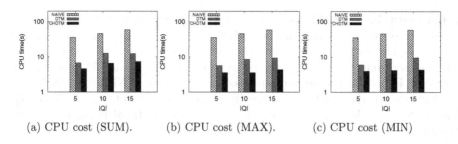

(a) CPU cost (SUM).   (b) CPU cost (MAX).   (c) CPU cost (MIN)

Fig. 18. Comparison results of varying $|Q|$ on NBA data with AR-k query (SUM, MAX, MIN functions), W: UN data, $|W| = 100K$, all with $k = 10$.

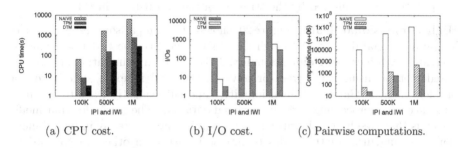

(a) CPU cost.   (b) I/O cost.   (c) Pairwise computations.

Fig. 19. Scalability on varying $|P|$ and $|W|$, P: UN data, W: UN data, all with $k = 10$, $|Q| = 5$, $d = 3$.

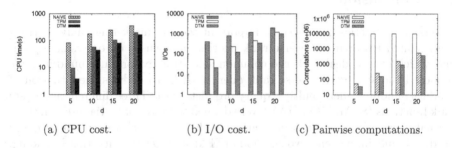

(a) CPU cost.   (b) I/O cost.   (c) Pairwise computations.

Fig. 20. Comparison results of varying d on high-dimensional UN data with AR-k query (SUM function), $|P| = |W| = 100K$, all with $|Q| = 5$, $k = 10$.

HOUSE Data. Figure 17 shows the comparison results of CPU time, I/O cost, and pairwise computations for all algorithms with the HOUSE dataset and different k (10–50). DTM again performed the best. We also investigated the distribution of the HOUSE dataset and found that it is similar to an exponential distribution.

NBA Data. Using the NBA dataset, the AR-k query can answer such practical questions as "who likes a team more than others?" We selected five, ten, and fifteen players from the same team as Q and then generated the dataset W as various user preferences. The three *ARank* functions represent different ways of thinking: To find the people who care about all players of an NBA team (SUM) or are just concerned about the most favorite/unlike player in a team (MAX/MIN). Figure 18 shows the results of NBA data. As expected, DTM (CHDTM) found the answer the fastest.

Scalability. Figure 19 shows the scalable property for varying $|P|$ and $|W|$. We show the results of $|P| = |W| = 100K$, 500K, 1M. The CPU cost of DTM increased slightly with increasing $|P|$ and $|W|$ because the majority of pairwise computations were filtered by the strategy of the two R-trees in DTM.

High-Dimensional Data. Figure 20 shows the comparison results on the high-dimensional dataset. Although the DTM is still the best, outperformance decreases with increasing dimensionality. This results in a limitation of the proposed method using an R-tree (or any other spatial indexes) suffers from a problem named "Curse of Dimensionality," and subsequently leads to low performance when processing high-dimensional data sets. The reason for that inefficiency is that tree-based algorithms cannot divide data correctly in high dimensions, causing most of the nodes to intersect with each other. In conclusion, finding a better solution with high-dimensional data is important.

10   Conclusion

Reverse rank queries have become important tools in marketing analysis. However, related research on reverse rank queries has focused on only single product, which cannot deal with the common sale strategy, product bundling. We proposed the aggregate reverse rank query (AR-k) to address the situation of product bundling where multiple query products exist. Three different aggregate rank functions (SUM, MIN, MAX) were defined to target potential users in three normal views. To solve AR-k efficiently, we devise a novel way to bound query products, and implement two methods (TPM and DTM) with this bounding. TPM is a tree-based pruning method that prunes unnecessary products with the help of an R-tree. DTM uses two R-trees to manage and prune products and user preferences. We compared the methods through experiments on both synthetic data and real data and the results show that DTM is the most efficient.

As future work, we first plan to extend approaches for other aggregate rank functions, such as evaluating the aggregate rank by the harmonic average of each rank. We also want to consider approximate solutions for AR-k queries.

Acknowledgement. This research was partly supported by the program "Research and Development on Real World Big Data Integration and Analysis" of RIKEN, Japan.

References

1. Beladev, M., Rokach, L., Shapira, B.: Recommender systems for product bundling. Knowl. Based Syst. **111**, 193–206 (2016)
2. Chang, Y., Bergman, L.D., Castelli, V., Li, C., Lo, M., Smith, J.R.: The onion technique: indexing for linear optimization queries. In: Proceedings of the 2000 ACM SIGMOD International Conference on Management of Data, 16–18 May 2000, Dallas, Texas, USA, pp. 391–402 (2000)
3. Cheema, M.A., Lin, X., Zhang, W., Zhang, Y.: Influence zone: efficiently processing reverse k nearest neighbors queries. In: Proceedings of the 27th International Conference on Data Engineering, ICDE 2011, 11–16 April 2011, Hannover, Germany, pp. 577–588 (2011)
4. Dellis, E., Seeger, B.: Efficient computation of reverse skyline queries. In: Proceedings of the 33rd International Conference on Very Large Data Bases, 23–27 September 2007, pp. 291–302. University of Vienna, Austria (2007)
5. Dong, Y., Chen, H., Furuse, K., Kitagawa, H.: Aggregate reverse rank queries. In: Hartmann, S., Ma, H. (eds.) DEXA 2016. LNCS, vol. 9828, pp. 87–101. Springer, Cham (2016). https://doi.org/10.1007/978-3-319-44406-2_8
6. Ilyas, I.F., Beskales, G., Soliman, M.A.: A survey of top-k query processing techniques in relational database systems. ACM Comput. Surv. **40**(4), 11 (2008)
7. Korn, F., Muthukrishnan, S.: Influence sets based on reverse nearest neighbor queries. In: Proceedings of the 2000 ACM SIGMOD International Conference on Management of Data, 16–18 May 2000, Dallas, Texas, USA, pp. 201–212 (2000)
8. Lian, X., Chen, L.: Monochromatic and bichromatic reverse skyline search over uncertain databases. In: Proceedings of the ACM SIGMOD International Conference on Management of Data, SIGMOD 2008, Vancouver, BC, Canada, 10–12 June 2008, pp. 213–226 (2008)
9. Papadias, D., Shen, Q., Tao, Y., Mouratidis, K.: Group nearest neighbor queries. In: Proceedings of the 20th International Conference on Data Engineering, ICDE 2004, 30 March–2 April 2004, Boston, MA, USA, pp. 301–312 (2004)
10. Papadias, D., Tao, Y., Mouratidis, K., Hui, C.K.: Aggregate nearest neighbor queries in spatial databases. ACM Trans. Database Syst. **30**(2), 529–576 (2005)
11. Stanoi, I., Agrawal, D., El Abbadi, A.: Reverse nearest neighbor queries for dynamic databases. In: ACM SIGMOD Workshop, pp. 44–53 (2000)
12. Stanoi, I., Agrawal, D., El Abbadi, A.: Reverse nearest neighbor queries for dynamic databases. In: ACM SIGMOD Workshop on Research Issues in Data Mining and Knowledge Discovery, pp. 44–53 (2000)
13. Tao, Y., Papadias, D., Lian, X., Xiao, X.: Multidimensional reverse kNN search. VLDB J. **16**(3), 293–316 (2007)
14. Vlachou, A., Doulkeridis, C., Kotidis, Y., Nørvåg, K.: Reverse top-k queries. In: Proceedings of the 26th International Conference on Data Engineering, ICDE 2010, 1–6 March 2010, Long Beach, California, USA, pp. 365–376 (2010)
15. Vlachou, A., Doulkeridis, C., Kotidis, Y., Nørvåg, K.: Monochromatic and bichromatic reverse top-k queries. IEEE Trans. Knowl. Data Eng. **23**(8), 1215–1229 (2011)
16. Vlachou, A., Doulkeridis, C., Nørvåg, K.: Monitoring reverse top-k queries over mobile devices. In: Proceedings of the Tenth ACM International Workshop on Data Engineering for Wireless and Mobile Access, MobiDE 2011, 12 June 2011, Athens, Greece, pp. 17–24 (2011)

17. Vlachou, A., Doulkeridis, C., Nørvåg, K., Kotidis, Y.: Identifying the most influential data objects with reverse top-k queries. PVLDB **3**(1), 364–372 (2010)
18. Vlachou, A., Doulkeridis, C., Nørvåg, K., Kotidis, K.: Branch-and-bound algorithm for reverse top-k queries. In: Proceedings of the ACM SIGMOD International Conference on Management of Data, SIGMOD 2013, New York, NY, USA, 22–27 June 2013, pp. 481–492 (2013)
19. Wang, S., Cheema, M.A., Lin, M.A., Zhang, Y., Liu, Y.: Efficiently computing reverse k furthest neighbors. In: 32nd IEEE International Conference on Data Engineering, ICDE 2016, 16–20 May 2016, Helsinki, Finland, pp. 1110–1121 (2016)
20. Yang, S., Cheema, M.A., Lin, X., Wang, W.: Reverse k nearest neighbors query processing: experiments and analysis. PVLDB **8**(5), 605–616 (2015)
21. Yang, S., Cheema, M.A., Lin, X., Zhang, Y.: SLICE: reviving regions-based pruning for reverse k nearest neighbors queries. In: IEEE 30th International Conference on Data Engineering, Chicago, ICDE 2014, March 31–April 4, 2014, IL, USA, pp. 760–771 (2014)
22. Yao, B., Li, F., Kumar, P.: Reverse furthest neighbors in spatial databases. In: Proceedings of the 25th International Conference on Data Engineering, ICDE 2009, March 29– April 2 2009, Shanghai, China, pp. 664–675 (2009)
23. Zhang, Z., Jin, C., Kang, Q.: Reverse k-ranks query. PVLDB **7**(10), 785–796 (2014)

Syntactic Anonymisation of Shared Datasets in Resource Constrained Environments

Anne V. D. M. Kayem[1(✉)], C. T. Vester[2], and Christoph Meinel[1]

[1] Hasso-Plattner-Institute, Potsdam, Germany
anne@mykayem.org
[2] Department of Computer Science, University of Cape Town,
Cape Town, South Africa
http://hpi.de/meinel/lehrstuhl.html

Abstract. Resource constrained environments (RCEs) describe remote or rural developing world regions where missing specialised expertise, and computational processing power hinders data analytics operations. Outsourcing to third-party data analytics service providers offers a cost-effective management solution. However, a necessary pre-processing step is to anonymise the data before it is shared, to protect against privacy violations. Syntactic anonymisation algorithms (k-anonymisation, l-diversity, and t-closeness) are an attractive solution for RCEs because the generated data is not use case specific. These algorithms have however been shown to be NP-Hard, and as such need to be re-factored to run efficiently with limited processing power. In previous work [23], we presented a method of extending the standard k-anonymization and l-diversity algorithms, to satisfy both data utility and privacy. We used a multi-objective optimization scheme to minimise information loss and maximize privacy. Our results showed that the extended l-diverse algorithm incurs higher information losses than the extended k-anonymity algorithm, but offers better privacy in terms of protection against inferential disclosure. The additional information loss (7%) was negligible, and did not negatively affect data utility. As a further step, in this paper, we extend this result with a modified t-closeness algorithm based on the notion of clustering. The aim of this is to provide a performance-efficient algorithm that maintains the low information loss levels of our extended k-anonymisation and l-diversity algorithms, but also provides protection against skewness and similarity attacks.

Keywords: Data anonymisation · k-anonymity · l-diversity
t-closeness · Clustering · Privacy · Information loss

1 Introduction

One of the challenges that emerges in resource constrained environments (RCEs) is that of effectively, and efficiently analysing data. For instance, studies from

© Springer-Verlag GmbH Germany, part of Springer Nature 2018
A. Hameurlain et al. (Eds.): TLDKS XXXVIII, LNCS 11250, pp. 27–60, 2018.
https://doi.org/10.1007/978-3-662-58384-5_2

the United Nations (UN) and World Bank (WB) [39] estimate that annually, violent crime costs developing world countries about 10% of their Gross Domestic Product (GDP). In the 2007 year alone, Guatemala lost 7.3% of her Gross Domestic Product (GDP), and Mexico estimated the costs of violence in terms of lost investment from local business and jobs at \$9.6 billion. While corruption is a major reason behind the failure to resolve reported crime cases, the lack of crime data analytics also plays a key role [19, 43].

In order to address this data analytics issue, Burke et al. [6] proposed outsourcing the data to third-party data analytics service providers as a cost effective management solution. The Burke et al. [6] anonymisation framework is based on using low-cost mobile devices to collect the crime data, which is then transferred to a law enforcement agency where the data is anonymised before it is outsourced. However, manual anonymisation is a time-consuming process that is prone to error, and information disclosure. A further concern is protecting subsequent anonymised datasets from being combined with historical data to provoke linking and inferential attacks.

We addressed this issue by proposing an automated anonymisation scheme that extends the standard k-anonymisation and l-diversity algorithms by using multi-objective optimization to maximize information utility (minimize information loss) [23]. Weighting based on information exposure severity was used to ensure privacy by protecting against linking and inference attacks. Our results indicated that l-diverse datasets incur worse information loss (7% on average) than k-anonymised data, but offer better privacy (protection against linking and inference attacks) with a diversity of between 9–14% in comparison to 10–30% in k-anonymised datasets. Therefore, by augmenting k-anonymisation with l-diversity, we improve privacy at a negligible cost to utility. Our approach however, remains vulnerable to similarity and skewness attacks which could become an issue as the sizes of the datasets grow [29].

In this paper, we handle the potential for similarity and skewness attacks by extending our automated anonymisation scheme to handle t-closeness anonymisation. However, Liang and Yuan [30] have shown, the t-closeness problem is NP-Hard, and as we show in Sect. 4.3, the average time complexity of t-closeness anonymisation is in $2^{O(n^2)} \cdot O(m)$ where n is the number of tuples and m, the number attributes in the dataset. Therefore, to make t-closeness applicable to RCEs, we propose a performance efficient alternative based on using the notion of clustering to classify tuples. Each cluster of size k is centered around a tuple, that is selected such that there exist at $k-1$ tuples with a similar quasi-identifier. In order to satisfy the properties of t-closeness anonymisation, that is to prevent skewness and similarity de-anonymisations of data, we ensure that the distance between the cluster centroid and the classified tuples is no greater than a threshold value of t. We determine the degree of similarity on the basis of the severity ranking (cost to privacy due to attribute exposure) of the SA, and the distance of the tuples' quasi-identifiers from the cluster centroid's quasi-identifier. The Jaccard coefficient is used to evaluate categorical attributes, and the Euclidean distance for numerical attributes in the quasi-identifier. A high degree of similarity, is expressed by a small distance from the cluster centroid, and the reverse is true for a low similarity degree. Our proposed t-clustering algorithm has a average time complexity of $O(m^2 \log n)$ where n and m are the number of tuples and attributes, respectively. Experimental results indicate that our proposed scheme is practically feasible performance-wise for large datasets, and inherits the privacy protection properties of the t-closeness anonymisation algorithm.

In addition to RCEs, other potential applications of our work emerge in the Internet-of-things (e.g. opportunistic, and Fog computing networks). In this context, personal data is sometimes collected unintentionally and so it makes sense to have methods of anonymising data before it is transferred to a forwarding device.

The outline of the paper is as follows. In Sect. 2 we provide an overview of the literature on privacy preserving data publishing from the syntactic data anonymisation perspective. We proceed in Sect. 3 with a summary of the Kayem et al. [23] multi-objective scheme to support k-anonymisation and l-diversity in automated data anonymisation. In Sect. 4, we present the t-clustering scheme [22] and show that t-clustering has an average time complexity of $O(m^2 \log n)$ in comparison to $2^{O(n^2)} \cdot O(m)$ for t-closeness. In Sect. 5, we present experimental results based on data obtained from a prototype implementation platform [6,38], and offer conclusions in Sect. 6.

2 Related Work

Privacy preserving data publishing is aimed at making data available for data analytics tasks [5,17,21,29,34,44,48]. There are two general approaches to privacy preserving data publishing. The first is to anonymise and then mine the data [2,3,5,17], while the second, is to mine and then anonymise the released query results [1–3]. The first approach is better suited to RCEs where the data is often shared with untrusted services providers who might be "honest-but-curious". As such, we focus our related work discussion on privacy preserving data publishing schemes where the data is anonymised and then shared.

Following Sweeney's k-anonymity model for protecting data privacy [40], several solutions have been proposed to effectively anonymise data [1,5,21,29,34]. Existing anonymisation algorithms can generally be classified into two main groups namely, syntactic and semantic models [9]. Syntactic models have a well defined data output format, such that for small data sets privacy traits can often be confirmed by visually inspecting the data. Examples of syntactic anonymisation models include k-anonymity [1,5,21], l-diversity [34], and t-closeness [29]. On the other hand, semantic privacy models employ data perturbations based primarily on noise additions to distort the data [9,46]. Examples of semantic data anonymisation models include differential privacy and its variants [9,14,46].

On the other hand, probabilistic privacy models employ data perturbations based primarily on noise additions to distort the data [9,46]. Perturbation approaches have been critiqued for being vulnerable to inferential attacks based on adversarial knowledge of the true underlying distributions of the data [33].

Dwork et al. [14] proposed addressing this caveat with the notion of differential privacy. Differential privacy basically requires that the adversary learns no more from a published data set when one record (or individual) is present in, or removed from, the data set [46]. Attempts have also been made to combine attributes from both syntactic and probabilistic models to form hybrid anonymisation approaches. Examples include probabilistic k-anonymity [2], and differential privacy with t-closeness [9]. Both syntactic and semantic data anonymisation algorithms transform the data using a combination of *generalisation, suppression*, and *perturbation*. These data transformation methods fall into one of two categories namely, *randomisation* and *generalisation* which we explain in some detail below.

Randomization algorithms operate by altering the veracity of the data. This is done by modifying attributes that strongly link the data to an individual. The modifications are achieved either by noise injections, permutations, or statistical shifting [20]. For instance, in differential privacy, this is done by determining at the runtime of a query, how much noise injections to add to the resulting dataset to ensure anonymity in each case [12]. Additionally, differential privacy uses the exponential mechanisms to release statistical information about a dataset without revealing private details of individual data entries [35]. Furthermore, the Laplace mechanism for perturbation, supports statistical shifting in differential privacy, by employing controlled random distribution sensitive noise additions [13,24]. It is worth noting here that the discretized version [18,32] is known as the matrix mechanism because both sensitive attributes and quasi-identifiers are evaluated on a per-row basis during anonymisation [28,29].

By contrast, *generalization* describes a group of techniques that modify dataset values according to a hierarchical model where each value progressively loses uniqueness as one moves upwards in the hierarchy. Several generalisation algorithms have been used effectively in combination with k-anonymity, l-diversity, as well as t-closeness. In k-anonymity the concept is to place each person in the data set together with at least $k-1$ similar data records, such that there is no possibility of distinguishing between them. This is done by assimilating the $k-1$ nearest neighbors based on their describing attributes through generalization and suppression [40]. Generalisation is vulnerable to homogeneity and background knowledge attacks [34], which l-diversity alleviates by considering the granularity of sensitive data representations to ensure a diversity of a factor of l for each quasi-identifier within a given equivalence class (usually a size of k) [10,11,25,31]. For instance, l-diversity considers that sensitive attribute distributions are the main reason behind disclosures of information used to provoke inferential attacks [8,31,37]. Further extensions of t-closeness, handle skewness and background knowledge attacks by considering the relative distributions of sensitive values both in individual equivalence classes and in the entire dataset [29]. In all three syntactic anonymisation algorithms, and their extensions [5,36], generalisation and suppression are used to support transforming the data [16].

In k-anonymity and l-diversity, efficiently obtaining usable but privacy preserving data sets is provably NP-Hard [47] and so, optimisation heuristics have been proposed to improve on the basic l-diversity scheme [10,11,37,47]. We note that l-diversity has the drawback of being dependent on the distribution of sensitive attributes in the data set and so, sensitive attribute values with high probability mass functions (that is some values have a very high frequency and others a very low frequency of occurrence) are prone to provoking high information loss in the anonymised data set. In addition l-diversity only considers the frequency of specific values within independent ECs and not in the dataset as a whole which can result in inadvertent inferential disclosure. t-closeness addresses this caveat but requires a high degree of computational resources and so is not practical for use in low resource settings. Other issues are centred on the semantics of generalisations and the effect these generalisations have on enabling information disclosures [10,29,34].

Perturbation is conceptually similar to generalization but instead of building groups or clusters of similar attributes without falsifying the data, perturbation modifies the actual value to the closest similar value. This is done by introducing an aggregated value or using a similar value such that only one value needs modification rather than multiple values. As such, finding such a value can take longer, due to the effect of having to iteratively recheck the newly created value(s), making such an approach - in terms of perfomance - unsuitable for RCEs.

Further work on data transformation for anonymity appears in the data mining field, where a variety of work exists on addressing privacy related constraints in publishing anonymised datasets. Some of this work includes but is not limited to regression models [15], clustering [41], and naive Bayes classification [42]. These methods are strongly focused on data mining tasks in specific application areas with well-defined privacy models and constraints. This is the case particularly when merging various distributed data sets to ensure privacy in each partition [49].

Data anonymization inherently leads to a loss of information that has an impact on query use cases [45]. While [27] leverage modern classification and regression based algorithms in the anonymization procedure and [50] use Bayesian networks for effective noise injection in the context of differential privacy applications, this work goes back to traditional methods of identifying and transforming quasi-identifiers (Fig. 1). Anonymisation by clustering also stems from the data mining field and has been studied as an approach to improving the performance of k-anonymisation by alleviating the cost of information loss [34,37]. The idea behind these clustering schemes is to cluster quasi-identifiers in equivalence classes of size k, and to avoid using generalisation hierarchies when this impacts negatively on information loss. This property of clustering lends itself well to t-closeness anonymisation as an approach to alleviating the performance demands of anonymising large datasets, particularly when this is done on low-powered, low-processing devices. In the next section we describe our proposed clustering algorithm.

In the following section, we consider the augmented k-anonymity and l-diversity schemes to support automated data anonymisation in RCEs [23] as

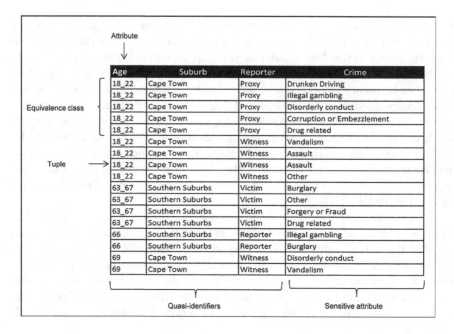

Fig. 1. An anonymised crime dataset: example

a basis for the t-clustering algorithm that we present in Sect. 4. The idea is to use the notion of Pareto optimality [4] that has the quality of considering that no optimal solution exists for a given problem but rather that the solution space consists of a set of optimal points [4]. This quality, is useful in designing an automated anonymisation scheme for RCEs in that it allows the best optimal with respect to data utility and privacy can be selected at some given instant without having to wait for an overall optimal solution.

3   Multi-objective Data Anonymisation (MOA)

In this section we present a description of the multi-objective anonymisation (MOA) scheme [23] as a basis for our proposed t-clustering algorithm. The MOA scheme extends k-anonymization (CG-Kanon) and l-diversity (CG-Diverse), by weighting sensitive attributes in terms of severity of privacy disclosure, and works to find the optimal bucket size (value of k in terms of equivalence class size) to minimize the rate of information loss (maximize data utility). We begin by providing some preliminary background information on k-anonymisation as a basis for the CG-Kanon, CG-Diverse, and t-clustering anonymisation algorithms that we study in this paper. For reference, a notation table containing the symbols used is provided in Appendix 6.

3.1   Preliminaries

Before we delve into the description of the CG-Kanon, CG-Diverse, and t-clustering algorithms, it is important to provide some definition of what k-anonymity is, because all three algorithms inherit the properties of k-anonymity. Let $D(A_1, A_2, ..., A_n)$ be a dataset with a finite number of tuples. The attribute space A of D (columns of D) is such that $\{A_1, A_2, ..., A_n\}$ where $a \in A$ represents a specific attribute value in A. A tuple in D is denoted by d such that $d\{v_1, v_2, ..., v_n\}$ denotes a projection of the sequence of values in d.

Definition 1. Quasi-identifier
Given a dataset $D(A_1, A_2, ..., A_n)$, a quasi-identifier Q_T of D is a set of attributes $\{A_i, ..., A_j\} \subset \{A_1, A_2, ..., A_n\}$ such that $\forall d \in D$, $d\{v_i, ..., v_j\} \subset d\{v_1, ...v_n\}$, $Q_T\{t\}$ is a set of attributes whose values can be mapped to at least one $d \in D$.

This definition describes quasi-identifiers as attributes which independently or when combined can be used to uniquely identify an individual or entity. Most often such identification is done by combining external data with the published dataset. To prevent such de-identifications, the notion of k-anonymity can be used to classify tuples. We define k-anonymity as follows:

Definition 2. k-anonymity
Let DT be a dataset $DT(A_1, A_2, ..., A_n) \subset D(A_1, A_2, ..., A_n)$, with a quasi-identifier $Q_T\{d\}$ associated to DT. DT is said to satisfy k-anonymity if and only if each $Q_T\{d\}$ appears in at least k tuples in DT, where the size of DT is bounded by k.

Definition 3. Equivalence Class
An equivalence class EC, is a set of tuples $\{d_i, ..., d_j\}$ such that $\forall\{d_j, d_j\}$, $Q_T(d_i) = ... = Q_T(d_j)$.

Finally, we define what disclosure and sensitive attributes are in this context. Disclosure is the unintended loss or reduction of privacy for an individual or entity resulting from a publication of anonymised data. In [29], Li et al. note that two types of information disclosure can be identified namely, identity disclosure and attribute disclosure. Identity disclosure occurs when an individual is linked to a particular record in the released table. Attribute disclosure occurs when new information about some individual is revealed. The released data then makes it possible to infer the characteristics of an individual more accurately than it would be possible before the data release. On the other hand, a sensitive attribute, is an attribute which contains a value that when combined with a quasi-identifier, could result in disclosure. Example 1, provides some clarifications of these concepts based on crime data.

Example 1. 2-Anonymity Dataset As shown in Fig. 2, the equivalence class adheres to 5-anonymity (k = 5), and has a quasi-identifier Q_T = $\{Age, Suburb, Reporter\}$. For the tuples contained in the equivalence class, the values that comprise the quasi-identifier appear at five times. We note in this case that the "Crime" attribute is sensitive.

However, we note that a closer examination of the equivalence class in Fig. 2 indicates that it is possible to provoke linking attacks on the data either by inference or by combining the anonymised dataset with available data from other sources. For instance, if an 18 year old happened to have been mentioned in the news for involvement in a corruption scandal, it is easy to deduce from our equivalence class that the individual at d_4 (tuple 4), is likely to be the person mentioned in the news. Likewise, an equivalence class in which all sensitive attributes equal "Corruption or Embezzlement" could lead to inference that the members of this equivalence class are infact all or most of those who were involved in the scandal from the news. In order to address this issue Machanavajjhala et al. [34] proposed l-diversity as an extension to k-anonymity. l-diversity requires that the most frequently occurring sensitive attribute in any equivalence class should not occur more frequently than $\frac{1}{l}$. If we consider the equivalence class in Fig. 2 with 5 tuples with "Corruption or Embezzlement" as the most common crime, to achieve 2-diversity "Corruption or Embezzlement" cannot occur more than twice in this equivalence class. Note that another interpretation of this is that there should be at least 2 distinct sensitive values per equivalence class, since any given sensitive value cannot appear more than twice. This definition is referred to as *distinct l-diversity*. Two other stronger forms of diversity, include *entropy l-diversity* and *recursive l-diversity*. *Entropy l-diversity* is based on information entropy, but Machanavajjhala et al. [34] show that this can be too restrictive as it requires a minimum aggregate level of entropy across the whole dataset. *Recursive l-diversity* on the other hand ensures that the most frequent sensitive value occurs frequently enough but the most infrequent value not too infrequently.

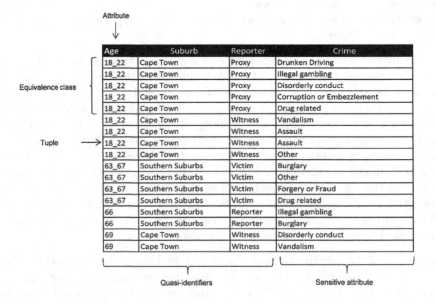

Fig. 2. k-anonymisation: example

Since, both of these versions of l-diversity are computationally expensive (in terms of searching through the entire space of sensitive attributes to find suitable SA distributions or combinations), we opted to use a heuristic that focuses on categorising SA in terms of exposure impact.

We now discuss the notions of generalisation and suppression to show how CG-Kanon, CD-Diverse, and t-clustering employs these notions to transform the data.

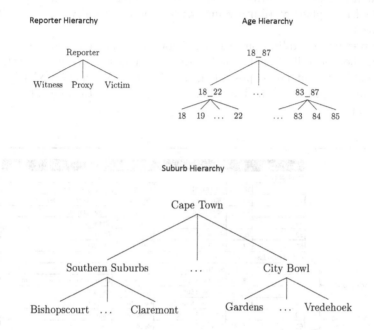

Fig. 3. Generalisation hierarchy: Reporter, Age, and Suburb Taxonomies

3.2   Generalisation and Suppression

We denote $T(a)$ as the generalisation tree for numerical attributes and $K(a)$ is the generalisation tree for categorical attributes. Furthermore, $T(a)_{max}$ and $T(a)_{min}$ denote the upper and lower limits respectively for numerical attribute generalisations. While $t_{d,i}(a)_{max}$ and $t_{d,i}(a)_{min}$ represent the upper and lower limits of the generalisation of an attribute a in tuple d during the ith iteration of the anonymisation algorithm. This is because as we show in the CG-Kanon and CG-Diverse schemes, each anonymised dataset obtained is evaluated to determine the cost-benefit tradeoff between information loss and privacy. Only when a suitable dataset is obtained, is the anonymised dataset transferred to the third-party service provider for analysis.

$K(a)_{total}$ is the total number of leaf nodes generated for $K(a)$ and P is the number of nodes created by $K(a)$. $k(a)_p$ is a sub-tree of $K(a)$ rooted at a node $p \in P$ and $k(a)_{p,total}$ is the number of leaf nodes in $k(a)_p$.

In anonymising data, we must determine a generalisation hierarchy for the quasi-identifiers (Q_T). This enables the anonymisation algorithm to achieve a higher degree of classification accuracy whilst minimising the amount of information loss. In order to facilitate classification, each quasi-identifier of a tuple must match at leat $k - 1$ other tuples in any of the given clusters. Generalisation is used to replace attribute values with a more general values to facilitate classification.

We represent generalisation hierarchies for each quasi-identifier as shown in Fig. 3. In the generalisation hierarchy, the leaf nodes represent the attribute values and the parent nodes possible generalisations. We handle NULL values without any pre-processing by including a node with a NULL value at each level of the hierarchy [7].

Report ID	Age	Suburb	Reporter	Crime
Original data				
56	18	Claremont	Victim	Illegal gambling
57	18	Claremont	Witness	Corruption or Embezzlement
58	18	Claremont	Proxy	Illegal gambling
59	22	Rosebank	Victim	Illegal gambling
60	22	Green Point	Victim	Rape
61	22	Sea Point	Victim	Murder
Global recoding				
56	18_23	Southern Suburbs	Reporter	Illegal gambling
57	18_23	Southern Suburbs	Reporter	Corruption or Embezzlement
58	18_23	Southern Suburbs	Reporter	Illegal gambling
59	18_23	Southern Suburbs	Reporter	Illegal gambling
60	18_23	Atlantic Seaboard	Reporter	Rape
61	18_23	Atlantic Seaboard	Reporter	Murder
Local recoding				
56	18	Claremont	Reporter	Illegal gambling
57	18	Claremont	Reporter	Corruption or Embezzlement
58	18_23	Southern Suburbs	Reporter	Illegal gambling
59	18_23	Southern Suburbs	Reporter	Illegal gambling
60	22	Atlantic Seaboard	Victim	Rape
61	22	Atlantic Seaboard	Victim	Murder

Equivalence class 1, Equivalence class 2 (Global recoding)

Equivalence class 1, Equivalence class 2, Equivalence class 3 (Local recoding)

Fig. 4. Local versus global recoding: example

Generalisation is usually accompanied by suppression of portions or whole parts of attribute values, or whole rows in order to prevent linking attacks. For instance, we suppress explicit identifiers like "names" and "telephone numbers" from the data. In suppression the previous attribute value is replaced by "*". For instance $firstname = $ "John" is replaced by $firstname = $ "*"; likewise to alter portions of attribute values, and $ZIPCODE = $ "47982" could be transformed to $ZIPCODE = $ "479**".

Attribute generalisation can be done either by using a *global/full domain* generalisation model, or a *local recoding* generalisation model. In global generalisation [26], the occurrence of a specific attribute value is always generalised to the same level. For example, if age 18 is generalised to 18–87 for one tuple, then all tuples with a value of 18 for the age attribute are generalised to 18–87. In local recoding models [40] generalisations are contextualised to ECs. For example, attribute age 18 might be recoded to 18–87 in one EC and to 18–23 in another EC. Once the data has been processed and generalised, the next step is to find a suitable balance between information loss and privacy. Minimising information loss is useful in ensuring data usability while maximising privacy ensures adequate data protection from adversarial access. Since high levels of information loss impact negatively on data utility, we need a method of minimising information loss in the CG-Kanon, CG-Diverse, and *t*-clustering algorithms. We discuss our proposed information loss model in the following section.

3.3 Information Loss and Severity Weighting

Once the data has been pre-processed by generalisation and suppression, our next step is to find a balance between the levels of information loss and privacy. Minimising information loss is useful for data usability in terms of querying, while maximising privacy ensures data protection. In line with our goal of multi-objective optimisation, we employ a piece-wise function to handle information loss on both categorical and numerical data.

$$IL_{d,i}(a) = \begin{cases} \frac{k(a)_{p,total} - 1}{P - 1} & \text{if categorical} \\ \frac{t_{d,i}(a)_{max} - t_{d,i}(a)_{min}}{T(a)_{max} - T(a)_{min}} & \text{if numerical} \end{cases} \tag{1}$$

where the Information Loss Metric is given by:

$$LM_i(a) = \sum_{d \in D} \sum_{a \in A} IL_{d,i}(a) \tag{2}$$

To minimise information loss, we employ a weighting scheme for the loss metric which enables authorised end users to prioritise specific attributes during anonymisation. By this we mean that the data owner can decide to specify the Quasi-Identifiers (QIDs) that should contain more information without negatively impacting on data privacy. The weighting scheme acts as a sort of utility function that can be adjusted dynamically to allow the data owner decide what levels of privacy to sacrifice in favour of query result accuracy without negatively impacting on the overall privacy of the data. The weighted information loss metric ($LM_{CG,i}$) at the ith iteration of the CG-Kanon algorithm (that is we evaluate different attribute combinations for Q_T to determine which one produces the lowest information loss and highest privacy at some given point) is computed as follows.

$$LM_{CG,i} = \sum_{d \in D} \sum_{a \in A} w_a \times IL_{d,i}(a) = w_a \times LM_i(a) \tag{3}$$

where w_a is the weight assigned to attribute $a \in A$ by the data owner. Finally, to facilitate automated anonymisation we use a sensitive attribute severity weighting $S(c)$ where $c \in SA$. SA is the list of sensitive attributes and $S(\cdot)$ maps the sensitive attribute category to its weight.

Example 2. In Table 3, SA denotes the list of offences (sensitive attribute) and $S(\cdot)$ maps the crime category to its weight, which in this case is simply the guideline sentence duration (in time - months, years...) for a given crime. So, $S(\text{Theft}) = 5$ indicates a sentence of 5 years. We note that following this scale, the risk of privacy loss for a tuple containing *"Robbery"* is higher than for a tuple with *"Disorderly Conduct"*.

Table 1. Crime severity weightings

Crime	Severity
Embezzlement	3
Disorderly conduct	3
Theft	5
Drunken driving	5
Robbery	7

We now describe our automated anonymisation algorithms, namely CG-Kanon and CG-Diverse that are extensions of the k-anonymisation and l-diversity algorithms respectively (Table 1).

3.4   CG-Kanon Algorithm

Our proposed CG-Kanon scheme uses the severity weighting and bucketisation (as is the case in k-anonymisation, classifying tuples based on quasi-identifier similarity), to hide tuples with highly sensitive values in larger equivalence classes (ECs) while tuples of lower sensitivity are classified in smaller ECs. For instance, a tuple concerning a "Robbery" is classified in a 20-anonymity EC while "theft" could be placed in a lower level EC say, 5-anonymity. This idea of hiding more sensitive values in larger ECs does not affect the absolute level of k-anonymity for different sensitive attribute categories. It is instead a relative statement regarding the level of k-anonymity required for different sensitive attributes in the anonymised dataset.

The CG-Kanon algorithm begins by determining a set of quasi-identifiers $Q_T = \{q_T(1), ..., q_T(y)\}$ which are basically a series of different attribute combinations that when combined with SA, can be used to uniquely identify individual tuples in the dataset. Based on these q_T, generalisation and suppression are applied as described in Sect. 3.2. Once generalisation is complete, we obtain a series of candidate datasets namely $D'(q_T)$ for each quasi-identifier combination. We must now proceed to define the sizes of equivalence classes (ECs) in order to classify the data for anonymity. To do this, we compute an absolute required minimum level of k-anonymity (k_{min}) for the dataset and use k_{min} to guarantee a global minimum level of k-anonymity that all ECs must adhere to in the dataset. We compute k_{min} as follows:

$$k_{min} = \max\left(k_{cons}, \min\left(S_D(\cdot)\right)\right) \tag{4}$$

where k_{cons} is a fixed minimum level of k and $S_D(\cdot)$ is the set of all severities for the dataset D. The definition of k_{min} shows that the global minimum level of k-anonymity is fixed at k_{cons} or at the lowest level of attribute sensitivity in the dataset when $\min\left(S_D(\cdot)\right) > k_{cons}$. If $k_{cons} = 5$ and $\min\left(S_D(\cdot)\right) = 3$ then $k_{min} = 5$. However if $\min\left(S_D(\cdot)\right) = 7$ then $k_{min} = 7$ instead. The CG-Kanon scheme uses k_{min} as the k-anonymity baseline when deciding on appropriate ECs for tuples based on severity weighting. Once k_{min} has been computed, we compute

---

Algorithm 1. CG-Kanon

1: **function** ANONYMISE(D, D', Q_T)
2:     $Q_T = \{q_T(1), ..., q_T(y)\}$ - set of quasi-identifier combinations
3:     **for** $i = 1$ to y **do**
4:         $\forall q_T(i) \in Q_T$ - Generalisation and suppression on D
5:         Generate $D'(q_T(i))$ - Candidate datasets for classification
6:         $k_{min} = max(k_{cons}, min(S'_D(\cdot)))$
7:         $\forall D'(q_T(i)$ - compute $SP_{d,i} = \frac{S_d(c)}{e_{d,i}}$ and $SP_{tot,i} = \sum_{d \in D} SP_{d,i}$
8:         $FF_i^{CG-Kanon} = \frac{1}{max(SP_{tot,i}, LM_{CG,i})}$
9:     $\forall q_T(i)$ return most fit $D'(q_T(i))$ - low information loss and high privacy

---

the severity penalty for each classification since the CG-Kanon scheme requires this information to optimise the information loss and privacy cost-benefit trade-off. The severity penalty determines the level of loss of privacy for a single tuple $d \in D(\cdot)$ and is computed as follows.

$$SP_{d,i} = \frac{S_d(c)}{|e_{d,i}|} \tag{5}$$

where $D(\cdot)$ is the dataset, $S_d(c)$ is the severity weight of sensitive attribute $c \in d$, and E is the set of ECs such that $|e_{d,i}|$ is the size of the EC that a tuple d is classified in during the ith iteration of the CG-Kanon scheme (that is when CG-Kanon evaluates $D'(q_T(i))$).

Example 3. From the severity penalty computation, highly sensitive attributes in small ECs result in high penalties and vice versa. So, if a "murder" report with a severity weighting of 25 were located in a 5-anonymity EC, a penalty of $\frac{25}{5} = 5$ is generated. An incident of "theft" with a severity weighting of 5 generates a severity penalty of 1, indicating that this information is comparatively less sensitive. The CG-Kanon scheme uses the severity penalty as a criterion besides, information utility, to determine tuple placement in ECs to minimise the overall sensitive information exposure risk.

Finally, the CG-Kanon scheme must compute the aggregate severity penalty, $SP_{tot,i}$, for the entire dataset, to determine whether the obtained anonymised dataset satisfies at least the threshold goals of privacy and utility. $SP_{tot,i}$ is computed as follows:

$$SP_{tot,i} = \sum_{d \in D} SP_{d,i} \tag{6}$$

and expresses the total severity penalty for the dataset as the summation of the severity penalties of the individual tuples. The $SP_{tot,i}$ is then feed into a fitness function to decide whether each tuple in D satisfies both objectives. We express the fitness function as follows:

$$FF_i^{CG-Kanon} = \frac{1}{\max\left(SP_{tot,i}, LM_{CG,i}\right)} \tag{7}$$

So, the result for $FF_i^{CG-Kanon}$ at iteration i is the inverse of the maximum of $SP_{tot,i}$ and $LM_{CG,i}$. Recall that a high $SP_{tot,i}$ indicates a strong risk of privacy exposure, while a high $LM_{CG,i}$ indicates a high level of information loss. Therefore, it is desirable that the fitness function generates results that iteratively converge towards a high value for $FF_i^{CG-Kanon}$, expressed by low values of $SP_{tot,i}$ and $LM_{CG,i}$ respectively. Algorithm 1, summaries our description of how CG-Kanon works.

The main drawback of the CG-Kanon algorithm is that, depending on tuple distribution, the diversity of the sensitive attributes in large ECs can be quite low and this negatively impacts on privacy. As well, a large proportion of tuples are suppressed to satisfy the minimum level of k-anonymity which results in high information loss. We addressed this by limiting the size of ECs to a pre-defined threshold size and as we discuss in Sect. 5, found that this reduces the number of suppressions to satisfy k_{min}-anonymity. We still have the caveat of inferential attacks and so augment our CG-Kanon scheme with the CG-Diverse scheme (l-diversity algorithm inspired) to help circumvent these attacks.

3.5   CG-Diverse Scheme

In CG-Diverse we extend CG-Kanon by using $SP_{tot,i}$ instead, to classify tuples into ECs. The CG-Diverse scheme computes the average severity, AS_D, for D as well as the EC average severity weighting AS_e. The AS_D is computed for D and is used to start the anonymisation process to ensure that the target level of l-diversity in D is such that $l = AS_D$. We compute AS_D as follows:

$$AS_D = \frac{\sum_{d \in D} S_d(c)}{|D|} \tag{8}$$

A high AS_D implies a higher level of diversity in the entire dataset. As a stopping criterion for deciding when an acceptable level of k_{min} and AS_D has been satisfied by all the ECs, we bound the l-diversity range with the severity weighting scale and use AS_D to compute the fitness of the dataset with respect to privacy and utility. We employ the following modified fitness function, expressed as follows:

$$FF_i^{CG-Diverse} = \frac{1}{\max\left(AS_{D,i}, LM_{CG,i}\right)} \tag{9}$$

However, as mentioned before suppressing the ECs that fail to meet the required

---

Algorithm 2. CG-Diverse

1: **function** ANONYMISE(D, D', Q_T)
2:     $Q_T = \{q_T(1), ..., q_T(y)\}$ - set of quasi-identifier combinations
3:     **for** $i = 1$ to y **do**
4:         $\forall q_T(i) \in Q_T$ - Generalisation and suppression on D
5:         Generate $D'(q_T(i))$ - Candidate datasets for classification
6:         $k_{min} = max(k_{cons}, min(S'_D(\cdot)))$
7:         $\forall D'(q_T(i)$ - compute $AS_{D'(q_T(i))} = \frac{\sum_{d \in D'(q_T(i))} S_d(c)}{D'(q_T(i))}$
8:         $FF_i^{CG-Diverse} = \frac{1}{max(AS_{D'(q_T(i))}, LM_{CG,i})}$
9:         $\forall q_T(i)$ return most fit $D'(q_T(i))$ - low information loss and high privacy
10:        $\forall e \in D'(q_T(i))$ compute $AS_e = \frac{\sum_{d \in D'(q_T(i))} S_d(c)}{\|e\|}$ - Ensure diversity

---

levels of AS_D and k_{min} would result in a high level of information loss. Therefore, we alleviate this problem by identifying ECs with a lower average severity (but adequate relative diversity) to avoid high suppression rates. This is achieved by assessing the privacy of individual ECs that do not meet the global AS_D-diversity requirement. To this end the EC average severity weighting AS_e is computed as follows:

$$AS_e = \frac{\sum_{d \in D} S_d(c)}{|e|} \tag{10}$$

The AS_e of an EC is compared to the relative diversity l_e, and if $AS_e > l_e$ the tuples in the EC are generalised to the highest possible level to avoid suppression. Alternatively, when the diversity is higher than AS_e no changes are made. We note that this procedure is computationally inexpensive since it simply requires comparing AS_e with the actual observed diversity of the EC. Algorithm 2, summaries the operation of the CG-Diverse algorithm.

Example 4. Table 2 shows the average severity measures calculated for a given sample dataset. The $AS_e = 5$ is calculated as follows: $\frac{5+3+7+5+5}{5}$ using the crime severity weightings given in Table 3. By considering Table 3, and Eqs. 8 and 10, the l-diversity range can be restricted to between 3–25, depending on the underlying dataset. Yet requiring ECs to satisfy the global level of AS_D-diversity might be too restrictive. We alleviate this issue by moving tuples between ECs to minimise the information loss due to suppression. For instance, in Table 2 we observe that in the 5-anonymity EC, "Robbery" has a severity of 7 which implies an inference risk. CG-diverse handles such cases by using the AS_e to move the tuple to the more appropriate 7-anonymity EC as highlighted in Table 2.

Table 2. Average severity versus diversity

Age	Crime	Diversity (Equivalence Class)	AS_D (Dataset)	AS_e (Equivalence Class)
18 - 22	Theft	4	11	5.0
18 - 22	Embezzlement	4	11	5.0
18 - 22	Robbery	4	11	5.0
18 - 22	Drunken Driving	4	11	5.0
18 - 22	Theft	4	11	5.0
18 - 87	Rape	8	11	7.0
18 - 87	Vandalism	8	11	7.0
18 - 87	Robbery	8	11	7.0
18 - 87	Assault	8	11	7.0
18 - 87	Murder	8	11	7.0

We are now ready to discuss our proposed t-clustering algorithm, which draws on t-closeness principles but uses clustering as the classification mechanism for forming equivalence classes.

4 t-Closeness Anonymisation as a Clustering Problem

The t-closeness anonymisation approach provides data anonymity by ensuring that the distance between the distribution of a sensitive attribute in an equivalence class and the distribution of sensitive attributes in the dataset is no greater than a threshold value of t. As mentioned before, this approach to privacy enforcement on shared micro-data is performance intensive. We address this problem by using clustering to classify the data to ensure anonymity. This results in an improved time complexity of $O(m^2 \log n)$ in comparison to $2^{O(n^2)O(m)}$ in the number of operations required for the average case standard t-closeness algorithm.

t-closeness anonymisation builds on k-anonymisation [29] where the principle is to categorise tuples into equivalence classes of size $k \geq 2$ such that every combination of quasi-identifier values can be indistinctly matched to at least k individuals. A high value of k makes it harder for the adversary to de-anonymise the data but also results in a high level of information loss thereby negatively impacting the utility of the dataset. So, a tradeoff between privacy and information loss is needed to generate usable anonymised datasets. We begin by providing some notations and definitions of the terminology we will be using to support our algorithm.

4.1   Notation for t-clustering

We extend CG-Kanon and CG-Diverse to adhere to t-closeness properties such that all the ECs in D are formed by ensuring that the distance between the distribution of sensitive attributes $S(a)$ in each EC and the distribution of $S(a)$ in D is less than or equal to the threshold value t [29]. Building on this, we describe t-closeness as a clustering problem as follows:

Definition 4 (t-Clustering). Given a micro-data set D, a distance measure $dist(t_i, t_j)$ that describes the similarity between the two tuples t_i and t_j, where t_j is the centroid of a cluster (equivalence class) e_l, $S(a_{e_l})$ the entropy of the severity weighting of a sensitive attribute in e_l, and $S(a_D)$ the cross-entropy of the severity weighting of a sensitive attribute in e_l and D. We define the t-clustering as a mapping of t_i to e_l, such that $e_l \cap e_y = \emptyset$, and $\|e_l\| \geq k$, such that $\forall t_i, t_j \in e_l$, $Dist(t_i, t_j) \leq Dist(t_i, t_l)$ and $Dist(S(a_{e_l}), S(a_D))) \leq Dist(S(a_{e_y}), S(a_D))$.

Based on the definition of the t-clustering problem, we express the optimal solution to the t-clustering problem as follows:

Definition 5 (Optimal t-Clustering). Given a micro-data set D, a distance measure $dist(t_i, t_j)$, and a distance measure $Dist(S(a_e), S(a_D))$ we define optimal t-clustering as a mapping of t_i to e, such that in addition to satisfying t-clustering (Definition 1), cluster sizes are maximised, while at the same time minimising $Dist(S(a_e), S(a_D))$, and $dist(t_i, t_j)$.

4.2 t-Clustering Anonymisation

We ensure t-closeness anonymity with clustering, by computing the minimum cluster size required to guarantee a global minimum level of t-closeness for all clusters. Drawing from CG-Kanon, the clustering algorithm uses a value k_{min} as the minimum cluster size and moves tuples into appropriate clusters based on the calculated severity weighting as well as the distance measure (distance between a given tuple and the tuple representing the cluster centroid). This ensures that a minimum cluster size will be adhered to by all the clusters created and in addition a minimum level of anonymity for the tuples within each cluster is guaranteed.

Based on the cluster size, we must determine which tuples to either include or exclude from a cluster. As a first step from the definition a clusters, we evaluate the relative distance between tuples to decide on which tuples to classify in the same cluster. In order to compute the inter-tuple distance, we consider both categorical and numerical attributes. The distance between categorical attributes is measured using the Jaccard's coefficient and is defined as follows:

$$sim_{d_x, d_y} = \frac{Q_{d_x} \cap Q_{d_y}}{Q_{d_x} \cup Q_{d_y}} \tag{11}$$

where d_x, d_y are two given tuples, Q_{d_x} and Q_{d_y} are the respective quasi-identifiers for d_x and d_y, and d_y represents the centroid of the cluster into which d_x is classified. We note that the value of $\sim (d_x, d_y)$ varies between 0 and 1, with 1 indicating a strong similarity (small) distance between the tuples, and 0 indicating a strong dissimilarity (high distance) between the tuples, based on the quasi-identifier attributes.

However, looking solely at attribute similarity to decide on classifications, can result in a high number of outliers (information loss due to misclassification/inability to classify) that get suppressed from the generated anonymised dataset. Suppressions increase the rate of information loss, so we also look at numerical values and compute the Euclidean distance to compare the difference between attributes by using an n-dimensional space function which is represented as follows:

$$Dist(d_x, d_y) = \sqrt{\left(d_x\,(a_1) - d_y\,(a_1))^2 + \dots. + (d_i\,(a_m) - d_y\,(a_m))^2 \right)} \qquad (12)$$

where a_i represents an attribute in Q. Tuples separated by a small Euclidean distance are classified in the same cluster. The next step requires us to consider the sensitive attribute severity weightings. To this end, we compute the average severity weighting AS_D for D and the average severity weighting AS_e for e for a given cluster (equivalence class). We use both values in the same way that t-closeness is used to decide on tuple classifications based on statistical distributions of sensitive attributes, and also to prevent skewness as well as similarity attacks.

We then evaluate the level of loss of privacy with respect to information loss in forming the clusters. This is in line with using the t parameter in the t-closeness scheme as a method of optimising the utility of the dataset, while at the same time enforcing privacy. To this end, we use a fitness function to decide on the value of t to use in the clustering algorithm and express the fitness function as follows:

$$FF_i^{t-clustering} = \frac{1}{Max\,(AS_{D,i}, LM_{CG,it})} = t \qquad (13)$$

when t is low this implies a high degree of loss of either privacy or information, while a high value is an indication of a reasonably good balance between privacy and data utility. Finally, to evaluate the level of diversity of sensitive attributes in e with respect to D, we compute the Kullback-Leibler distance between AS_e and AS_D, to determine whether or not the variation of sensitive attributes in e enforces enforces information utility and privacy. We use the Kullback-Leibler distance (divergence) to provide a measure of entropy which is important in determining the maximum likelihood of inference leading to privacy disclosures due to skewness and similarity attacks. So the Kullback-Leibler distance provides a standard measure for assessing anonymised datasets from the statistical perspective. An added advantage is that because it is not as cost intensive to compute as the Earth mover's distance measure used in the t-closeness scheme [29, 30], we are able to make performance gains in computing the anonymised dataset. We note also at this stage that our added severity weighting metric for the sensitive attributes, compensates for any weaknesses the Kullback-Leibler

---

Algorithm 3. CG-Diverse

1: **function** ANONYMISE(D, D', Q_T)
2:     $Q_T = \{q_T(1), ..., q_T(y)\}$ - set of quasi-identifier combinations
3:     **for** $i = 1$ to y **do**
4:         $\forall q_T(i) \in Q_T$ - Generalisation and suppression on D
5:         Generate $D'(q_T(i))$ - Candidate datasets for clustering
6:         $k_{min} = max(k_{cons}, min(S'_D(\cdot)))$ - minimum cluster size
7:         $\forall e \in D'(q_T(i))$ compute $centroid(d_e)$
8:         $\forall d \in e$ compute $sim(d, d_e)$ and $Dist(d, d_e)$
9:         $\forall D'(q_T(i)$ - compute $AS_{D'(q_T(i))} = \frac{\sum_{d \in D'(q_T(i))} S_d(c)}{D'(q_T(i))}$
10:         $FF_i^{t-clustering} = \frac{1}{max(AS_{D'(q_T(i))}, LM_{CG,i})}$
11:         $\forall e \in D'(q_T(i))$ compute $Dist(AS_e, AS_{D'(q_T(i))}) = \sum AS_e \log \frac{AS_e}{AS_{D'(q_T(i))}}$
12:         **if** $Dist(AS_e, AS_{D'(q_T(i))}) \leq FF_i^{t-clustering}$ **then**
13:             Return $D'(q_T(i))$ - low information loss and high privacy

---

divergence may represent in terms of accounting for the semantics of the dataset in ensuring privacy. We compute this as follows:

$$Dist\,(AS_e, AS_D) = \sum AS_e \log \frac{AS_e}{AS_D} \leq t \qquad (14)$$

where

$$\sum AS_e \log \frac{AS_e}{AS_D} = H(AS_e) - H(AS_e, AS_D)$$

such that $H(AS_e) = \sum AS_e \log AS_e$ is the entropy of AS_e and $H(AS_e, AS_D)$ is the cross entropy of AS_e as well as AS_D

When $Dist\,(AS_e, AS_D) \leq t$ the anonymised dataset mimics t-closeness by ensuring that sensitive attributes are classified according to severity of exposure. So for example, we would classify $S\,(Cancer)$ in a larger equivalence class and together with values that allow for a mixed distribution of sensitive attributes. In this way the chance of identifying users based on similar chronic or serious illnesses is reduced, in comparison to classifying $S\,(Cancer)$ in a cluster that is dominated by minor illnesses. When $Dist\,(AS_e, AS_D) \not\leq t$, we rerun the algorithm from the top (Generalisation Algorithm - Algorithm 1) to re-compute cluster structures. Algorithm 2, provides a summarised version of our clustering scheme.

In the next section we provide a complexity analysis of the average case running time for our proposed scheme and compare this to the t-closeness scheme.

4.3 t-Closeness and t-Clustering: Complexity Analysis

In terms of the complexity analysis of the t-closeness anonymisation algorithm, we know from Liang and Yuan's work [30] that the t-closeness anonymisation problem is NP-Hard. In fact computing the number of operations required to search the dataset is on the $O(n^2)$ where n is the number of tuples in the dataset D. This is due to the fact that we make the comparisons for each tuple with respect to every other tuple in the dataset. So this essentially requires going through the dataset on a power of 2. In addition, considering attributes we a complexity of $O(m)$ where m is the number of attributes. This happens because the attributes are bound to the tuples and tuple comparisons involve attribute comparisons. Finally because we compare both within equivalence classes and within the dataset the overall time requires for the various operations involved is $2^{O(n^2)}O(m)$.

With respect to t-clustering, we know that clustering problems are in general NP-Hard. However, with our heuristics we are able to drop the performance cost to $O(n^2 \log m)$ where n and m represent the tuples and attributes in the dataset D. We achieve this by dividing up D into at most n clusters, computations required for classification are in $O(n)$ and the fraction of attributes that are critical for classification are in $O(\log m)$, which results in a total time complexity of $O(n^2 \log m)$. We are now ready to discuss our experimental platform, results and analysis.

5 Results and Analysis

We demonstrate the feasibility of our proposed automated data anonymisation scheme with results from experiments conducted on a prototype crime data collection application [38]. A host server with an Ubuntu server 12.04 operating system running on a 64 bit machine with 8GB RAM and a processor speed of 3.2GHz (Intel Xeon E3-1230 Quad Core) was used. The algorithms were implemented in Java 1.7.0_65 while Python 2.7.3 was used to run the web server. A PostgreSQL 9.1 database management system and a Postfix email server were used to store the dataset, both plain and anonymised.

ID	Firstname	Lastname	Gender	Age	Address	Suburb	Region	Cell number	Reporter type	Occurrence	Time	Crime type
1	Heather	Cornish	F	30	Franklin Court	Tamboerskloof	City Bowl	0893068604	Victim	Bishopscourt	9	Drug related
2	Matt	Brown	M	49	Route 30	Maitland	Northern Suburbs	0866103857	Victim	Monte Vista	14	Theft
3	Anna	James	F	63	Durham Road	Schotse Kloof (Malay Quarter)	City Bowl	0898842854	Victim	University Estate	15	Corruption or Embezzlement
4	Joe	Simpson	M	26	Virginia Street	Edgemead	Northern Suburbs	0874702036	Victim	Kenilworth	8.5	Illegal gambling
5	Virginia	Dyer	F	67	Overlook Circle	Kreupelbosch	Southern Suburbs	0812064642	Victim	Oranjezicht	16	Illegal gambling
6	Andrea	Ellison	F	62	Front Street North	Bishopscourt	Southern Suburbs	0812559236	Witness	Maitland	12.5	Drunken Driving
7	Alan	Butler	M	23	2nd Avenue	Tamboerskloof	City Bowl	0826338733	Victim	Observatory	6.5	Burglary

Fig. 5. Crime dataset: example

Our dataset consisted of 250000 records as an average of the number of crime reports per police station in a month. This is considering the fact that the crime data was generated with South Africa as an example scenario where crime report rates are estimate at approximately 2–3 million per year [19]. The attributes considered included "Age", "Suburb", "Reporter", "Crime" and "Reporter".

Sensitive attributes such as "Names" and "Date of Birth" were removed during pre-processing. Figure 5 provides an example of the composition of our crime dataset.

Age	Suburb	Reporter	Crime	Diversity (equivalence class)	AS (dataset)	AS (equivalence class)
Equivalence class 1						
18_22	Cape Town	Proxy	Drunken Driving	6	11	5.5
18_22	Cape Town	Proxy	Drug related	6	11	5.5
18_22	Cape Town	Proxy	Disorderly conduct	6	11	5.5
18_22	Cape Town	Proxy	Theft	6	11	5.5
18_22	Cape Town	Proxy	Corruption or Embezzlement	6	11	5.5
18_22	Cape Town	Proxy	Robbery	6	11	5.5
18_22	Cape Town	Proxy	Robbery	6	11	5.5
Equivalence class 2						
18_22	Cape Town	Reporter	Drunken Driving	4	11	5.0
18_22	Cape Town	Reporter	Corruption or Embezzlement	4	11	5.0
18_22	Cape Town	Reporter	Robbery	4	11	5.0
18_22	Cape Town	Reporter	Theft	4	11	5.0
18_22	Cape Town	Reporter	Theft	4	11	5.0
Equivalence class 3						
18_22	Cape Town	Witness	Other	8	11	7.5
18_22	Cape Town	Witness	Family or Domestic Violence	8	11	7.5
18_22	Cape Town	Witness	Other	8	11	7.5
18_22	Cape Town	Witness	Theft	8	11	7.5
18_22	Cape Town	Witness	Rape	8	11	7.5
18_22	Cape Town	Witness	Burglary	8	11	7.5
18_22	Cape Town	Witness	Drug related	8	11	7.5
18_22	Cape Town	Witness	Assault	8	11	7.5
18_22	Cape Town	Witness	Vandalism	8	11	7.5
Equivalence class 4						
18_87	City Bowl	Proxy	Theft	11	11	8.5
18_87	City Bowl	Proxy	Other	11	11	8.5
18_87	City Bowl	Proxy	Murder	11	11	8.5
18_87	City Bowl	Proxy	Arson	11	11	8.5
18_87	City Bowl	Proxy	Drunken Driving	11	11	8.5
18_87	City Bowl	Proxy	Other	11	11	8.5
18_87	City Bowl	Proxy	Forgery or Fraud	11	11	8.5
18_87	City Bowl	Proxy	Family or Domestic Violence	11	11	8.5
18_87	City Bowl	Proxy	Drug related	11	11	8.5
18_87	City Bowl	Proxy	Burglary	11	11	8.5
18_87	City Bowl	Proxy	Drug related	11	11	8.5
18_87	City Bowl	Proxy	Illegal gambling	11	11	8.5
18_87	City Bowl	Proxy	Drunken Driving	11	11	8.5
18_87	City Bowl	Proxy	Disorderly conduct	11	11	8.5
Equivalence class 5						
58_62	Atlantic Seaboard	Reporter	Disorderly conduct	6	11	5.5
58_62	Atlantic Seaboard	Reporter	Theft	6	11	5.5
58_62	Atlantic Seaboard	Reporter	Drunken Driving	6	11	5.5
58_62	Atlantic Seaboard	Reporter	Drug related	6	11	5.5
58_62	Atlantic Seaboard	Reporter	Corruption or Embezzlement	6	11	5.5
58_62	Atlantic Seaboard	Reporter	Robbery	6	11	5.5
Equivalence class 6						
58_62	Cape Town	Reporter	Vandalism	5	11	5.0
58_62	Cape Town	Reporter	Drunken Driving	5	11	5.0
58_62	Cape Town	Reporter	Illegal gambling	5	11	5.0
58_62	Cape Town	Reporter	Burglary	5	11	5.0
58_62	Cape Town	Reporter	Assault	5	11	5.0

Fig. 6. Average severity weighting distribution: example

Referring to Figs. 4, 5, and 6, quasi-identifiers which more closely match the k-anonymity requirement for CG-Kanon were generated before the anonymisation process. This was done by generalising attributes to the highest node in the generalisation hierarchy (tree) for ECs that do not meet the k-anonymity requirement. We qualitatively assessed the anonymised data produced by the CG-Kanon and the CG-Diverse algorithms, by considering aspects such as information loss, classification accuracy and the impact of the weighting scheme on linking and inference attacks. In order to obtain the data shown in Fig. 7, we transformed the data in Fig. 6 by using an adjustment factor to compensate for biases introduced through the data reporting and collection process [6]. Bias is basically what w consider to be the difference between the reported frequency distribution of crime reports and the true (real-life) frequency distribution. This idea is based on the fact that we are able to determine the true distribution of crime and we assume that third party data analytics service providers are interested in the true underlying statistics of crime in general not only that gathered through our crime reporting framework. In practice, we may take the true underlying distribution of crime to be historical data gathered by law enforcement agencies over several years. Admittedly in the developing world, such data may have been tampered or destroyed but we do not take this into consideration in this paper.

Crime	Generated / Observed data	True distribution	z_c	adj_c
Corruption or Embezzlement	555	650	13.88	4
Rape	574	600	1.13	1
Disorderly conduct	561	500	7.44	3
Drug related	729	760	1.26	1
Murder	777	300	758.43	28
Burglary	699	1700	589.41	24
Drunken Driving	605	620	0.36	1
Robbery	648	1000	123.90	11
Forgery or Fraud	627	650	0.81	1
Family or Domestic Violence	611	550	6.77	3
Illegal gambling	670	650	0.62	1
Vandalism	656	600	5.23	2
Assault	593	600	0.08	0
Arson	535	500	2.45	2
Theft	634	1200	266.96	16
Other	526	500	1.35	1

Fig. 7. Data distributions and adjustment factors: example

From hypothesis testing we know that the random variable Z_c as defined below, has a normal ($N(0,1)$) distribution:

$$z_c = \frac{(O_c - E_c)^2}{E_c}$$

where E_c is the expected frequency, and O_c is the observed frequency. The summation across all crime categories then gives a χ^2 random variable to be used for goodness-of-fit. based on this we calculated the adjustment factor for each crime category as $adj_c = \sqrt{z_c}$ (see Fig. 7).

Throughout the discussion of the results we refer to an anonymisation based on the weightings of the quasi-identifiers (QIDs) used during the anonymisation. This will be denoted as $A_{w_{Age}} : S_{w_{Suburb}} : R_{w_{Reporter}}$. Figure 8 provides information on the classification accuracy of the CG-Kanon and CG-Diverse anonymisation schemes to support the claims we make about the efficiency in terms of low information loss for the modified k-anonymisation and l-diversity schemes that we proposed.

For example where equal weights were assigned to the QIDs this will be denoted as an $A1 : S1 : R1$ anonymisation, similarly where we use $A10 : S5 : R1$ weights of 10, 5, and 1 were used for the Age, Suburb, Reporter attributes respectively. $k_{constant}$ was set to 5 for all results on CG-Kanon anonymisation.

Our minimum crime severity level for the data was set to 3 and in this case, $k_{min} = 5$. For CG-Diverse, we set our lowest diversity level to 3 for all anonymisation runs as a standard minimum privacy level. Since on average,

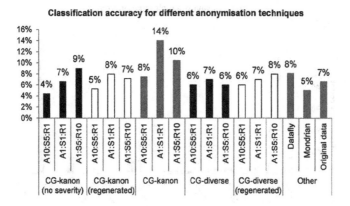

Fig. 8. Classification accuracy of CG-Kanon and CG-Diverse

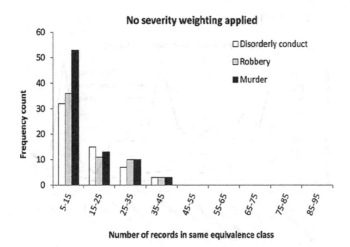

Fig. 9. Severity impact on dataset (No Severity Weighting)

the lower severity crimes were located in such ECs, this was acceptable. All algorithms were allowed to run for 30 min after which the algorithm was stopped.

Pre-experiment sampling revealed that running for shorter periods, say 15 min resulted in high severity penalties and information loss for larger ECs, while running for resulted in only between 3–6% of tuples meeting the minimum anonymity level. Running for much longer resulted in better success rates, but at the price of time.

Once stopped the anonymised data was checked for compliance with the desired level of privacy. Tuples not satisfying the privacy criteria on termination were processed further according to the respective CG-Kanon and CG-Diverse algorithms. Figure 9 shows the CG-Kanon algorithm classifying data using ECs only with no severity weighting support. We note that the crimes are clustered

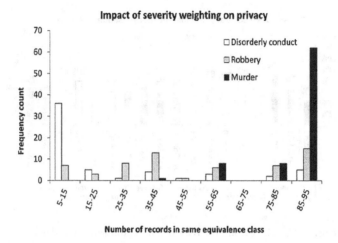

Fig. 10. Impact of severity weighting on privacy

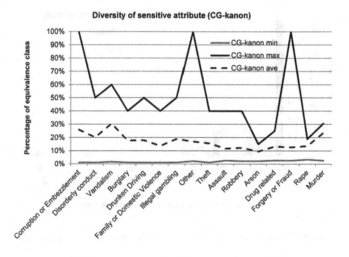

Fig. 11. Sensitive attributes frequency for CG-Kanon using A1:S1:R1

around smaller sized ECs which is good for protection against inference attacks, but bad for information loss. When the severity penalty is applied, we note as shown in Fig. 10 that more severe crimes are classified in larger ECs but this has the caveat of introducing inferential disclosure. For instance, from Fig. 10 one can see directly that more severe crime has a higher frequency with *"Murder"* being as high as 31%. We address this with the CG-Diverse scheme.

Furthermore, as shown in Figs. 11 and 12, based on the $A1 : S1 : R1$ weighting and an average severity level of 11, the global diversity and average severity of each EC is evaluated before suppressing the QIDs. When compared to Figs. 9 and 10, we note that the average diversity in CG-Kanon varies between 10% and

30% while that of CG-Diverse is much lower at 9% to 14% and in t-clustering the diversity is between 7% and 12%. This implies that risk of inferential disclosure is lower in t-clustering than in the CG-Kanon and CG-Diverse schemes, because by using the severity weightings we are able to distribute highly sensitive records into equivalence classes that make distinguishing individual record lower.

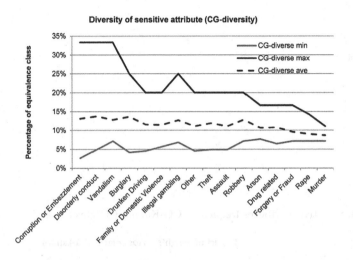

Fig. 12. Sensitive attributes frequency for CG-Diverse using A1:S1:R1

The desired lower frequency (i.e. higher diversity) for more severe crimes is evident in CG-diverse whereas in CG-Kanon there is no such correlation. More severe crimes (Rape and Murder) in this case actually have lower average diversity and consequently less risk of inferential exposure. In addition we see the deviation from the mean frequency for more severe crimes is lower as severity increases. So not only does the average diversity increase as crime severity increases but the variance decreases as well. This gives us more certainty that more severe crimes will be less vulnerable to inference attacks.

Finally, we note that l-diversity guarantees at least k-anonymity where $k = l$. We also consider the average diversity over all three schemes (CG-Kanon, CG-Diverse, and t-clustering) and note as expected that t-clustering has a higher diversity rate on average which is reflective of our expectations of protection against background attacks in line with the t-closeness anonymisation principle.

The lowest diversity of 3 may appear weak from the privacy perspective when compared to the global diversity of 11 but it is unlikely, practically speaking, that severe crime (sensitive data) will be included in such lower diversity ECs. For instance, if we revisit our earlier results for CG-Kanon where the most serious crime ("Murder") was in an EC of size 90 and still only achieved a 3-diversity.

Figures 13 and 14 show the aggregated information losses for different weighting schemes after termination of the algorithm. We selected three weighting schemes to monitor how the algorithms perform when attributes with varying

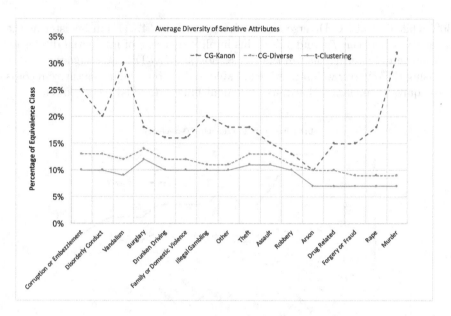

Fig. 13. Sensitive attributes frequency: CG-Kanon, CG-Diverse, and t-clustering

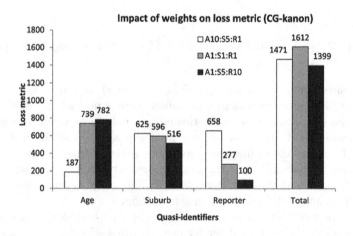

Fig. 14. Information loss for CG-Kanon

granularity are weighted differently. For instance the $A10 : S5 : R1$ scheme over-weights the *Age* attribute which is highly granular and under weighs the *Reporter* attribute, while $A1 : S5 : R10$ test the opposite scenario and $A1 : S1 : R1$ is equivalent to having no weighting scheme.

The marginal increase in information loss for CG-diverse relative to CG-Kanon seems quite acceptable given the improved privacy provided by CG-Diverse. For our results the information loss across the three weighting schemes

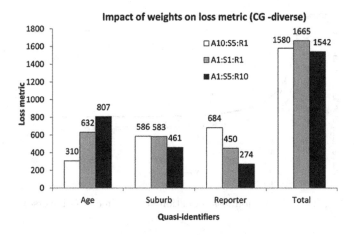

Fig. 15. Information loss for CG-Diverse

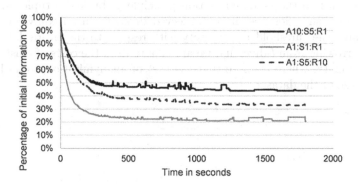

Fig. 16. Information loss reduction versus time (CG-Kanon)

was on average 7% higher for CG-diverse. However, this reduced data utility is acceptable given our desire for better anonymised data privacy.

One further insight relates to the number of parameters that are used for the fitness function in selecting QIDs. We see from Figs. 15 and 16 that information loss for CG-diverse is a much lower proportion of its starting value than for CG-Kanon. This is attributed to the fact that CG-Kanon searches for solutions that minimise both the information loss and the severity penalty, in addition to satisfying k-anonymity. While CG-diverse only minimises information loss and endeavours to meet the diversity requirement. The additional parameter (severity penalty) for CG-Kanon increases the search space and reduces the efficiency of the algorithm. For instance, at termination the reduction in the initial information loss for $A10 : S5 : R1$ in CG-diverse was 74% compared to 55% for CG-Kanon. In Fig. 17, we note that for an average cluster size (EC)

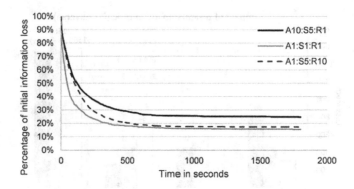

Fig. 17. Information loss reduction versus time (CG-Diverse)

of 7, information loss was on average 14.6% mainly because our t-clustering algorithm relies on the k-anonymisation principle to bucketise tuples and only seeks to establish t-closeness if the observed diversity in an equivalence class is less than t the threshold for diversity with respect to the entire dataset. As well by borrowing from l-diversity, we are able to drop the costs of clustering as shown in Fig. 18, where we note that the cost of anonymisation grows linearly with the size of the dataset.

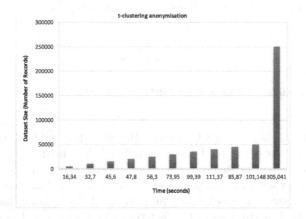

Fig. 18. t-Clustering time

We now present concluding statements and propose some ideas for future work.

6   Conclusions

We presented three algorithms namely, CG-Kanon, CG-diverse, and t-clustering that augment the standard k-anonymity and l-diverse algorithms to facilitate automatic classification and anonymisation of data. In particular, we considered crime data because it contains a large volume of sensitive data and is vulnerable to linking and inferential attacks. To match privacy with utility, we used a random sampling approach without replacement so, historical released reports were excluded from being selected in subsequent releases. The sampling approach also offers the advantage of reduced computational complexity and therefore runtime for our algorithms which is a plus for use in computationally constrained environments. To reduce information loss, we also used a fitness function to improve classification accuracy, and privacy. Our results demonstrate that CG-diverse incurs an average information loss of 7% over CG-Kanon, but with a diversity of between 9–14% in comparison to 10–30% CG-Kanon. So, we can conclude that, since CG-Diverse offers anonymity levels that are at least equal to CG-Kanon's, the percentage of information loss incurred does not significantly affect query response accuracy and in addition, provides stronger privacy guarantees than CG-Kanon.

We also considered a t-clustering scheme as a method of alleviating the performance cost of t-closeness anonymisation while at the same time offering better privacy protection than CG-Kanon and CG-Diverse, which is an advantage for low resource settings. Basically, what we did was build on the method of ranking sensitive attributes by a severity weighting proposed for the CG-Kanon and CG-Diverse scheme. The ranking system was used to classify tuples to enforce diversity, so that we do not always have to compute statistical distributions to satisfy t-closeness. The tuples are classified to minimise the risk of privacy disclosure of tuples containing high severity weight sensitive attributes. Clustering has the advantage of reducing the need for extensive attribute generalisation in order to classify tuples based on similarity. This is good, in addition, because it reduces the cost of information loss. As we have mentioned earlier, high levels of information loss make datasets unusable in practical situations. By considering severity weightings both for individual clusters and the entire dataset, we mimic the t-closeness principle, of seeking to distribute tuples in ways that ensure that the difference in distributions both within the equivalence classes and the entire dataset, does not surpass a threshold value of t. In this way, our proposed scheme also offers protection against skewness and similarity attacks. Finally, a further benefit of our scheme is that because it is not performance intensive, it can be used on low-powered, low-processing networks for guaranteeing privacy of data under data forwarding schemes.

Appendix A Notations: Summary

see Table 3.

Table 3. Notation

Symbol	Explanation
A	Attribute Space (set of attributes)
a	An attribute $\forall a \in A$
d	A tuple in the dataset D
$T(a)$	Generalisation hierarchy for numerical attributes
$K(a)$	Generalisation hierarchy for categorical attributes
$T(a)_{max}$	Upper limit for numerical attribute generalisations in D
$T(a)_{min}$	Lower limit for numerical attributes generalisations in D
$t(a)_{min}$	Lower limit for numerical attributes generalisations in d
$t(a)_{max}$	Upper limit for numerical attribute generalisations in d
$K(a)_{total}$	Total number of leaf nodes generated for $K(a)$
P	Number of parent nodes in $K(a)$
$K(a)_p$	sub-tree of $K(a)$ rooted at node $p \in P$
$K(a)_{p,total}$	Total number of leaf nodes in $K(a)_p$
$D(A_1, A_2, ..., A_n)$	Dataset with attributes
Q_T	Quasi-identifier
w_a	weighted attribute
$LM_{CG,i}$	weighted information loss for dataset at ith iteration
$IL_{d,i}(a)$	Information loss on categorical and numerical data
$LM_i(a)$	Information loss metric for attribute a
c	sensitive attribute (crime value)
AS_D	Average severity weighting for a dataset D
AS_e	Average severity weighting for an equivalence class e
$SP_{tot,i}$	Aggregate severity penalty for the dataset D
$SP_{d,i}$	Severity penalty for each tuple classification in e
$e_{d,i}$	An equivalence class associated with tuple d at the ith iteration
$S_d(c)$	Severity penalty for an attribute c, where c is a crime
$Dist(AS_e, AS_D)$	Distance between AS_e and AS_D
$H(AS_e)$	Entropy of AS_e
$H(AS_e, AS_D)$	Cross-entropy of AS_e and AS_D

References

1. Aggarwal, C.C.: On k-anonymity and the curse of dimensionality. In: Proceedings of the 31st International Conference on Very Large Data Bases, VLDB 2005, pp. 901–909. VLDB Endowment (2005)
2. Aggarwal, C.C.: On unifying privacy and uncertain data models. In: Proceedings of the 2008 IEEE 24th International Conference on Data Engineering, ICDE 2008, pp. 386–395. IEEE Computer Society, Washington, DC, USA (2008)
3. Aggarwal, C.C., Yu, P.S.: Privacy-Preserving Data Mining: Models and Algorithms, 1st edn. Springer Publishing Company Incorporated, New York (2008). https://doi.org/10.1007/978-0-387-70992-5
4. Aytug, H., Koehler, G.J.: New stopping criterion for genetic algorithms. Eur. J. Oper. Res. **126**(3), 662–674 (2000)
5. Bayardo, R.J., Agrawal, R.: Data privacy through optimal k-anonymization. In: 21st International Conference on Data Engineering (ICDE 2005), pp. 217–228, April 2005
6. Burke, M., Kayem, A.V.D.M.: K-anonymity for privacy preserving crime data publishing in resource constrained environments. In: 28th International Conference on Advanced Information Networking and Applications Workshops, AINA 2014 Workshops, Victoria, BC, Canada, 13–16 May 2014, pp. 833–840 (2014)
7. Ciglic, M., Eder, J., Koncilia, C.: k-anonymity of microdata with NULL values. In: Decker, H., Lhotská, L., Link, S., Spies, M., Wagner, R.R. (eds.) DEXA 2014. LNCS, vol. 8644, pp. 328–342. Springer, Cham (2014). https://doi.org/10.1007/ 978-3-319-10073-9_27
8. Ciriani, V., Vimercati, S.D.C., Foresti, S., Samarati, P.: k-Anonymous data mining: a survey. In: Aggarwal, C.C., Yu, P.S. (eds.) Privacy-Preserving Data Mining: Models and Algorithms, vol. 34, pp. 105–136. Springer, Boston (2008). https:// doi.org/10.1007/978-0-387-70992-5_5
9. Clifton, C., Tassa, T.: On syntactic anonymity and differential privacy. Trans. Data Priv. **6**(2), 161–183 (2013)
10. Dewri, R., Ray, I., Ray, I., Whitley, D.: Exploring privacy versus data quality trade-offs in anonymization techniques using multi-objective optimization. J. Comput. Secur. **19**(5), 935–974 (2011)
11. Dewri, R., Whitley, D., Ray, I., Ray, I.: A multi-objective approach to data sharing with privacy constraints and preference based objectives. In: Proceedings of the 11th Annual Conference on Genetic and Evolutionary Computation, GECCO 2009, pp. 1499–1506. ACM, New York (2009)
12. Dwork, C.: Differential privacy: a survey of results. In: Agrawal, M., Du, D., Duan, Z., Li, A. (eds.) TAMC 2008. LNCS, vol. 4978, pp. 1–19. Springer, Heidelberg (2008). https://doi.org/10.1007/978-3-540-79228-4_1
13. Dwork, C., McSherry, F., Nissim, K., Smith, A.: Calibrating noise to sensitivity in private data analysis. In: Halevi, S., Rabin, T. (eds.) TCC 2006. LNCS, vol. 3876, pp. 265–284. Springer, Heidelberg (2006). https://doi.org/10.1007/11681878_14
14. Dwork, C., Roth, A.: The algorithmic foundations of differential privacy. Found. Trends Theor. Comput. Sci. **9**(3–4), 211–407 (2014)
15. Fienberg, S.E., Jin, J.: Privacy-preserving data sharing in high dimensional regression and classification settings. J. Priv. Confid. **4**(1), 10 (2012)
16. Fredj, F.B., Lammari, N., Comyn-Wattiau, I.: Abstracting anonymization techniques: a prerequisite for selecting a generalization algorithm. Procedia Comput. Sci. **60**, 206–215 (2015)

17. Ghinita, G., Karras, P., Kalnis, P., Mamoulis, N.: Fast data anonymization with low information loss. In: Proceedings of the 33rd International Conference on Very Large Data Bases, VLDB 2007, pp. 758–769. VLDB Endowment (2007)
18. Ghosh, A., Roughgarden, T., Sundararajan, M.: Universally utility-maximizing privacy mechanisms. SIAM J. Comput. **41**(6), 1673–1693 (2012)
19. Gould, C., Burger, J., Newham, G.: The SAPS crime statistics: What they tell us and what they don't. S. Afr. Crime Quaterly, December 2012. https://www.issafrica.org/uploads/1crimestats.pdf
20. Islam, M.Z., Brankovic, L.: Privacy preserving data mining: a noise addition framework using a novel clustering technique. Knowl. Based Syst. **24**(8), 1214–1223 (2011)
21. Iyengar, V.S.: Transforming data to satisfy privacy constraints. In: Proceedings of the Eighth ACM SIGKDD International Conference on Knowledge Discovery and Data Mining, KDD 2002, pp. 279–288. ACM, New York (2002)
22. Kayem, A.V.D.M., Meinel, C.: Clustering heuristics for efficient t-closeness anonymisation. In: Benslimane, D., Damiani, E., Grosky, W.I., Hameurlain, A., Sheth, A., Wagner, R.R. (eds.) DEXA 2017. LNCS, vol. 10439, pp. 27–34. Springer, Cham (2017). https://doi.org/10.1007/978-3-319-64471-4_3
23. Kayem, A.V.D.M., Vester, C.T., Meinel, C.: Automated k-anonymization and l-diversity for shared data privacy. In: Hartmann, S., Ma, H. (eds.) DEXA 2016. LNCS, vol. 9827, pp. 105–120. Springer, Cham (2016). https://doi.org/10.1007/978-3-319-44403-1_7
24. Koufogiannis, F., Han, S., Pappas, G.J.: Optimality of the laplace mechanism in differential privacy. arXiv preprint arXiv:1504.00065 (2015)
25. Last, M., Tassa, T., Zhmudyak, A., Shmueli, E.: Improving accuracy of classification models induced from anonymized datasets. Inf. Sci. **256**, 138–161 (2014). Business Intelligence in Risk Management
26. LeFevre, K., DeWitt, D.J., Ramakrishnan, R.: Incognito: efficient full-domain k-anonymity. In: Proceedings of the 2005 ACM SIGMOD International Conference on Management of Data, SIGMOD 2005, pp. 49–60. ACM, New York (2005). http://doi.acm.org/10.1145/1066157.1066164
27. LeFevre, K., DeWitt, D.J., Ramakrishnan, R.: Workload-aware anonymization techniques for large-scale datasets. ACM Trans. Database Syst. (TODS) **33**(3), 17 (2008)
28. Li, C., Miklau, G., Hay, M., McGregor, A., Rastogi, V.: The matrix mechanism: optimizing linear counting queries under differential privacy. VLDB J. **24**(6), 757–781 (2015). http://dx.doi.org/10.1007/s00778-015-0398-x
29. Li, N., Li, T., Venkatasubramanian, S.: t-closeness: privacy beyond k-anonymity and l-diversity. In: 2007 IEEE 23rd International Conference on Data Engineering, pp. 106–115, April 2007
30. Liang, H., Yuan, H.: On the complexity of t-closeness anonymization and related problems. In: Meng, W., Feng, L., Bressan, S., Winiwarter, W., Song, W. (eds.) DASFAA 2013. LNCS, vol. 7825, pp. 331–345. Springer, Heidelberg (2013). https://doi.org/10.1007/978-3-642-37487-6_26
31. Lin, J.L., Wei, M.C.: Genetic algorithm-based clustering approach for k-anonymization. Expert. Syst. Appl. **36**(6), 9784–9792 (2009)
32. Liu, F.: Generalized Gaussian mechanism for differential privacy. arXiv preprint arXiv:1602.06028 (2016)

33. Liu, K., Giannella, C., Kargupta, H.: A survey of attack techniques on privacy-preserving data perturbation methods. In: Aggarwal, C.C., Yu, P.S. (eds.) Privacy-Preserving Data Mining: Models and Algorithms, vol. 34, pp. 359–381. Springer, Boston (2008). https://doi.org/10.1007/978-0-387-70992-5_15
34. Machanavajjhala, A., Kifer, D., Gehrke, J., Venkitasubramaniam, M.: L-diversity: privacy beyond k-anonymity. ACM Trans. Knowl. Discov. Data 1(1), Article no. 3 (2007)
35. McSherry, F., Talwar, K.: Mechanism design via differential privacy. In: 48th Annual IEEE Symposium on Foundations of Computer Science, FOCS 2007, pp. 94–103. IEEE (2007)
36. Meyerson, A., Williams, R.: On the complexity of optimal k-anonymity. In: Proceedings of the Twenty-Third ACM SIGMOD-SIGACT-SIGART Symposium on Principles of Database Systems, pp. 223–228. ACM (2004)
37. Nergiz, M.E., Tamersoy, A., Saygin, Y.: Instant anonymization. ACM Trans. Database Syst. 36(1), 2:1–2:33 (2011)
38. Sakpere, A.B., Kayem, A.V.D.M., Ndlovu, T.: A usable and secure crime reporting system for technology resource constrained context. In: 29th IEEE International Conference on Advanced Information Networking and Applications Workshops, AINA 2015 Workshops, Gwangju, South Korea, 24–27 March 2015, pp. 424–429 (2015)
39. Seckan, B.: Violent crime in the developing world: research roundup. In: Journalist's Resource: Research on today's New topics, October 2012. http://journalistsresource.org/studies/international/development/crime-violence-developing-world-research-roundup
40. Sweeney, L.: K-anonymity: a model for protecting privacy. Int. J. Uncertain. Fuzziness Knowl. Based Syst. 10(5), 557–570 (2002)
41. Vaidya, J., Clifton, C.: Privacy-preserving k-means clustering over vertically partitioned data. In: Proceedings of the Ninth ACM SIGKDD International Conference on Knowledge Discovery and Data Mining, pp. 206–215. ACM (2003)
42. Vaidya, J., Kantarcıoğlu, M., Clifton, C.: Privacy-preserving Naive Bayes classification. VLDB J. Int. J. Very Large Data Bases 17(4), 879–898 (2008)
43. Website: South africa's police: Something very rotten. The Economist: Middle East and Africa, June 2012. http://www.economist.com/node/21557385
44. Wicker, S.B.: The loss of location privacy in the cellular age. Commun. ACM 55(8), 60–68 (2012)
45. Wimmer, H., Powell, L.: A comparison of the effects of k-anonymity on machine learning algorithms. In: Proceedings of the Conference for Information Systems Applied Research ISSN, vol. 2167, p. 1508 (2014)
46. Xiao, Q., Reiter, M.K., Zhang, Y.: Mitigating storage side channels using statistical privacy mechanisms. In: Proceedings of the 22nd ACM SIGSAC Conference on Computer and Communications Security, CCS 2015, pp. 1582–1594. ACM, New York (2015)
47. Xiao, X., Yi, K., Tao, Y.: The hardness and approximation algorithms for l-diversity. In: Proceedings of the 13th International Conference on Extending Database Technology, EDBT 2010, pp. 135–146. ACM, New York (2010)
48. Xu, J., Wang, W., Pei, J., Wang, X., Shi, B., Fu, A.W.C.: Utility-based anonymization using local recoding. In: Proceedings of the 12th ACM SIGKDD International Conference on Knowledge Discovery and Data Mining, KDD 2006, pp. 785–790. ACM, New York (2006)

49. Zhang, B., Dave, V., Mohammed, N., Hasan, M.A.: Feature selection for classification under anonymity constraint. arXiv preprint arXiv:1512.07158 (2015)
50. Zhang, J., Cormode, G., Procopiuc, C.M., Srivastava, D., Xiao, X.: Privbayes: private data release via Bayesian networks. In: Proceedings of the 2014 ACM SIGMOD International Conference on Management of Data, pp. 1423–1434. ACM (2014)

Towards Faster Similarity Search by Dynamic Reordering of Streamed Queries

Filip Nalepa[✉], Michal Batko, and Pavel Zezula

Faculty of Informatics, Masaryk University, Brno, Czech Republic
f.nalepa@gmail.com

Abstract. Current era of digital data explosion calls for employment of content-based similarity search techniques, since traditional searchable metadata like annotations are not always available. In our work, we focus on a scenario where the similarity search is used in the context of stream processing, which is one of the suitable approaches to deal with huge amounts of data. Our goal is to maximize the throughput of processed queries while a slight delay is acceptable. We propose a technique that dynamically reorders the queries coming from the stream in order to use our caching mechanism in huge data spaces more effectively. We were able to achieve significantly higher throughput compared to the baseline when no reordering and no caching were used. Moreover, our proposal does not incur any additional precision loss of the similarity search, as opposed to some other caching techniques. In addition to the throughput maximization, we also study the potential of trading off the throughput for low delays (waiting times). The proposed technique allows to be parameterized by the amount of the throughput that can be sacrificed.

Keywords: Stream processing · Similarity search

1 Introduction

Huge amounts of unstructured data are being produced nowadays resulting from the current digital media explosion. Many tasks targeting at processing such data involve, in some form, searching in the data. Traditional search techniques based on exact match of data attributes cannot be often applied to such data types. Instead, content-based search that treats the data by similarity can be an appropriate option. Such search then usually uses *k-nearest-neighbors (kNN) queries*, which retrieve the k objects that are the most similar to a given query object. The level of similarity is measured by a metric distance function.

Due to the nature of the data and applications that use them, it can be desired to deal with the data as with a potentially infinite stream that is continuously being created. For example, consider a text search-engine crawler that

© Springer-Verlag GmbH Germany, part of Springer Nature 2018
A. Hameurlain et al. (Eds.): TLDKS XXXVIII, LNCS 11250, pp. 61–88, 2018.
https://doi.org/10.1007/978-3-662-58384-5_3

gathers images from the web and needs to continuously annotate them by textual descriptions according to the image content. As another example, a news notification system needs to compare the newly published articles to the profiles of all the subscribed users to find out who should be notified.

A subtask of these applications is processing the streamed data items by some form of content-based searching. An important characteristic of the applications is that the data do not need to be processed immediately as in interactive applications, but some delay is acceptable. The performance of these applications is mostly determined by the number of processed data items in a given time interval; that is, the throughput is the most important property. The individual query search times can be improved by applying some similarity indexing techniques that have efficient algorithms based on the metric model of similarity [20]. As opposed to interactive applications focusing on the single query optimization, in our scenario, we can afford to postpone processing of some queries if the overall throughput of the system is improved.

I/O costs typically have a significant effect on the performance of similarity search techniques. In our work, we exploit the fact that if a sequence of queries is processed in an appropriate order, we can achieve considerably lower I/O costs and overall processing times than if the order of the queries is random. This is possible if two similar queries need to access similar data of the search index, which is a common property of the indexes. By obtaining an appropriate ordering of queries, the accessed data can be cached in the main memory and reused for evaluation of similar queries lowering down the I/O costs.

The first contribution of the paper is a technique to dynamically reorder the incoming queries, which allows to achieve a significant improvement of the throughput according to our experiments. One of the features of the approach is that it does not influence the quality of query results as other approximation techniques do.

In the paper, we also present a way to trade off the throughput for the delays of the processed queries. In other words, we balance the number of queries processed per a time unit and the waiting times of individual queries. We show how the proposed technique for the throughput maximization can be modified to increase the number of queries processed until a given time limit while maintaining sufficient throughput to be able to keep up with the rate of incoming new query objects.

The presented approach is built upon our previous work [14]. In this paper, we present more effective reordering technique, which allows to achieve even higher throughput. We add formalization of the approach to the query reordering as a problem of traversing a graph. The throughput-delay trade-off is another new contribution of this paper.

The proposed technique is implemented as an extension of the M-Index [15] used for indexing metric-space data, and its performance is compared to the basic version of the M-Index. We used the Profimedia dataset of images [6] represented as high-dimensional vectors (4,096 and 256 dimensions) and measured the throughput and other throughput-related properties of kNN queries. We were able to significantly improve the throughput compared to the basic version of the M-Index. We also experimented with balancing the throughput and the delays of the processed queries.

The rest of the paper is organized as follows. First, we formally define our problem in Sect. 2. In Sect. 3, we present related work on caching and query reordering in similarity search. A deep look into the proposed technique is presented in Sect. 4. It explains details of the caching system and the principles of dynamic query reordering based on underlying graph model. The experimental evaluation of our approach can be found in Sect. 5. We show modifications of the proposed technique to tradeoff throughput for delays in Sect. 6. Our results are summarized in Sect. 7.

2 Problem Definition and Objectives

Suppose there is a set of complex objects D (e.g., images represented as high-dimensional vectors) and a large database $X \subseteq D$ ($|X| \geq 10^6$). Let $s = (d_1, d_2, \ldots)$ be a stream, that is, a potentially infinite sequence of data items. Each item of the stream is a pair $d_i = (q_i, t_i)$ where $q_i \in D$ is a query object and t_i is the time when it was created (became available). We suppose the data items of the stream are ordered from the oldest ones; that is, it holds that $t_i \leq t_{i+1}$ for each i and $t_1 = 0$.

There is a defined metric space (D, md), which is a universal model of similarity [20]. md is a total distance function $md : D \times D \to \mathbb{R}$, where $\mathbb{R}$ is the set of real numbers. The distance function satisfies these postulates for all $o, p, q \in D$:

- $md(o, p) \geq 0$ (non-negativity),
- $md(o, p) = 0 \iff o = p$ (identity),
- $md(o, p) = md(p, o)$ (symmetry),
- $md(o, q) \leq md(o, p) + md(p, q)$ (triangle inequality).

The distance between any two objects from D corresponds to the level of their dissimilarity; the higher the distance, the higher the dissimilarity.

For each query object q_i in the stream s, a k-nearest-neighbors query $NN(q_i, k)$ is executed, which returns the k nearest objects from the database X to the query object q_i according to the distance function md. We consider the scenario when X is stored on a disk and a subset of its data needs to be accessed in order to evaluate a query. We also suppose I/O operations constitute a significant cost considering all the needed data have to be read from the disk during the query evaluation. Specifically, we target the situations when the time to evaluate a query by this approach is higher than the average time gap between two subsequent data items in the stream.

It is allowed to change the order of the processed query objects. More precisely, at the time t, any query object q_i, where (q_i, t_i) is a data item of the stream and $t_i \leq t$, can be processed.

The goal is to process the query objects of the stream so that the given criteria are optimized. There can be various criteria that can be a subject to optimization depending on a specific application. The criterion we focus on in this paper is throughput maximization. So the goal is to maximize the number of processed query objects of a given stream until a given time T. Alternatively, the criterion can be defined as the minimization of the number of unprocessed query objects at the time T, that is, the number of (q_i, t_i) from the stream s where $t_i \leq T$ and q_i is not processed.

We propose a technique that can be used to improve the throughput of similarity search processing. The technique is based on reordering of the query objects in the stream combined with a caching of the data that were accessed during the evaluation of previous queries.

3   Related Work

The usage of a caching mechanism in similarity search has been proposed in several papers to reduce the time spent by I/O operations. Unlike traditional caching, which is based on exact matches only (e.g., the one exploited by web search engines [9]), the similarity caching also has to manage similar matches.

Existing caching techniques used to speed up processing of a stream of similarity search queries assume that the queries are appropriately ordered. In particular, they assume that similar queries are placed nearby in the stream. This ensures that the cached values can be actually used before they are overwritten by different queries. However, such a characteristic applies to specific scenarios only, e.g., when there exist some popular objects that are frequently searched. In our approach, we do not consider any specific ordering of queries within a stream. Instead, we reorder the queries so that we obtain the sequences that are desired.

In [10], the authors deal with kNN queries to search for similar images in a metric space. They build their approach on the assumption that there exists a set of popular images, which are queried by users significantly more often than the other images. They propose an approach where the result sets of individual kNN queries are stored in a cache and they are reused to produce approximate results of subsequent queries.

The concept of caching in similarity search is also used in [16], where it is applied to contextual advertising systems. If there is a cache miss for a kNN query q, then a larger set of objects than are actually needed is retrieved from the disk and stored in the cache. When a similar query to the cached query q comes to the system, the cached values of q are explored to obtain results for the new query. In this way, an approximate answer is returned.

Static/Dynamic caching is presented in [19]. The cache consists of two parts. The static part stores queries (along with their results) that remain popular over time. The dynamic cache keeps queries that are popular for a short period of time. A combination of both is used to speedup the evaluation of queries. Several strategies are proposed to select the suitable queries to be stored in the cache based on analysis of past queries.

The paper [5] presents an index structure that serves as a cache and as an index at the same time. The index is built and reorganized dynamically as new queries are evaluated. The advantage of the proposed approach is that if the cache is not able to provide an answer, the data computed up to that moment are used by the index.

Caching of data partitions loaded from a disk during query evaluation is presented in [8] complemented with caching previous answers, which serves to set initial search radius for similar kNN queries.

The authors of the paper [18] target the situations when the distance computation itself is an expensive operation. They propose D-cache, which stores distances computed during previous queries to spare some distance computations of subsequent queries. The Snake Table presented in [2] uses a cache of distances to avoid some distance computations when processing streams of queries with snake distribution (i.e., consecutive query objects are similar). Since the Snake Table needs a space proportional to the size of the dataset, it is suitable for medium-sized databases.

Another way to improve the throughput of a stream of kNN queries, is to reorder the queries. In [17], the authors optimize nearest neighbor search for videos when each video is represented by a sequence of high-dimensional vectors. Given a query video containing n vectors, a search for each vector is performed and the overall similarity is computed at last. The authors make use of the fact that vectors of subsequent video frames are similar with respect to the Euclidean distance and they propose dynamic query ordering for advanced optimization of both I/O and CPU costs. They make an observation that the candidates of a previous query may help to further reduce the candidates shared with a subsequent query. The algorithm aims at progressively finding a query order such that the common candidates among queries are fully utilized to maximally reduce the total number of candidates. Also, this approach builds on the assumption that the subsequent kNN queries in the stream are similar to each other. Moreover, the ordering technique is designed for low-dimensional vector spaces (tested on 32 dimensions) and for a short sequence of queries (tested on sequences of the length of 60 queries). In our work, we target more complex metric spaces (e.g., high-dimensional vector spaces with thousands of dimensions), in which case it is highly improbable that similar queries can be found in such short sequences.

4   Principles of the Proposed Approach

To speed up a similarity query evaluation, a metric index is often used. In our approach, we consider a generic metric index that uses data partitioning $P = \{p_1, \ldots, p_n\}$ where $p_i \subseteq X$, $p_i \cap p_j = \emptyset$ for any two partitions p_i, p_j, and $\bigcup_{i=1}^{n} p_i = X$. When processing a query object q, a subset of the partitions $I(q) \subseteq P$ needs to be accessed. The partitions are typically stored on a disk [20]. A frequent bottleneck of similarity search techniques is the reading of the partitions from the disk during a query evaluation. Our solution aims to decrease the number of disk accesses, which consequently decreases the time to process the queries.

The aim of data partitioning methods is to generate the partitions in such a way that any two objects p, q of a partition are similar to each other; that is,

$md(p,q)$ is small. When a query is to be evaluated, a score is assigned to each partition according to estimated distances of the query to the objects of the partition. Based on the scores, only the objects of the most promising partitions are directly examined. The definition of the score is dependent on a specific metric index.

Let $I(q) \subseteq P$ be the set of data partitions accessed during the evaluation of the query object q. Taking into account the properties of data partitioning methods, the following holds:

$$md(q_1, q_2) \leq \epsilon \implies |I(q_1) \ominus I(q_2)| \leq \delta \qquad (1)$$

where ϵ is a small non-negative real number; δ is a small non-negative integer. That means if two query objects are very similar to each other (their distance is at most ϵ), the sets of accessed data partitions are also very similar (the number of elements in their symmetric difference is at most δ). This property can be used to speed up the processing of query objects q_1 and q_2. First, q_1 is evaluated and the accessed data partitions are kept in the main memory cache. When q_2 is being evaluated, the data partitions stored in the cache can be reused to avoid expensive disk accesses.

However, the caching itself is not typically enough for the speedup. Suppose there is a database of millions of objects indexed in a metric space. In practice, the metric space is often defined as a vector space of a high number of dimensions. Due to such a huge search space, there is very low probability that two subsequent query objects in the stream are similar enough to access overlapping sets of data partitions during their evaluation. For the cache to be sufficiently utilized, the query objects in the stream need to be reordered so that sequences of similar query objects are obtained.

To sum it up, our approach consists of two parts. The first one is the in-memory caching of recently loaded data partitions and reusing them for evaluation of subsequent queries. The second one is the query object reordering allowing to process sequences of similar query objects to maximize the cache utilization.

In Sect. 4.1, we describe the architecture of the system used for processing a stream of query objects. Details of the caching system are presented in Sect. 4.2. In Sect. 4.3, we model the problem of query object ordering from the perspective of graphs and we define a query graph with query objects as the vertices. Section 4.4 discusses ways to construct the query graph; we present principals of traversing the graph in order to maximize the throughput in Sect. 4.3; a specific algorithm is provided in Sect. 4.6.

4.1   Architecture

In this section, we describe the architecture of the whole system. The schema of the architecture is depicted in Fig. 1.

Let us have a stream $((q_1, t_1), (q_2, t_2), \ldots)$. A query object q_i arrives at the application at the time t_i and it is inserted into a component called a buffer. The buffer

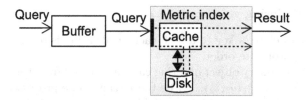

Fig. 1. Architecture

is used to temporarily store the incoming query objects that are waiting for processing. This is the component where the query reordering takes place.

Another part of the architecture is the metric index, which takes care of the query object evaluation. It contains a disk where the database of objects is stored and a main memory cache is used to store the recently loaded data partitions from the disk.

When the metric index is ready for processing another query, a query object is picked from the buffer according to a strategy described in following parts of this paper. During processing of the query, the metric index looks into the cache to possibly use any data partitions obtained while evaluating recent queries. If the data are not in the cache, they are loaded from the disk.

4.2   Cache

The cache is defined as a set of partitions $cache = \{p_1, \ldots, p_m\} \subseteq P$. The size of the cache is limited by the number of objects within the cached partitions:

$$\sum_{p \in cache} |p| \leq cacheLimit.$$

To measure the utility of the cache during evaluation of a given query object q, we define the following function.

$$cacheUtility(q, cache) = \frac{|I(q) \cap cache|}{|I(q)|} \qquad (2)$$

where $cache$ represents the content of the cache and $I(q) \subseteq P$ is the set of partitions accessed during the evaluation of q. We suppose $I(q)$ is a non-empty set.

To keep track of the content of the cache, we define the function $updateCache(q, cache)$ returning the content of the cache after processing the query object q where $cache$ represents the content of the cache before executing q. In our implementation, we use the *least recently used* policy [12]. In particular, the partitions with the oldest last access time are discarded and replaced with the new partitions of the last query while obeying the $cacheLimit$.

The $queryTime(q, cacheUtility)$ represents the time to process the given query object q using the given cache utility. The desired property of the function is that the time should be decreasing with increasing cache utility due to a lower I/O cost.

$$cu_1 \leq cu_2 \iff queryTime(q, cu_1) \geq queryTime(q, cu_2) \qquad (3)$$

where cu_1, cu_2 are cache utilities.

4.3   Query Ordering

As it was stated before, a key to a high cache utilization is to process the query objects in an appropriate order.

The problem of query object ordering can be modeled from the perspective of graphs. Let $s = ((q_1, t_1), (q_2, t_2), \ldots)$ be the stream to be processed. Let us consider just the portion of the stream available at the time t: $((q_1, t_1), \ldots, (q_k, t_k))$ so that $t_k \leq t$ and $t_{k+1} > t$. We define the undirected *query graph* $G_t = (V, E)$ at the time t in the following way. The set of vertices is comprised of the subsequence items $V = \{(q_1, t_1), \ldots, (q_k, t_k))\}$. In other words, each query object of the stream subsequence represents a vertex in the query graph.

The graph is complete; that is, there is an edge between every pair of vertices (q_i, t_i) and (q_j, t_j) where $i \neq j$. A value is associated with each edge denoting an upper bound of the query time to process q_i right after q_j or q_j right after q_i. We denote the value assigned to the edge (referred to as the *edge value* in the rest of the paper) between the vertices (q_i, t_i) and (q_j, t_j) as $e((q_i, t_i), (q_j, t_j))$.

The edge value between the vertices (q_i, t_i) and (q_j, t_j) is determined as follows:

$$e((q_i, t_i), (q_j, t_j)) = max\{queryTime(q_i, cu_i), queryTime(q_j, cu_j)\} \quad (4)$$

where $cu_i = cacheUtility(q_i, I(q_j))$ and $cu_j = cacheUtility(q_j, I(q_i))$. That is, the upper bound of the query time is the maximum of the query times when q_i is processed right after q_j or q_j right after q_i, while the cache contains only the partitions needed by one previous query. If the cache contains more partitions rather than those needed by the previous query, the cache utility does not decrease and therefore, the query time does not increase according to Formula 3.

The query graph G_t is defined at each time t where t is a non-negative integer. The graph continuously grows by adding new vertices and edges as new query objects become available in the stream. G_t is a subgraph of G_k where $k > t$; $G_{t+1} = G_t$ if and only if there does not exist an item $(q_i, t + 1)$ in the stream; that is, no new item becomes available at the time $t + 1$. An example of the graph evolution can be seen in Fig. 2.

Our objective is to find such an ordering in which the query objects are processed so that the throughput is maximized. Regarding the query graph, we want to find an acyclic path (i.e., a sequence of the vertices) that determines

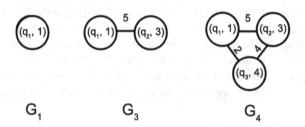

Fig. 2. Query graph evolution example

the ordering of the query objects. Formally, given the time limit T, the task is to find the longest path $((q_{i_1}, t_{i_1}), \ldots, (q_{i_k}, t_{i_k}))$ in G_T so that $start_k < T$ where $start_k$ is the time when the last query object q_{i_k} starts to be evaluated. The length of the path is measured as the number of vertices, that is, the number of processed query objects.

A query object is processed as soon as the preceding query object is processed or as soon as it becomes available in the stream, whichever occurs later. This strategy is applied in order to improve the throughput.

Algorithm 1 describes the generic processing of a stream of query objects. The input is the stream of query objects arriving continuously to the application and the time limit T. The algorithm repeatedly calls the *addNewQueryObjects* function to add newly arrived query objects to the query graph and the *getQueryToProcess* function that returns a query object that is to be processed next according to the query graph and according to the path of query objects generated so far. The returned query object is processed and added to the path. The loop finishes when the time limit T is exceeded.

Algorithm 1. Generic algorithm

Input: stream of query objects $stream = (q_1, q_2, \ldots)$ and the time limit T
Output: *path*: the order in which the stream objects are processed
> **function** PROCESSSTREAM(*stream*, T)
>> $path \leftarrow ()$
>> $G \leftarrow$ empty graph
>> **while** $T \leq now$ **do**
>>> $G.addNewQueryObjects(stream)$
>>> $q \leftarrow getQueryToProcess(G, path)$
>>> **if** $q \neq null$ **then**
>>>> $process(q)$
>>>> $path.add(q)$
>> **return** *path*

4.4   Query Graph Construction

To process the stream in the described manner, the query graphs have to be generated from the raw stream of query objects. In particular, the edge values have to be assigned. According to the definition, they should denote an upper bound of the time to process a query object at one side of the edge right after processing the query object on the other side. The question is how to predict the query times. Usually, it is not possible to obtain the precise query times in advance. In practice, we are likely to end up with a method for computing the expected times to execute the queries.

The query time greatly depends on the cache utility (see Formula 3), that is, on the number of data partitions loaded from the disk during query evaluation. The problem is that it is not typically possible to precisely determine the set of needed data partitions without the actual query evaluation. The underlying metric index usually works with a priority queue of data partitions, which is being updated dynamically as the individual data partitions are examined [20]. Therefore, the approach based on precise computation of the cache utility is not usable in practice.

Data partitions that are needed during the processing of a query are generally determined by their distance to the query object in the metric space. So the size of the intersection of data partitions needed during processing of two query objects is influenced by the metric distance of the query objects. Pairs of close query objects are assumed to share more data partitions than pairs of distant ones.

Therefore, a straightforward way to approximate edge values of the query graph can be based on the metric distances between query objects. When a new query object arrives, the distances to all the other query objects of the graph are computed. From the practical point of view, it is actually not necessary to assign the edge values to already processed query objects (except for the last one) because they are not used to generate the path (the details are described later). Despite this practical consequence, the edge value assignment can be very time consuming if there are a lot of query objects (e.g., tens of thousands as in our experiments) that are still waiting for their processing. This is because the metric distance computation can be a computationally intensive operation. If the computational complexity of adding a new query object to the graph is measured by the number of metric distance computations, the complexity is linear with respect to the number of unprocessed query objects already in the graph.

Instead, we use a pivot based technique to estimate the metric distances and the query times [7]. In particular, let there be a fixed set of objects in the metric space; we will denote them as pivots. When a new query object q is to be added to the graph, distances between the query object q and all the pivots are computed. The pivots are ordered from the nearest to the farthest one, which defines a permutation of the pivots. This pivot permutation is stored for each query object. The edge value between two query objects is determined according to the length of the common prefix of their pivot permutations, the longer the common prefix, the lower the edge value. The length of the common prefix of two permutations $(p_{i_1}, p_{i_2}, \ldots, p_{i_m})$ and $(p_{j_1}, p_{j_2}, \ldots, p_{j_m})$ is determined as the maximum number k $(\leq m)$ such that $i_r = j_r$ for all $1 \leq r \leq k$. The pivot based technique was also shown to work well in high-dimensional vector spaces [15], which is essential for our scenario.

We can either stay with such relative edge values, or absolute edge values can be assigned based on empirical measurements. Specifically, we can construct a function that for a length of a common prefix of two query objects assigns an average query time $estimatedQueryTime(prefLength) = qt_{pl}$. Since there is a fixed set of pivots, the cost to insert a new query object in the query graph is constant. As we consider the scenarios when the rate of incoming query objects is high, the number of pivots is typically much lower than the number of query objects waiting for their processing.

Many strategies for pivot selection have been proposed [1]. According to the comparison of pivot selection techniques for permutation-based indexing provided in [1], there is no universally best pivot selection technique, but rather different techniques are optimal for different purposes. The authors also state that "the random chosen pivots is never a bad idea even if it is also never the smartest decision". In our experiments, we use the M-Index [15] to evaluate the similarity search queries, which is also a permutation-based access method. From the efficiency point of view, it is beneficial to use the same set of pivots for building the query graph and for indexing the dataset, since it helps to save some distance computations. The authors of the M-Index claim that the random pivot selection results in similar performance of query evaluations as other selection methods. Due to these statements, we use a random selection of the pivots to build the query graph.

4.5   Query Path Search

As we are now able to efficiently construct the query graphs, let us focus on the throughput maximization criterion. The goal is to generate an appropriate path in the graph. The path is generated whenever a next query object can be processed. The query object that is to be processed needs to be chosen very efficiently so that it does not impose much overhead. To be able to do that, we apply a greedy approach trying to find a path with minimal average edge values.

Let us first define the term of the density of a subgraph $SG = (V_S, E_S)$, where $|V_S| > 1$: Let $(v_{i_1}, v_{i_2}, \ldots, v_{i_{|V_S|}})$ be the shortest path going through all the vertices V_S; $v_{i_j} \in V_S$ for $1 \leq j \leq |V_S|$ where the length of the path is computed as the sum of the edge values between the subsequent vertices in the path. Then $density(SG) = \frac{|V_S|}{\sum_{j=1}^{|V_S|-1} e(v_{i_j}, v_{i_{j+1}})}$; that is, the density is determined by the average edge value in the corresponding shortest path.

The proposed greedy approach relies on finding subgraphs of high density. Such a dense subgraph is determined by the existence of a path through all the vertices of the subgraph with a low average edge value. Since new vertices are continuously added to the graph, the density of the subgraphs changes. The search for dense subgraphs is intended to identify the parts of the query graph that are at the current time possible to be processed with high cache utility. The dense subgraph strategy is combined with the nearest-neighbor strategy [4], which is a simple heuristic technique for the traveling salesman problem: Start at an arbitrary vertex. The next vertex to visit is the one that has the lowest-value edge to the current vertex among the unvisited vertices. This step is repeated until all the vertices of the given subgraph are visited. In summary, the greedy approach repeatedly finds a dense subgraph and processes all the query objects in the subgraph in the nearest-neighbor manner.

This gets us to another problem to solve: how to efficiently identify dense subgraphs. First, we construct a hierarchical clustering of the vertices. Dense subgraphs are then found by exploring individual clusters rather than the whole graph.

Let $G_t = (V, E)$ be the query graph at the time t. The set of clusters $C_t = \{c_{L_1}, c_{L_2}, \ldots, c_{L_k}\}$ is a decomposition of the set of vertices V so that $L_i = max\{e(v_a, v_b) \mid v_a, v_b \in c_{L_i}\}$ for $1 \leq i \leq k$. It means that all the vertices are decomposed into disjoint groups (clusters). Each cluster c_{L_i} defines an upper limit L_i on the edge value between any two vertices, that is, a query time limit. Note that there can be multiple valid decompositions given a set of clusters with their distance limits. This forms the lowest level of the hierarchical clustering. Another level of clusters is constructed by a decomposition of the set of clusters on a lower level and by assigning query time limits to the new clusters so that the limits are obeyed. Eventually, the *tree of clusters* T_t is generated. The vertices of the original query graph (i.e., the query objects) are added as leaf nodes to the corresponding bottom clusters.

For the decomposition of a set of vertices and subsequently clusters, we reuse the pivot based technique that is applied for the query graph construction in Sect. 4.4. Each internal node on the level k of the tree is of the form $n = ((p_{i_1}, \ldots, p_{i_{k-1}}), L_n)$ where $(p_{i_1}, \ldots, p_{i_{k-1}})$ is the pivot permutation prefix shared by all the descending nodes; L_n is the upper limit on the edge value between any two descending leaf nodes. Each leaf node is of the form (q, t), where q denotes the query object; t denotes its time of arrival.

An example can be seen in Fig. 3. Suppose there is the stream $((q_1, 1), (q_2, 3), (q_3, 4), (q_4, 7), (q_5, 11), \ldots)$. Let p_1, p_2, p_3 be the pivots. Let the pivot permutations for the first four items of the stream be (p_1, p_2, p_3), (p_3, p_1, p_2), (p_1, p_3, p_2) and (p_1, p_2, p_3) in the respective order. Let the estimated query times for individual common prefix lengths be 8, 2, 1 for the prefix lengths 0, 1, 2, respectively (see the function *estimatedQueryTime* in Sect. 4.4). On the left side of the figure, there is the query graph G_7 with the query times on the edges. On the right side, there is the generated tree. Individual levels of the tree correspond to the length of the common pivot permutation prefix of the descending leaf nodes. The upper bound of the query time of q_i processed right after q_j is determined by the query time limit of their lowest common parent node. For example, the maximum query time limit of q_3 when processed right after q_4 is determined by the lowest common parent $((p_1), 2)$.

Contrary to the generic Algorithm 1, we actually work with the tree of clusters in the implementation of the proposed approach. However, the structure of the algorithm does not change; that is, there is a loop in which new query objects are added to the tree and a next-to-process query object is selected and processed.

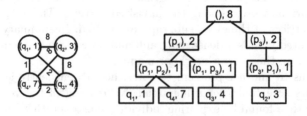

Fig. 3. Query graph and corresponding tree of clusters

A pseudo code of the function inserting a new query object into the tree of clusters is shown in Algorithm 2, which applies the pivot based technique. In the next section, we will describe details of the function that traverses the tree and selects a next query object to be processed.

Algorithm 2. Query object insertion algorithm

Input: tree of clusters *tree*, a query object *q* to insert and a set of pivots *P*
   function ADDNEWQUERYOBJECT(*tree*, *q*)
     pp ← *computePivotPermutation*(*q*, *P*)
     tree.addQueryObject(*q*, *pp*)

4.6 Tree Traversal

Let us describe how the tree of clusters T_t is traversed in accordance with the dense subgraph and nearest-neighbor heuristics. The depth-first search is applied. Suppose q is the last processed query object so far. First, we look for a set of near neighbors by finding the lowest nonempty parent p of q. A node is considered nonempty if and only if it has descending unprocessed leaf nodes (query objects). After that, a child of p is selected based on some given strategy. Recursively, a grandchild and other descendants are selected until a leaf is reached and processed. This is captured in the pseudo code in Algorithm 3.

Algorithm 3. Tree traversal algorithm

Input: tree of clusters *tree* and path *path* representing the order of already processed
   query objects
Output: the next query object to be processed
   function GETQUERYTOPROCESS(*tree*, *path*)
     lastQO ← *path.lastQueryObject*
     node ← *tree.findLowestNonEmptyParent*(*lastQO*)
     while *node* ≠ *null* and *node* is not a leaf **do**
       node ← *tree.selectChild*(*node*)
     return *node*

A general strategy for selecting a particular child c (i.e., the subtree with the root c) is to identify dense subtrees (dense clusters) in order to achieve high throughput. A possible way is to select the subtree that minimizes the average query time of processing all its leaf nodes. This way we select the subtree with the largest immediate contribution to the throughput.

Let us illustrate the algorithm with an example. Consider the tree in Fig. 3. Suppose that the currently processed query object is q_2; the other query objects have not been processed yet. Let us find the lowest nonempty parent of $(q_2, 3)$, which is the root $((), 8)$. There is only one possible child to select, which is

$((p_1), 2)$. Now, there are two possible children of $((p_1), 2)$. In order to select one child or the other, the average query time is estimated for each of the two subtrees as follows. The subtree of $((p_1, p_3), 1)$ contains just one leaf node $(q_3, 4)$ and the maximum query time is 8, since the lowest common parent of the last query q_2 and q_3 is $((), 8)$. The maximum time to process the first leaf of the subtree $((p_1, p_2), 1)$ is 8. The second leaf needs at most 1 time unit for processing, since the lowest common parent of $(q_1, 1)$ and $(q_4, 7)$ is $((p_1, p_2), 1)$. Therefore, the $((p_1, p_2), 1)$ subtree is selected, since it minimizes the average query time. Subsequently both its leaves are processed.

Let us formalize the estimation of the average query time. Let $n = (pref_n, qt_n)$ be a nonempty internal node of the tree and $m = (pref_m, qt_m)$ be the lowest common parent of n and of the last processed leaf node. We suppose the leaf node is not a descendant of n.

The maximum time to process all the leaf nodes of the subtree n equals

$$qt_m + childrenQueryTime(n)$$

where qt_m is the maximum query time of the first query object q of n. $childrenQueryTime(n)$ is the maximum time to process all the other descending leaf nodes:

$$childrenQueryTime(n) =$$

$$= max\{|n.children| - 1, 0\} \cdot qt_n + \sum_{c \in n.children} childrenQueryTime(c)$$

where $n.children$ is the set of nonempty direct children of n; qt_n is the maximum time to process a leaf node of n when the lowest common parent of the last and the next processed leaf is n. $childrenQueryTime$ is applied recursively for individual children of n.

The described strategy when the subtree minimizing the average query time is selected possesses two possible caveats. It takes only the current state of the tree to make the decision without considering evolution of the tree. The other caveat is the possibility of starvation because some subtrees may never be chosen for processing.

Let us explain the evolution of the tree of clusters caveat. Let p be a subtree that at a time t contains a set of leaf nodes C_t that are all unprocessed and at a time u it contains a set of leaf nodes C_u such that $t < u$ and $C_t \subset C_u$. Let us consider two scenarios. In the first one, p is selected as the subtree to be processed at the time t and again at the time u. In the second one, p is selected just at the time u. The set of processed leaf nodes is the same for both the scenarios (C_u), but the query time is lower in the second one, since all the leaves of p are processed in a row achieving higher cache utility. It implies that it pays off to process p as few times as possible to achieve low query times, since the subtree "switches" introduce processing overhead.

For illustration purposes, see the Fig. 3 again and let us consider the subtree $((p_1, p_2), 1)$. If both the children are processed in a row, the maximum query time to process the second one is one, since their lowest common parent is $((p_1, p_2), 1)$.

However, if just $(q_1, 1)$ is processed, then another subtree is processed and $(q_4, 7)$ is processed later. The maximum overall time to process $(q_1, 1)$ and $(q_4, 7)$ is then higher than in the first scenario, since $((p_1, p_2), 1)$ is not the lowest common parent of $(q_4, 7)$ and of the previous leaf node. Thus the cost of processing $(q_4, 7)$ is higher than one.

When also considering the starvation problem, a suitable strategy is to choose the subtree that contains the oldest unprocessed leaf node among the considered subtrees. This way the starvation problem is diminished and also the number of times a subtree is chosen for processing is limited.

In fact, the starvation is not really eliminated. There can be a situation when the processing gets stuck in a single subtree if there are always query objects to be processed in this subtree and it cannot be completely emptied. Such a situation can be solved by setting a time limit during which a single subtree of the root node can be continuously processed. When the time limit is reached, the tree traversal is reset to the root node.

The two presented implementations of the *selectChild* function (minimal average query time and oldest leaf) are experimentally compared later in this paper.

5   Experiments

In this section, we experimentally evaluate the proposed techniques for the throughput maximization. We start by describing the setup of the experiments in Sect. 5.1. The impact of the cache utility on the query time is explored in Sect. 5.2. We show how the buffer size influences the throughput in Sect. 5.3. In Sect. 5.4, we experiment with different rates of incoming query objects in the stream. The cache size impact is evaluated in Sect. 5.5. Different ways of constructing the query graph are experimentally compared in Sect. 5.6.

5.1   Setup of Experiments

We use the M-Index [15] structure to index the metric-space data. It employs practically all known principles of metric space partitioning, pruning, and filtering, thus reaching high search performance. The actual data are separated into partitions, which are stored as separate files on a disk and read into the main memory during query evaluations. To partition the data, M-Index uses a set of pivots. To insert an object into the index, the pivots are sorted based on the distance to the object. In this way, a pivot permutation is obtained, which identifies the data partition to insert the object. During a similarity search, mutual distances between the query object and the pivots are used to reduce the set of data partitions that need to be accessed. The M-Index supports executing approximate kNN queries among other operations. One of the stop conditions of a query evaluation is given by the maximum number of accessed objects (the size of a candidate set). Such a stop condition is used in our experiments.

One of the reasons why we chose to use the M-Index is that it can use the same set of pivots as are used for the query graph construction in Sect. 4.4. This is beneficial for the effectiveness of the query ordering. It also improves efficiency because the distances from a query object to the pivots can be computed just once and used both in the query graph and in the M-Index. Another reason for selecting the M-Index is that it also achieves high search performance in high-dimensional vector spaces.

For the experiments, we use the Profimedia dataset of images [6], which is a freely-available large-scale dataset for evaluation of content-based image retrieval systems. We created two different subsets of the images and extracted their visual-feature descriptors. The generated datasets are: 1 million Caffe descriptors [11] (4096 dimensional vectors) and 10 million MPEG-7 descriptors. Separately, we created streams of images represented by corresponding descriptors. During each experiment, images from the respective collection are continuously streamed and stored in the buffer from which they are processed by approximate 10-NN queries. For the approximate kNN queries, we used candidate sets of size 1,000 for the Caffe dataset and size 2,000 for the MPEG-7 dataset. We applied the Euclidean distance and the weighted Euclidean distance as the distance functions for the metric space with Caffe and MPEG-7 descriptors, respectively. For both datasets, we use 160 randomly selected objects as pivots. In the M-Index, this pivot selection strategy was observed to provide similar search performance as other more sophisticated strategies [15].

If not said otherwise, the maximum size of the cache is set to 40,000 descriptors for the Caffe dataset (i.e., 4% of the database); up to 90,000 descriptors are stored for the MPEG-7 dataset (i.e., 0.9% of the database). The least recently used policy is used when inserting to the full cache. In particular, the data partitions with the oldest last access time are discarded and replaced with the new partitions of the current query so that the maximum size of the cache is maintained. To traverse the tree of clusters, the oldest leaf approach is used (see Sect. 4.6) if not stated otherwise.

The tested applications are implemented using Java programming language with the use of the MESSIF library [3] providing an implementation of the M-Index. The experiments were run on Intel Xeon 2.00 GHz with 8 GB RAM. The datasets are stored on a HDD (access time 5 ms, transfer rate 90 MBps). We have run each of the experiments multiple times (at least three) and we have taken the median values where appropriate.

5.2   Cache Utility vs. Query Time

At first, the impact of the cache utility on the query time is explored to validate Formula 3. We ran approximate 10-NN queries for each dataset and we were continuously changing the percentage of the data partitions that could be obtained from the cache. The results are shown in Fig. 4a. The x-axis shows the percentage of the cached values of all the data needed for processing of a particular query; the y-axis represents the percentage of the time to process the query compared to the situation when the cache is not used. It can be observed

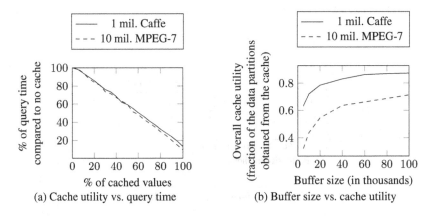

Fig. 4. Cache utility experiments

that the processing time can be improved dramatically (below 10% of the original time) if the cache is filled with appropriate values, thus the assumption in Formula 3 is valid.

5.3   Buffer Size Impact

In the next group of experiments, we explore the impact of the size of the buffer on the cache utility and the throughput. The buffer size denotes the number of query objects that are waiting for their processing and thus are a subject to reordering. The size of the buffer was fixed during the experiments. At the beginning, the buffer was filled with the query objects from the stream up to the given size; then another query object was loaded whenever a query has been processed to keep the size of the buffer constant. Exactly 100,000 query objects were processed during each experiment. We can observe that with a growing size of the buffer, both the cache utility and the throughput grow because the processed subgraphs (clusters) are denser and the cached values are reused more often, see Figs. 4b and 5. The throughput speedup was computed as the ratio of the processing time using a given buffer size and the processing time when the query objects were processed in their original order without the caching mechanism.

The results when the query objects were processed in their original order (i.e., there is no reordering) are captured by Table 1. Average query times were measured with and without use of the cache. The cache utility was very low, which means the reordering of query objects significantly influences the efficiency.

5.4   Input Frequency Experiments

In the following experiments, we set a fixed frequency f of the incoming query objects of the stream. It means the stream follows the pattern $((q_1, 0), (q_2, f), \ldots, (q_i, (i-1) \cdot f), \ldots)$. We measured the throughput by observing the size of the buffer (i.e., the number of unprocessed query objects). Each experiment was run with a different frequency of streamed query objects.

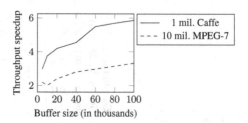

Fig. 5. Buffer size vs. throughput

Table 1. Processing query objects in their original order

Dataset	Cache	Cache utility	Avg. query time [ms]
10 mil. MPEG-7	Yes	0.01	103
10 mil. MPEG-7	No	-	113
1 mil. Caffe	Yes	0.03	65
1 mil. Caffe	No	-	69

The processing was run for two hours for the Caffe dataset and for four hours for the MPEG-7 dataset. The two approaches presented in Sect. 4.6 are compared. In particular, these are the strategies for ordering the subtrees during the depth-first traversal of the tree of clusters, namely, the oldest leaf (OL) approach and the minimal average query time ($MAQT$) approach. The oldest leaf strategy selects the subtree containing the oldest unprocessed query object, while the minimal average query time strategy selects the subtree minimizing the average query time to process all the unprocessed query objects of the subtree.

The results are shown in Fig. 6. For the oldest leaf approach, we show the results for input frequencies of 5 ms, 10 ms, 20 ms, 30 ms, and 60 ms. For the $MAQT$ approach, the results are shown just for the 30 ms frequency. It can be observed that the size of the buffer grows at the beginning because the query graph does not contain dense subgraphs, which are essential for the processing speedup. As soon as the subgraphs are dense enough, the processing is more efficient and eventually the buffer size stabilizes once the average query time equals the input frequency. The results are in compliance with the results regarding the buffer size: as the input rate of the streamed items increases, the buffer size also increases to keep up with the incoming query objects. It can be seen the OL approach gives a little better results than the $MAQT$ one. Moreover OL does not have the disadvantage of the starvation.

In all the cases except for the 5 ms and 10 ms frequencies, it was possible to achieve sufficient throughput so that the buffer size was practically stable. It means that, for example, the average query time was 20 ms for the 20 ms input frequency after the initial phase. The experiments with 5 ms were stopped after reaching the size of the buffer of 200,000 or 700,000 for the Caffe or MPEG-7 dataset, respectively.

Tables 2 and 3 show comparison of delays for individual input frequencies. The delay is the time since a query object enters the buffer until it is processed by the metric index. As expected, the median and the maximum delays are greater for more rapid streams because the buffer sizes are higher and it takes a longer time until a particular query object can be processed. The maximum delay for the *MAQT* approach is very high because it has no starvation prevention. The tables also present the overall cache utility computed as the ratio of the number of data partitions loaded from the cache and of all the data partitions needed during the processing. The cache utility correlates with the size of the buffer as was already seen in Fig. 4b.

Exact distribution of the delays for the experiment with the MPEG-7 dataset and 30 ms input frequency can be observed in Fig. 7. The graph shows the percentage of queries that were processed until a given delay. So for example, we can see that 50% of queries were delayed maximally by 13 min, while about 10% of queries were kept in the buffer for more than 25 min.

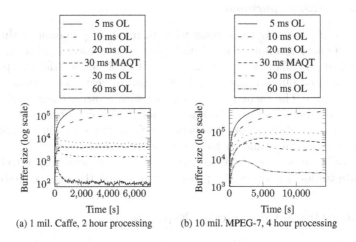

(a) 1 mil. Caffe, 2 hour processing   (b) 10 mil. MPEG-7, 4 hour processing

Fig. 6. The buffer size evolution in time during fixed input frequency experiments

Table 2. Fixed input frequency statistics for Caffe dataset

Input frequency [ms]	10	20	30	30	60
	OL	OL	OL	MAQT	OL
Max delay [s]	2721	309	169	7036	59
Median delay [s]	740	117	47	38	7
Cache utility	0.87	0.65	0.44	0.48	0.08

Table 3. Fixed input frequency statistics for MPEG-7 dataset

Input frequency [ms]	10 OL	20 OL	30 OL	30 MAQT	60 OL
Max delay [s]	6409	4031	2988	6557	1565
Median delay [s]	2599	1525	894	1050	234
Cache utility	0.92	0.78	0.59	0.64	0.30

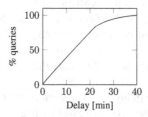

Fig. 7. Delay cumulative function; MPEG-7 dataset; 30 ms input frequency; OL approach; 4 h run time

5.5 Cache Size Experiments

The cache utility is likely to increase with an increasing amount of the cached data, since a query can reuse data of multiple previous queries. This expectation is validated by the following experiments. A set of 50,000 queries was processed using a fixed-sized buffer containing 20,000 query objects. The graphs in Fig. 8 depict the results. The cache utility increases with growing cache size; the processing time decreases as the cache size gets larger. We can observe that caching very large amount of data does not bring much improvement in the cache utility and the processing time so for the other experiments, we selected 40,000 and 90,000 objects for the Caffe and the MPEG-7 datasets, respectively, as an appropriate trade-off between the processing time and the storage space.

5.6 Query Graph Construction Experiments

In this section, we compare three approaches to the query graph construction (described in Sect. 4.4). The first one is the pivot based technique we use in the other experiments; that is, the edge values (maximum query times) of the query graph are estimated according to common pivot permutation prefix lengths of query objects. Another approach we consider is the one when the metric distances to all the query objects of the query graph are explicitly computed and the edge values correspond to the distances. The last one uses the knowledge of data partitions needed during evaluation of individual queries and the edge values are determined according to the number of common partitions.

In the experiments, we used the MPEG-7 dataset and a finite stream of 10,000 query objects $((q_1, 1), \ldots, (q_{10000}, 1))$; that is, all the query objects were

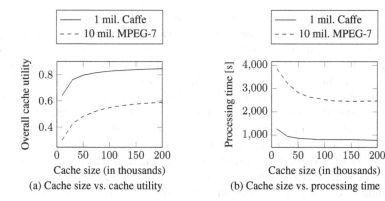

(a) Cache size vs. cache utility

(b) Cache size vs. processing time

Fig. 8. Cache size experiments; fixed-sized buffer of 20,000 query objects; 50,000 processed queries

available at once. For each approach, a path in the query graph was found going through all the 10,000 query objects. The query objects were processed in that order and the overall cache utility was acquired.

We considered two cache policies for each approach. In one case, the cache was used to keep only the data partitions that were needed to evaluate one previous query (OPP policy). This is the strategy that is used to set the upper bound of the query time in Sect. 4.3. The other policy is the one that is used for the other experiments; that is, the cache size is limited by 90,000 objects and the least recently used replacement strategy is applied (LRU policy).

For the explicit distance computations technique, the query graph was constructed so that the edge values were set to the metric distances between the query objects. Subsequently a path in the query graph was found using the 2-approximate minimum spanning tree heuristics designed for the traveling salesman problem [13]. Note that the definition of the query graph requires query times to be assigned to the edges. However, for the purposes of the experiments, we worked directly with the metric distances assigned to the edges.

The sum of the edges of the constructed minimum spanning tree was 12,816, which sets the minimal bound on the shortest path. The actual length of the path obtained from the minimum spanning tree was 15,583. We also took the path generated using the pivot based technique and computed its length in terms of the metric distances between query objects, which resulted in the length of 18,059. However, the achieved cache utility for the OPP policy using the pivot based technique was 9% compared to only 3% using the minimum spanning tree path. For the LRU policy, the cache utility using the pivot based technique was 32% compared to only 10% using the minimum spanning tree path. It means the metric distance is not strictly correlated with the cache utility (and the query time). The choice of the query graph construction approach should consider the properties of the used metric index so that the query times are estimated correctly and the query ordering is effective.

For the next approach, the data partitions needed for the evaluation of individual queries were obtained beforehand. The value of the query graph edge $q_i q_j$ was assigned according to the difference of the data partitions needed for processing q_i and q_j; specifically we took $max\{|I(q_i) - I(q_j)|, |I(q_j) - I(q_i)|\}$ where $I(q)$ is the set of the data partitions needed for processing q. The path was found using the minimum spanning tree heuristics, which resulted in the cache utility of 15% for the OPP policy and 29% for LRU. As for OPP, this approach achieves better cache utility than the pivot based approach. If LRU is used, the achieved results are similar to those obtained for the pivot based technique. However, the precise set of needed data partitions is not generally known prior to actual evaluation of the query so this approach is not usable in practice.

A summary of the results is captured by Table 4. We can conclude that from the practical point of view, the pivot based strategy is the most suitable.

Table 4. Query graph construction experiments

Constr. strat.	Cache policy	Cache util.
Pivot based	OPP	0.09
Pivot based	LRU	0.32
Metric dist.	OPP	0.03
Metric dist.	LRU	0.10
Data parts.	OPP	0.15
Data parts.	LRU	0.29

6   Delay Improvement

The proposed approaches so far were focused on the throughput maximization of the query processing and the delays of individual query objects were not targeted for optimization. To recall, the delay is the time since a query object was added into the stream until it was processed. In this section, we show how the throughput can be traded off for improving the delays.

In Fig. 7, which shows the delay cumulative function for the experiment with the MPEG-7 dataset and a fixed input frequency of 30 ms, we can observe that just 5% of the queries were processed with maximally 1 min delay. In this section, we explore the scenario when we want to process more queries until a given delay limit while maintaining sufficient throughput.

Formally, the problem is defined as follows. Given the time limit T, the task is to find a path $((q_{i_1}, t_{i_1}), \ldots, (q_{i_k}, t_{i_k}))$ in the query graph G_T so that $start_k < T$ where $start_j$ is the time when the query object q_{i_j} starts to be evaluated (for more details see Sect. 4.3). Given the delay limit DL, the optimal path maximizes the expression

$$w \cdot |beforeLimit| + |afterLimit|$$

where *beforeLimit* is the set of processed query objects with the delay of maximally *DL*; *afterLimit* is the set of the other processed query objects; $w \geq 1$ is a parameter determining the weight of the query objects processed until the given delay limit.

Such a criterion can also be imagined as weighted throughput. A certain number of points is received for each processed query object. If a query object is processed before the given delay limit, more points are obtained. The goal is to maximize the number of received points in a given time interval.

Let us define *beforeLimit* and *afterLimit* sets formally. We start with the definition of the delay as the time since a query object was added into the stream until it was processed:

$$delay((q_{i_j}, t_{i_j})) = start_j + qt_{i_j} - t_{i_j} \text{ for } j \geq 1$$

where qt_{i_j} is the time to process q_{i_j}.

$$beforeLimit = \{(q_{i_j}, t_{i_j}) - delay((q_{i_j}, t_{i_j})) \leq DL\}$$
$$afterLimit = \{(q_{i_j}, t_{i_j}) - delay((q_{i_j}, t_{i_j})) > DL\}$$

To address the specified criterion, we modify the strategy for ordering the children subtrees in the depth-first traversal of the tree of clusters (presented in Sect. 4.6). Instead of choosing the subtree containing the oldest query object, a score for each subtree candidate is computed:

$$a \cdot oldestItemDelay + b \cdot beforeLimitCount$$

where *oldestItemDelay* is the time since the oldest unprocessed query object of the subtree entered the stream; *beforeLimitCount* is the number of unprocessed query objects of the subtree that have been in the stream for at most *DL* time; a and b are the weights influencing the trade-off of the delays and the throughput. When $b = 0$, we get the original oldest leaf approach. As b grows, the subtrees possessing newest query objects are more and more prioritized over the ones containing the oldest leaves. The optimal value of b correlates with the value of the weight w. The influence of the parameters is studied experimentally.

6.1   Delay Improvement Experiments

The following experiments were conducted for different values of b to see how the throughput and the number of queries processed before the given delay limit change. The value of a was fixed to 1. The 10 mil. MPEG-7 dataset was used; the delay limit *DL* was set to 1 min; a new query object entered the buffer every 30 ms. Every experiment was run for 4 h.

The results are depicted in Fig. 9. By increasing the weight of the newest query objects, it is possible to increase the number of query objects with the delay below 1 min. On the other hand, the overall throughput decreases, since subtrees with lower densities are prioritized (see Fig. 9a). The graph in Fig. 9b

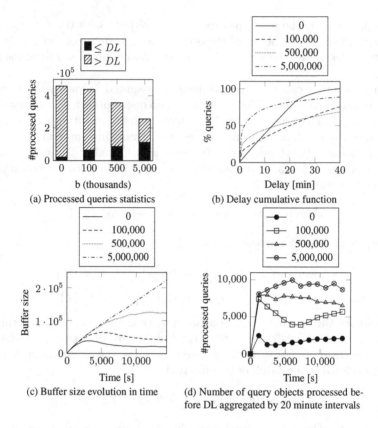

Fig. 9. Throughput delay trade-off for various b values; DL = 1 min; MPEG-7 dataset; 30 ms input frequency

depicts the percentage of queries processed until a corresponding delay. The percentage of low delayed queries gets higher with the growing weight b; on the other hand, the percentage of high delayed queries also increases because of the lower throughput. Figure 9c shows the evolution of the buffer size for individual weights. The larger the weight is, the larger the buffer size has to be in order to keep up with the rate of the incoming query objects. When the weight is too high, the buffer grows to very large sizes, since the average query time is very high.

Figure 9d captures the numbers of query objects processed within the delay limit throughout the time. The runs with nonzero b reach approximately the same value after the first 20 min. After that, we can observe the influence of b, since some of the oldest query objects become prioritized.

As can be seen from the experiments, choosing inappropriate values of the parameters a and b can lead to unwanted results as the throughput drops to very low values. In the following, we present a modification of the approach for dynamical setting of the parameters according to the size of the buffer.

The application can be in one of two states. When the first state is active, the throughput maximization is aimed for (THRMAX state). When the other state is active, the number of query objects processed until the given delay limit is maximized (DELLIM state).

The behavior of the application in individual states differs in the setting of the weighting parameters. In the THRMAX state, the oldest leaf approach is applied, that is, $a = 1$, $b = 0$. For the DELLIM state, the subtree containing the largest number of unprocessed query objects that have spent at most DL (the delay limit) in the buffer is selected, that is, $a = 0$, $b = 1$.

The application switches from one state to the other according to the buffer size. In particular, there is a lower and an upper buffer size limit. When the upper limit is exceeded, the system goes to the THRMAX state to maximize the throughput so that the buffer size can be lowered down. When the size of the buffer drops below the lower limit, the DELLIM state is entered to maximize the number of query objects processed before the given delay limit.

Experiments addressing the state switch approach were run with the same settings as the first approach: that is, the MPEG-7 dataset, 1 min delay limit, 30 ms input frequency and four hour run time. Each experiment was run with different limits of the buffer size; the initial state was the DELLIM state. Figure 10 shows how the buffer size evolves in time. We can see that it oscillates between the upper and the lower limit. When the upper limit is hit, the throughput is enhanced by switching to the THRMAX state and the buffer size decreases. When the lower limit is reached, the DELLIM state is entered to increase the number of query objects processed until the given delay limit. However, the throughput is decreased and the buffer enlarges.

Table 5 provides an insight into the approach. Each row corresponds to one experiment with the given lower and upper switch limits of the buffer size. Individual statistics are computed from the second switch when the behavior of the buffer size evolution stabilizes (see Fig. 10) and relevant results can be obtained. In particular, the statistics are computed between the second time the application enters the DELLIM state and the last time the THRMAX state is exited. This ensures that the application was in each state the same number of times.

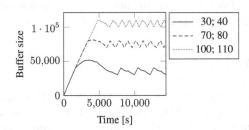

Fig. 10. Buffer size evolution in time for the state switch approach with various switch limits; DL = 1 min; 10 mil. MPEG-7 dataset; 30 ms input frequency; the legend is in the format "lower limit; upper limit" in thousands

Table 5. State switch approach statistics

Lower limit	Upper limit	Time in DS [%]	q in DS [%]	q < DL [%]	q < DL in DS [%]
30,000	40,000	26.4	10.6	13.4	78.4
70,000	80,000	43.9	17.2	18.4	92.1
100,000	110,000	47.5	18.0	18.8	94.3
65,000	85,000	43.6	17.3	18.6	91.5
75,000	80,000	42.6	16.7	17.9	91.8
79,000	80,000	39.8	16.5	17.9	91.0

The column *time in DS* contains the percentage of the time the application spent in the DELLIM state. When a larger buffer size is used, the percentage increases. This is because the average query time is low for large buffer sizes and so the buffer size grows slowly in the DELLIM state and falls fast in the THRMAX state.

The column *q in DS* contains the percentage of queries processed when the application was in the DELLIM state. It correlates with the time spent in the DELLIM state, but it is lower than the percentage of the time spent in the DELLIM state, since the average query time is higher in the DELLIM state than in the THRMAX state.

The column *q < DL* shows the percentage of queries that were processed until the given delay limit (1 min). Again, this correlates with the time spent in the DELLIM state. To compare the numbers with the oldest leaf approach, which is used for the throughput maximization, only 5% of queries were processed with the delay at most 1 min.

The last column *q < DL in DS* contains the percentage of the "before-limit" queries that were processed while the DELLIM state was active. In other words, all the queries that were processed within the delay limit form the whole (100%); the displayed value in the column is the percentage of those that were processed in the DELLIM state. It can be observed that most of the queries that were processed until the delay limit were in fact processed while the DELLIM state was active.

As it can be seen from the experiments, the presented approach can be successfully used for the throughput delay trade-off.

7   Conclusion

We have presented a novel approach to enhance the throughput of similarity search query processing. The technique is based on dynamic reordering of the incoming query objects combined with in-memory caching of the data partitions used to evaluate previous queries. The representation of the query reordering problem is simplified using a query graph thus allowing a theoretical analysis of the proposed techniques. An appropriate ordering of the queries is continuously created by generating a path in the query graph. The introduced methods are verified experimentally with positive results. The presented approach allows to achieve significantly better throughput than the baseline approach when the query objects are evaluated in their original order.

In addition to the throughput maximization, we also targeted optimization criterion trading off the throughput for low delays. The presented technique is based on modification of the query ordering strategy proposed for the throughput maximization. It is parameterized according to the amount of the throughput that can be sacrificed.

Acknowledgement. This work was supported by the Czech national research project GA16-18889S.

References

1. Amato, G., Esuli, A., Falchi, F.: A comparison of pivot selection techniques for permutation-based indexing. Inf. Syst. **52**, 176–188 (2015)
2. Barrios, J.M., Bustos, B., Skopal, T.: Analyzing and dynamically indexing the query set. Inf. Syst. **45**, 37–47 (2014)
3. Batko, M., Novak, D., Zezula, P.: MESSIF: metric similarity search implementation framework. In: Thanos, C., Borri, F., Candela, L. (eds.) DELOS 2007. LNCS, vol. 4877, pp. 1–10. Springer, Heidelberg (2007). https://doi.org/10.1007/978-3-540-77088-6_1
4. Bellmore, M., Nemhauser, G.L.: The traveling salesman problem: a survey. Oper. Res. **16**(3), 538–558 (1968)
5. Brisaboa, N.R., Cerdeira-Pena, A., Gil-Costa, V., Marin, M., Pedreira, O.: Efficient similarity search by combining indexing and caching strategies. In: Italiano, G.F., Margaria-Steffen, T., Pokorný, J., Quisquater, J.-J., Wattenhofer, R. (eds.) SOFSEM 2015. LNCS, vol. 8939, pp. 486–497. Springer, Heidelberg (2015). https://doi.org/10.1007/978-3-662-46078-8_40
6. Budikova, P., Batko, M., Zezula, P.: Evaluation platform for content-based image retrieval systems. In: Gradmann, S., Borri, F., Meghini, C., Schuldt, H. (eds.) TPDL 2011. LNCS, vol. 6966, pp. 130–142. Springer, Heidelberg (2011). https://doi.org/10.1007/978-3-642-24469-8_15
7. Chávez, E., Figueroa, K., Navarro, G.: Effective proximity retrieval by ordering permutations. IEEE Trans. Patt. Anal. Mach. Intell. **30**(9), 1647–1658 (2008)
8. Chung, Y., Su, I., Lee, C., Liu, P.: Multiple k nearest neighbor search. World Wide Web **20**(2), 371–398 (2017)
9. Fagni, T., Perego, R., Silvestri, F., Orlando, S.: Boosting the performance of web search engines: caching and prefetching query results by exploiting historical usage data. ACM Trans. Inf. Syst. **24**(1), 51–78 (2006)
10. Falchi, F., Lucchese, C., Orlando, S., Perego, R., Rabitti, F.: Similarity caching in large-scale image retrieval. Inf. Process. Manage. **48**(5), 803–818 (2012)
11. Jia, Y., et al.: Caffe: convolutional architecture for fast feature embedding. In: Proceedings of the ACM International Conference on Multimedia, MM 2014, Orlando, FL, USA, 03–07 November 2014, pp. 675–678. ACM (2014)
12. Karedla, R., Love, J.S., Wherry, B.G.: Caching strategies to improve disk system performance. IEEE Comput. **27**(3), 38–46 (1994)
13. Laporte, G.: The traveling salesman problem: an overview of exact and approximate algorithms. Eur. J. Oper. Res. **59**(2), 231–247 (1992)

14. Nalepa, F., Batko, M., Zezula, P.: Enhancing similarity search throughput by dynamic query reordering. In: Hartmann, S., Ma, H. (eds.) DEXA 2016. LNCS, vol. 9828, pp. 185–200. Springer, Cham (2016). https://doi.org/10.1007/978-3-319-44406-2_14

15. Novak, D., Batko, M., Zezula, P.: Metric index: an efficient and scalable solution for precise and approximate similarity search. Inf. Syst. **36**(4), 721–733 (2011)

16. Pandey, S., Broder, A.Z., Chierichetti, F., Josifovski, V., Kumar, R., Vassilvitskii, S.: Nearest-neighbor caching for content-match applications. In: Proceedings of the 18th International Conference on World Wide Web, WWW 2009, Madrid, Spain, 20–24 April 2009, pp. 441–450. ACM (2009)

17. Shao, J., Huang, Z., Shen, H.T., Zhou, X., Lim, E., Li, Y.: Batch nearest neighbor search for video retrieval. IEEE Trans. Multimedia **10**(3), 409–420 (2008)

18. Skopal, T., Lokoc, J., Bustos, B.: D-cache: universal distance cache for metric access methods. IEEE Trans. Knowl. Data Eng. **24**(5), 868–881 (2012)

19. Solar, R., Gil-Costa, V., Marín, M.: Evaluation of static/dynamic cache for similarity search engines. In: Freivalds, R.M., Engels, G., Catania, B. (eds.) SOFSEM 2016. LNCS, vol. 9587, pp. 615–627. Springer, Heidelberg (2016). https://doi.org/10.1007/978-3-662-49192-8_50

20. Zezula, P., Amato, G., Dohnal, V., Batko, M.: Similarity search - the metric space approach. In: Advances in Database Systems, vol. 32. Kluwer (2006)

SjClust: A Framework for Incorporating Clustering into Set Similarity Join Algorithms

Leonardo Andrade Ribeiro[1]([✉]), Alfredo Cuzzocrea[2],
Karen Aline Alves Bezerra[3], and Ben Hur Bahia do Nascimento[3]

[1] Instituto de Informática, Universidade Federal de Goiás, Goiânia, Goiás, Brazil
`laribeiro@inf.ufg.br`
[2] DIA Department, University of Trieste and ICAR-CNR, Trieste, Italy
`alfredo.cuzzocrea@dia.units.it`
[3] Departmento de Ciência da Computação, Universidade Federal de Lavras,
Lavras, Brazil
`karen.bezerra@posgrad.ufla.br`, `bhn@computacao.ufla.br`

Abstract. A critical task in data cleaning and integration is the identification of duplicate records representing the same real-world entity. *Similarity join* is largely used in order to detect pairs of similar records in combination with a subsequent clustering algorithm for grouping together records referring to the same entity. Unfortunately, the clustering algorithm is strictly used as a post-processing step, which slows down the overall performance, and final results are produced at the end of the whole process only. Inspired by this critical evidence, in this article we propose and experimentally evaluate *SjClust*, a framework to integrate similarity join and clustering into a single operation. The basic idea of our proposal consists in introducing a variety of cluster representations that are smoothly merged during the set similarity task carried out by the join algorithm. An optimization task is further applied on top of such framework. Experimental results derived from an extensive experimental campaign show that we outperform previous approaches by an order of magnitude in most settings.

1 Introduction

A critical task in data cleaning and integration is the identification of duplicate records representing the same real-world entity [14]. This topic is becoming more and more relevant in emerging *big data research* (e.g., [23, 34, 37]), as a plethora of real-life applications are characterized by the presence of multiple records representing the same real-world entity, which practically plagues every database in this context. Such records are often referred to as *fuzzy duplicates* [9] (duplicates, for short), because they might not be exact copies of one another. Duplicates arise due to a variety of reasons, such as typographical errors and misspellings, different naming conventions, and as a result of the integration of data sources storing overlapping information.

© Springer-Verlag GmbH Germany, part of Springer Nature 2018
A. Hameurlain et al. (Eds.): TLDKS XXXVIII, LNCS 11250, pp. 89–118, 2018.
https://doi.org/10.1007/978-3-662-58384-5_4

Duplicates degrade the quality of the data delivered to application programs, thereby leading to a myriad of problems. Some examples are misleading data mining models owing to erroneously inflated statistics, inability of correlating information related to a same entity, and unnecessarily repeated operations, e.g., mailing, billing, and leasing of equipment. Duplicate identification is thus of crucial importance in data cleaning and integration.

Duplicate identification is computationally very expensive and, therefore, typically done offline. However, there exist important application scenarios that demand (near) real-time identification of duplicates. Prominent examples are data exploration [18] and data integration [13]. In data exploration, new knowledge has to be efficiently extracted from databases without a clear definition of the information need; users need to get a quick sense about the results of each query and, thus, fast response time is essential. In virtual data integration, integrated data is not materialized and duplicates in the query result assembled from multiple data sources have to be identified—and eliminated—on-the-fly. Such scenarios have fueled the desire to integrate duplicate identification with processing of complex queries [2] or even as a general-purpose physical operator within a DBMS [10].

An approach to speed up duplicate identification is to employ *similarity join* in concert with a *clustering algorithm* [15]. Specifically, similarity join is used to find all pairs of records whose similarity is not less than a specified threshold; the similarity between two records is determined by a *similarity function*. In a post-processing step, the clustering algorithm groups together records using the similarity join results as input.

For data of string type, *set similarity join* is an appealing choice for composing a duplicate identification operator [10]. Set similarity join views its operands as sets—strings can be easily mapped to sets. The corresponding similarity function assesses the similarity between two sets in terms of their overlap and a rich variety of similarity notions can be expressed in this way [31]. Furthermore, a number of optimization techniques have been proposed over the years [5,10,30,31,36] yielding highly efficient and scalable similarity join algorithms.

However, the strategy of using a clustering algorithm strictly for post-processing the results of set similarity join has two serious drawbacks. First, given a group of n, sufficiently similar, duplicates, the set similarity join performs $\binom{n}{2}$ similarity calculations to return the same number of set pairs. While this is the expected behavior considering similarity join in isolation, it also means that repeated computations are being performed over identical subsets. Even worse, we may have to perform much more additional similarity calculations between non-duplicates because low threshold values are typically required for clustering algorithms to produce accurate results [15]. Existing filtering techniques are not effective at low threshold values and, thus, there is an explosion of the number of the comparisons at such values. Second, the clustering is a blocking operator in our context, i.e., it has to consume all the similarity join output before producing any cluster of duplicates as result element. This fact is particularly undesirable when duplicate identification is part of more complex data processing logic, possibly even with human interaction, because it prevents pipelined execution.

In this article, we propose and experimentally assess *SjClust*, a framework to integrate set similarity join and clustering into a single operation, which addresses the above issues. The main idea behind our framework is to represent groups of similar sets by a *cluster representative*, which is incrementally updated during the set similarity join processing. Besides effectively reducing the number similarity calculations needed to produce a cluster of n sets to $O(n)$, we are able to fully leverage state-of-the-art optimization techniques at high threshold values, while still performing well at low threshold values where such techniques are much less effective. Indeed, the resulting composed algorithm is even up to an order of magnitude faster than the original set similarity join algorithm for low threshold values. Moreover, we exploit set size information to identify when no new set can be added to a cluster; therefore, we can then immediately output this cluster and, thus, avoid the blocking behavior. Furthermore, there exists a plethora of clustering algorithms suitable for duplicate identification and no single algorithm is overall the best across all scenarios [15]. Thus, versatility in supporting a variety of clustering methods is essential. Our framework smoothly accommodates various cluster representation and merging strategies, thereby yielding different clustering methods for each combination thereof. We report extensive experiments on various datasets with different characteristics that confirm the accuracy and efficiency of our approach.

This article is a significantly and revised version of a previous conference paper [29]. As part of the new material, we discuss the state of the art in more depth and provide several application scenarios for our proposal. Furthermore, we include a comprehensive set of new experiments covering several aspects not discussed in [29]. In particular, we have evaluated our algorithms on unweighted sets. Note that an overview of *SjClust* appeared earlier in [28].

The remainder of this article is organized as follows. We discuss relevant related work in Sect. 2 and provide necessary background material in Sect. 3. The *SjClust* framework is presented in Sect. 4 and details of its main components are described in Sect. 5. Experimental results are reported and analyzed in Sect. 6. Finally, we wrap up with the conclusions and future work proposals in Sect. 7.

2   Related Work

The duplicate identification problem has a long history of investigation conducted by various research communities spanning databases, machine learning, and statistics, frequently under different names, including record linkage, deduplication, and near-duplicate identification. As a result, there is a plethora of proposals addressing many aspects of this problem from different perspectives, which has been covered in surveys, tutorials, and books [11,14,21]; an experimental evaluation of several techniques can be found in [20].

A simple and efficient approach to duplicate identification employs similarity join followed by clustering. *SjClust* encompasses both operations and, thus, can be straightforwardly used in this setting. On the other hand, obtaining high accuracy may require a quite complicated process, typically involving multiple steps. Our framework is related and can be integrated into a variety of duplicate identification approaches in different ways. We discuss some examples below.

- *Blocking:* A naive approach compares every pair of records, i.e., it requires a quadratic number of comparisons. Obviously, such approach is prohibitively expensive for large databases. Blocking methods aim at reducing the comparison space by dividing the input data into (possibly overlapping) blocks and comparing only records within the same block. Popular blocking methods are *sorted neighborhood* [17] and *canopies* [26]. *SjClust* can be employed to efficiently produce an initial set of non-overlapping blocks; afterwards, more accurate (and expensive) operations can be performed within each block to identify duplicates.
- *Crowdsourcing:* Human-based approaches employ crowdsourcing platforms (e.g., Amazon's Mechanical Turk) to improve accuracy [35]. In such platforms, people with little or no domain expertise get paid to execute a set of "microtasks" called Human Intelligence Tasks (HITs). For duplicate identification, the task is to classify records as duplicates or non-duplicates. In the variant known as cluster-based HIT, workers find duplicates among groups of records rather than pairs. *SjClust* can be used in this context to generate variable-sized, cluster-based HITs.
- *Probabilistic databases:* After having identified all duplicates, a typical next step is to produce a clean database by merging each set of duplicates into a single representation. This strategy may result in loss of information, especially if some records are erroneously classified as duplicates. An alternative is to keep all duplicates and interpret them as alternative representations of a real-world entity. A probabilistic database is then constructed with probabilities associated to each record. Andritsos et al. [3] modeled dirty databases as disjoint clusters of duplicates. For each cluster, record probabilities are calculated by first building a *cluster representative* and then measuring the similarity between each record and the cluster representative. This work was later extended by modeling the results obtained by different parametrization of the clustering algorithm [7]. *SjClust* is well-suited for these techniques: besides supporting multiple clustering methods, *SjClust* also maintains a representative for each cluster.

Furthermore, over the last years, there is growing interest in realizing duplicate identification on-the-fly. A query-driven approach is proposed in [1] to reduce the number of cleaning steps in simple selections queries over dirty data. The same authors presented a framework to answer complex Select-Project-Join queries [2]. Our work is complementary to these proposals as our algorithms can be encapsulated into physical operators to compose query evaluation plans.

There is long line of research on (exact) set similarity joins [5,10,24,30,31,36]. Aspects most relevant to our work are discussed at length in Sect. 3. To the best of our knowledge, integration of clustering into set similarity joins has not been previously investigated in the literature. In [25], the authors employ the concept of proximity} graph to cluster strings without requiring a predefined threshold value. The algorithm to automatically detected cluster borders was improved later in [19]. However, it is not clear how to leverage state-of-the-art set similarity joins in these approaches to improve efficiency and deal with large datasets. In [15], a large number of clustering algorithms are evaluated in the context of duplicate identification. These algorithms use similarity join to produce their input, but can start only after the complete similarity join execution.

By looking at the innovative context of duplicate detection over big data repositories, which is really emerging at now, some relevant state-of-the-art proposals are the following ones. The work in [37] proposes a data cleaning algorithm based on *MapReduce* that extracts relations from nodes in the target Cloud environment and, then, cleans data based on *an innovative weighted-based knowledge model*. The work in [23] evidences the relevance of data cleaning methodologies in big data scenarios, and harnesses both *context* and *usage patterns* of data entities to determine relationships among objects that are recognized as similar. Finally, reference [34] focuses the attention on the specific case of *big RDF data cleaning*, by also considering *semi-automatic methods*.

3   Fundamental Concepts and Background Knowledge

In this section, we first present important concepts and definitions related to set similarity joins before discuss important optimization techniques. Then, we describe a general set similarity join algorithm, which provides the basis for our framework.

3.1   Basic Concepts and Definitions

We determine the similarity between two strings by measuring the overlap of their set representations. Strings are first mapped to sets of elements referred to as *tokens*. We can optionally use a *weighting scheme* to quantify the relative importance of tokens for similarity assessment. Finally, set overlap can be measured in various ways to obtain different notions of similarity.

There are several methods of mapping strings to sets of tokens. A string can be split into a set of word tokens using delimiters such as white space characters. For example, the set of work tokens of the string *"set similarity"* is { *'set'*, *'similarity'*}. Another well-known method is based on the concept of *q-grams*, i.e., sub-strings of length q obtained by "sliding" a window over the characters of a given string. To this end, the string is (conceptually) extended by prefixing and suffixing it with $q - 1$ occurrences of a special character *"$"*, so all its characters participate in exact q q-grams. For example, the string *"token"* can be mapped to the set of *2*-gram tokens { *'$t'*, *'to'*, *'ok'*, *'ke'*, *'en'*, *'n$'*}. Note that the result of both mapping methods can be a multi-set. Thus, we append the symbol of a sequential ordinal number to each occurrence of a token to convert multi-sets into sets, e.g, the multi-set $\{a, b, b\}$ is converted to $\{a \circ 1, b \circ 1, b \circ 2\}$.

In the following, we assume that all strings in the database have already been mapped to sets.

A widely adopted weighting scheme is the Inverse Document Frequency (IDF) [4], which associates a weight $idf\,(t)$ to a token t as follows: $idf\,(t) = ln\,(1 + N/df\,(t))$, where $df\,(t)$ is the *document frequency*, i.e., the number of strings a token t appears in a database of N strings. The intuition behind using IDF is that rare tokens are more discriminative and, therefore, matches on such tokens would have greater contribution to similarity. We refer to the sets obtained after applying a weighting scheme such as IDF as *weighted sets*. We can also reduce to the unweighted case by trivially associating the value of 1 to each token; we refer to sets weighted in this way as *unweighted sets*. The weight of a token t is denoted by $w\,(t)$. The size of a set r, denoted by $|r|$, is given by the number of tokens in r, whereas the weight of r, denoted by $w\,(r)$, is given by the summation of the weights of its tokens, i.e., $w\,(r) = \sum_{t \in r} w\,(t)$; note that we have $|r| = w\,(r)$ for unweighted sets.

We consider a general class of set similarity functions. Given two sets r and s, a set similarity function $sim\,(r, s)$ returns a value in $[0, 1]$ to represent their similarity; larger value indicates that r and s have higher similarity. We assume that $sim\,(r, s)$ is commutative, i.e., $sim\,(r, s) = sim\,(s, r)$. Popular set similarity functions are defined as follows [10, 30, 36].

Definition 1 (Set Similarity Functions). *Let r and s be two sets. We have:*

- *Jaccard similarity: $J\,(r, s) = \frac{w(r \cap s)}{w(r \cup s)}$.*
- *Dice similarity: $D\,(r, s) = \frac{2 \cdot w(r \cap s)}{w(r) + w(s)}$.*
- *Cosine similarity: $C\,(r, s) = \frac{w(r \cap s)}{\sqrt{w(r) \cdot w(s)}}$.*

Example 1. Consider the sets r and s below

$$r = \{\mathbf{A}, \mathbf{B}, C, \mathbf{D}, \mathbf{E}\}$$
$$s = \{\mathbf{A}, \mathbf{B}, \mathbf{D}, \mathbf{E}, F\}$$

and the following token-IDF association table:

Considering r and s as unweighted sets, we have $w\,(r) = w\,(s) = 5$ and $w\,(r \cap s) = 4$; thus $sim\,(r, s) = \frac{4}{5+5-4} \approx 0.66$. Considering the IDF weights and, therefore, r and s as weighted sets, we have $w\,(r) = w\,(s) = 10$ and $w\,(r \cap s) = 8$; thus $sim\,(r, s) = \frac{8}{10+10-8} \approx 0.66$.

We now formally define the set similarity join operation.

tk	A	B	C	D	E	F
$idf\,(tk)$	1.5	2.5	2	3.5	0.5	2

Definition 2 (Set Similarity Join). *Given two set collections $\mathcal{R}$ and $\mathcal{S}$, a set similarity function sim, and a threshold τ, the set similarity join between $\mathcal{R}$ and $\mathcal{S}$ returns all scored set pairs $\langle (r, s), \tau' \rangle$ s.t. $(r, s) \in \mathcal{R} \times \mathcal{S}$ and $sim(r, s) = \tau' \geq \tau$.*

In this article, we focus on self-join, i.e., $\mathcal{R} = \mathcal{S}$; we discuss the extension for binary inputs in Sect. 3.3. We also focus on the Jaccard similarity, i.e., unless stated otherwise, $sim(r, s)$ denotes $J(r, s)$. For brevity, we use henceforth the term similarity function (join) to mean set similarity function (join).

3.2 Optimization Techniques

Similarity functions can be equivalently represented in terms of an *overlap bound* [10]. Formally, the overlap bound between two sets r and s, denoted by $O(r, s)$, is a function that maps a threshold τ and the set weights to a real value, s.t. $sim(r, s) \geq \tau$ iff $w(r \cap s) \geq O(r, s)$[1]. The similarity join can then be reduced to the problem of identifying all pairs r and s whose overlap is not less than $O(r, s)$. For the Jaccard similarity, we have $O(r, s) = \frac{\tau}{1+\tau} \times (w(r) + w(s))$.

Further, similar sets have, in general, roughly similar weights. We can derive bounds for immediate pruning of candidate pairs whose weights differ enough. Formally, the weight bounds of r, denoted by $min(r)$ and $max(r)$, are functions that map τ and $w(r)$ to a real value s.t. $\forall s$, if $sim(r, s) \geq \tau$, then $min(r) \leq w(s) \leq max(r)$ [31]. Thus, given a set r, we can safely ignore all other sets whose weights do not fall within the interval $[min(r), max(r)]$. For the Jaccard similarity, we have $[min(r), max(r)] = \left[\tau \times w(r), \frac{w(r)}{\tau} \right]$. We refer the reader to [32] for definitions of overlap and weight bounds of several other similarity functions, including Dice and Cosine.

We can prune a large share of the comparison space by exploiting the *prefix filtering principle* [10,31], which allows discarding candidate pairs by examining only a fraction of the input sets. We first fix a global order $\mathcal{O}$ on the universe $\mathcal{U}$ from which all tokens are drawn. A set $r' \subseteq r$ is a prefix of r if r' contains the first $|r'|$ tokens of r. Further, $pref_\beta(r)$ is the shortest prefix of r, the weights of whose tokens add up to more than β. The prefix filtering principle is defined as follows. It can be shown that if $w(r \cap s) \geq \alpha$, then $pref_{\beta_r}(r) \cap pref_{\beta_s}(r) \neq \varnothing$, where $\beta_r = w(r) - \alpha$ and $\beta_s = w(s) - \alpha$, respectively.

We can identify all candidate matches of a given set r using the prefix $pref_\beta(r)$, where $\beta = w(r) - min(r)$. We denote this prefix simply by $pref(r)$. It is possible to derive smaller prefixes for r, and thus obtain more pruning power, when we have information about the set weight of the candidate sets, i.e., if $w(s) \geq w(r)$ [5] or $w(s) > w(r)$ [30]. Note that prefix overlap is a condition necessary, but not sufficient to satisfy the original overlap constraint: an additional verification must be performed on the candidate pairs. Finally, the number of candidates can be significantly reduced by using the *inverse document frequency ordering*, $\mathcal{O}_{idf}$, as global token order to obtain sets ordered by

---

[1] For ease of notation, the parameter τ is omitted.

Algorithm 1. Similarity join algorithm

Input: A set collection $\mathcal{R}$ sorted in increasing order of the set weight; each set
is sorted according to $\mathcal{O}_{idf}$; a threshold τ

Output: A set S containing all pairs (r, s) s.t. $Sim(r, s) \geq \tau$

1 $I_1, I_2, \ldots I_{|U|} \leftarrow \varnothing, S \leftarrow \varnothing$

2 **foreach** $r \in \mathcal{R}$ **do**

3 $\quad$ $M \leftarrow$ empty map from set id to overlap score (os)

4 $\quad$ **foreach** $t \in pref(r)$ **do** $\qquad\qquad\qquad\qquad\qquad\qquad$ // can. gen. phase

5 $\quad\quad$ **foreach** $s \in I_t$ **do**

6 $\quad\quad\quad$ **if** $w(s) < min(r)$

7 $\quad\quad\quad\quad$ Remove s from I_t

8 $\quad\quad\quad$ **if** $filter(r, s, M(s))$

9 $\quad\quad\quad\quad$ $M(s).os \leftarrow -\infty$ $\qquad\qquad\qquad\qquad\qquad\qquad$ // invalidate s

10 $\quad\quad\quad$ **else** $M(s).os = M(s).os + w(t)$

11 $\quad$ $S \leftarrow S \cup Verify(r, M, \tau)$ $\qquad\qquad\qquad\qquad\qquad\qquad$ // verif. phase

12 $\quad$ **foreach** $t \in pref(r)$ **do** $\qquad\qquad\qquad\qquad\qquad\qquad$ // index. phase

13 $\quad\quad$ $I_t \leftarrow I_t \cup \{r\}$

14 **return** S

---

decreasing IDF weight[2]. The idea is to minimize the number of sets agreeing on prefix elements and, in turn, candidate pairs by shifting lower frequency tokens to the prefix positions. Note that an equivalent ordering is the *document frequency ordering*, which can be used to obtain sets ordered by increasing token frequency in the collection—recall that IDF weights and document frequency are inversely proportional.

Example 2. Consider the sets r and s in Example 1 and $\tau = 0.6$. For the unweighted case, we have $O(r, s) = 3.75$; $[min(r), max(r)]$ and $[min(s), max(s)]$ are both $[3, 8.3]$. For the weighted case, we have $O(r, s) = 7.5$; $[min(r), max(r)]$ and $[min(s), max(s)]$ are both $[6, 16.7]$. By ordering r and s according to $\mathcal{O}_{idf}$ based on the IDF weights in Example 1, we obtain:

$$r = \{D, B, C, A, E\}$$
$$s = \{D, B, F, A, E\}.$$

For unweighted sets, we have $pref(r) = pref(s) = \{D, B\}$; for weighted sets, we have $pref(r) = pref(s) = \{D\}$.

3.3 Similarity Join Algorithm

Algorithm 1 formalizes the general steps of a similarity join algorithm based on inverted lists, which exploits all the previous optimizations [5, 24, 30, 31, 36].

---

[2] A secondary ordering is used to break ties consistently (e.g., the lexicographic ordering).

It has a typical high-level structure following a filter-and-refine approach. The algorithm receives as input a set collection sorted in increasing order of set weights, where each set is sorted according to $\mathcal{O}_{idf}$. An inverted list I_t stores all sets containing a token t in their prefix; inverted lists together with the output set are constructed at beginning of the algorithm (line 1). The input collection $\mathcal{R}$ is scanned and, for each *probe set* $r \in \mathcal{R}$, its prefix tokens are used to find *candidate sets*, denoted in the algorithm by s, in the corresponding inverted lists (lines 4–10); this is the *candidate generation phase*, where the map M is used to associate candidates to its accumulated overlap score os (line 3). Each candidate s is dynamically removed from the inverted list if its weight is less than $min\,(r)$ (lines 6–7). Further filters, e.g., filter based on an overlap bound, are used to check whether s can be a true match for r (i.e., whether r and S can satisfy the overlap constraint), and then the overlap score is accumulated, or not, and s can be safely ignored in the following processing (lines 8–10). In the *verification phase*, r and its matching candidates, which are stored in M, are checked against the similarity predicate and those pairs satisfying the predicate are added to the result set. To this end, the *Verify* procedure (not shown) employs a merge-join-based algorithm exploiting the token order and the overlap bound to define break conditions (line 11) [30]. Finally, in the *indexing phase*, a *pointer* to set r is appended to each inverted list I_t associated with its prefix tokens (lines 12 and 13).

Algorithm 1 is actually a self-join on a single set collection. Its extension to binary joins is trivial: we first index the smaller collection and then go through the larger collection to identify matching pairs. For simplicity, several filtering strategies such positional filtering [36] and min-prefixes [30], as well as inverted list reduction techniques [5, 30] were omitted in the remainder of this article. Nevertheless, these optimizations are based on tighter bounds and shorter prefixes. While they allow discarding candidate pairs that cannot be similar earlier, there are no false negatives, i.e., no pair satisfying the overlap constraint is missed in the result. Therefore, our discussion in the following remains valid.

4   Our Proposal: The Innovative *SjClust* Framework

We now present an overview of *SjClust*, a general framework to integrate clustering methods into similarity joins algorithms; we delve into details of its main components in Sect. 5. The goals of our framework are threefold: (1) *flexibility and extensibility* by accommodating different clustering methods; (2) *efficiency* by fully leveraging existing optimization techniques and by reducing the number of similarity computations to form clusters; (3) *non-blocking behavior* by producing results before having consumed all the input, preferably much earlier.

The backbone of *SjClust* is the similarity join algorithm presented in Sect. 3. In particular, *SjClust* operates over the same input of sorted sets, without requiring any pre-processing, and has the three execution phases present in Algorithm 1, namely, candidate generation, verification, and indexing phases. Nevertheless, there are, of course, major differences between *SjClust* and Algorithm 1 as we discuss in the following.

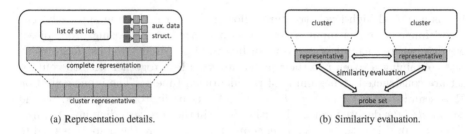

(a) Representation details.   (b) Similarity evaluation.

Fig. 1. Cluster representation.

The main objects are now cluster of sets, or simply clusters. Figure 1 illustrates the strategy adopted for cluster representation. The internal representation contains a list of its set element's ids, an (optional) auxiliary structure, and the cluster's *complete representation*, a set containing all tokens from all set elements. A cluster exports its external representation as the so-called *cluster representative* (or simply representative) (Fig. 1(a)). Representatives are comparable to input sets and similarity evaluations are always performed on the representatives, either between a probe set and a cluster or between two clusters (Fig. 1(b)). In the following, we use the terms cluster and representative interchangeably whenever the distinction is unimportant for the discussion.

Figure 2 depicts more details on the *SjClust* framework. In the candidate generation phase, prefix tokens of the current probe set are used to find cluster candidates in the inverted lists (Fig. 2(a)). Also, there is a *merging phase* between verification and indexing phases (Fig. 2(b)). The verification phase reduces the number of candidates by removing false positives, i.e., clusters whose similarity to the probe set is less than the specified threshold. In the merging phase, a new cluster is generated from the probing set and the clusters that passed through the verification are considered for merging with it according to a *merging strategy*. In the indexing phase, references to the newly generated cluster are stored in the inverted lists associated with its prefix tokens. Finally, there is the so-called *Output Manager*, which is responsible for maintaining references to all clusters—a reference to a cluster is added to the Output Manager right after its generation in the merging phase (Fig. 2(b)). Further, the Output Manager sends a cluster to the output as soon as it is identified that no new probing set can be similar to this cluster. Clusters in such situation can be found in the inverted lists during the candidate generation (Fig. 2(a)) as well as identified using the weight of the probe set (not shown in Fig. 2).

Note that *SjClust* can be smoothly integrated into similarity join algorithms following the high-level structure of Algorithm 1. Basically, one just needs to plug the merging component and the Output Manager into an existing algorithm. Because, clusters are represented as ordinary sets, any technique can be transparently applied during candidate generation, verification, and indexing phases.

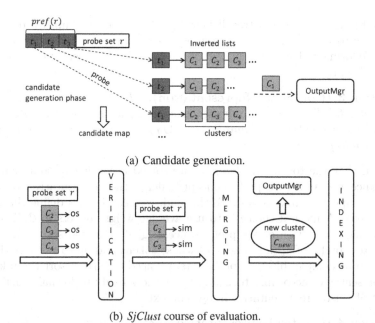

(a) Candidate generation.

(b) *SjClust* course of evaluation.

Fig. 2. *SjClust* framework components.

The aforementioned goals of *SjClust* are met as follows: flexibility and extensibility are provided by different combinations of cluster representation and merging strategies, which can be independently and transparently plugged into the main algorithm; efficiency is obtained by the general strategy to cluster representation and indexing; and non-blocking behavior is ensured by the Output Manager. Next, we provide details of each *SjClust* component.

5 *SjClust* Main Components

In this section, we present details of the main conceptual *SjClust* components, namely cluster representation, merging strategies, and the Output Manager.

5.1 Cluster Representation

Cluster representatives are used to compactly represent a cluster, while capturing the most significant features of its elements. In our context, there is the additional requirement that cluster representatives must be comparable with the original sets. Also, we want flexibility in obtaining different representation strategies.

We start by defining the complete representation of a cluster of sets, from which we extract the corresponding representative. Intuitively, the complete representation of a cluster is given by the union of its sets. We then order all tokens according to a *cluster ordering*, denoted by $\mathcal{O}_{cl}$. While $\mathcal{O}_{idf}$ is used to increase prefix filtering effectiveness (recall Sect. 3), $\mathcal{O}_{cl}$ is used to improve quality by sorting the tokens in the complete representation in decreasing order of importance. We formally define the concept of the complete representation of a cluster in the following.

Definition 3 (Complete Representation). *Let* $\mathcal{C} = \{r_1, r_2, \ldots, r_n\}$ *be a cluster of sets. The complete representation of* $\mathcal{C}$, *denoted by* $CompR_{\mathcal{C}}$, *is the union of its elements, i.e.,* $CompR_{\mathcal{C}} = r_1 \cup r_2 \cup \ldots \cup r_n$, *sorted in decreasing order according to* $\mathcal{O}_{cl}$.

Given that the tokens in $CompR_{\mathcal{C}}$ are sorted according to some notion of importance, we can use the prefix concept to derive the representative containing the most important tokens in $\mathcal{C}$. To this end, we need to first define the weight of the prefix. A natural choice is to use average weight of sets in $\mathcal{C}$. Then, we define a slight variation of the prefix concept: given a sorted set r, $pref'_\alpha(r)$ is the shortest prefix of r, the weights of whose tokens add up to *not less* than α. Finally, to be comparable with probe sets, we need to further sort the tokens in the representative according to $\mathcal{O}_{idf}$. We are now ready to formally define the concept of cluster representative in our context.

Definition 4 (Cluster Representative). *Let* $\mathcal{C} = \{r_1, r_2, \ldots, r_n\}$ *be a cluster of sets and* $CompR_{\mathcal{C}}$ *its complete representation according to Definition 3. The cluster representative of* $\mathcal{C}$, *denoted by* $CR_{\mathcal{C}}$, *is the following prefix of* $CompR_{\mathcal{C}}$:

$$CR_{\mathcal{C}} = pref'_\alpha(CompR_{\mathcal{C}}), where\ \alpha = \sum_{i=1}^{n} \frac{w(r_i)}{n},$$

ordered according to $\mathcal{O}_{idf}$.

Given a cluster $\mathcal{C}$, the (conceptual) steps for the construction of its representative is summarized as follows: the complete representation $CompR_{\mathcal{C}}$ is obtained by (1) unioning all sets in $\mathcal{C}$ and (2) sorting the tokens in the result in decreasing order according to $\mathcal{O}_{cl}$; the cluster representative $CompR_{\mathcal{C}}$ is then obtained by (3) extracting a prefix from $CompR_{\mathcal{C}}$ whose weight is not less than the average weight of the original sets and (4) sorting its tokens in decreasing order according to $\mathcal{O}_{idf}$.

We can now derive cluster different representation strategies by instantiating $\mathcal{O}_{cl}$. Specifically, $\mathcal{O}_{cl}$ can be defined by associating weights to tokens using a weighting scheme in the same fashion as $\mathcal{O}_{idf}$. A suitable weighting scheme to our context is the TF (Term Frequency), where the weight $tf(tk)$ of a token tk in a cluster $\mathcal{C}$ is directly given by the frequency of tk in $\mathcal{C}$. The intuition behind using TF-based ordering is to represent a cluster by its most frequent tokens. Such strategy requires the maintenance of a token-tf table for each cluster. Two sorting operations are needed after a merging between a probe set and one or more clusters: the first on the complete representation using the updated token-TF table and the second on the representative using IDF weights. Note that merging always occurs on the complete representation and the new representative is generated afterward.

Furthermore, except for $\mathcal{O}_{idf}$ and the more general definition in terms of weighted sets, this cluster representation is the same as the one used in [25]. A clear drawback of using TF is that frequent tokens in the collection, consequently with low IDF weights, tend to be also frequent within clusters. As opposed to rare tokens, such highly frequent tokens are often unimportant for similarity assessment, but can nevertheless appear in the representative owing to the TF-based ordering.

An alternative is to simply make $\mathcal{O}_{cl} = \mathcal{O}_{idf}$, i.e., the complete representation follows the same ordering of the input sets. A representative now is composed by tokens with the highest IDF values. This approach has a lower computational cost as compared to the previous representation: it does not require maintenance of an extra data structure such as the token-TF table, nor further sorting after merging clusters to probe sets. However, we now have the drawback that the representative may contain tokens that appear in only a few sets in the cluster.

Finally, we can avoid the issues of the previous strategies, while keeping their advantages, by using the TF-IDF weighting scheme: the weight *tf-idf* (tk) of a token tk is given by *tf-idf* $(tk) = (1 + ln\,(tf\,(tk))) \cdot idf\,(tk)$. Henceforth, we refer to the proposed representation strategies by their adopted weighting scheme, i.e., as TF, IDF, and TF-IDF representations.

Example 3. Consider the sets (or cluster representatives) r and s in Example 1. After the union of r and s, the resulting token-TF and token-TF-IDF association tables are as follows (for simplicity, we have not taken the logarithm of TF in the latter table).

The complete representation and the corresponding cluster representative for strategies TF, IDF, and TF-IDF are shown in Table 1—for the complete representation using TF and TF-IDF, ties are broken using the IDF-based ordering.

tk	A	B	C	D	E	F
tf (tk)	2	2	1	2	2	1
tf-idf (tk)	3	5	2	7	1	2

5.2 Merging Strategies

We now discuss strategies for the merging phase. The output of the verification phase is the current probe set r and a set of clusters S, where each cluster in S is similar to r. After generating a new (singleton) cluster $\mathcal{C}_r$ from the probe set, and before sending it to the indexing phase, there are three cases to consider in the merging phase.

(1) S is empty: the probe set is not similar to any previously generated cluster and $\mathcal{C}_r$ goes directly to the indexing phase.

Table 1. Cluster representations from Example 3 for strategies TF, IDF, and TF-IDF.

TF	**Complete representation**					
	D	B	A	E	C	F
	Representative					
	D	B	C	A	E	—
IDF	**Complete representation**					
	D	B	C	F	A	E
	Representative					
	D	B	C	F	—	—
TF-IDF	**Complete representation**					
	D	B	A	C	F	A
	Representative					
	D	B	A	C	F	—

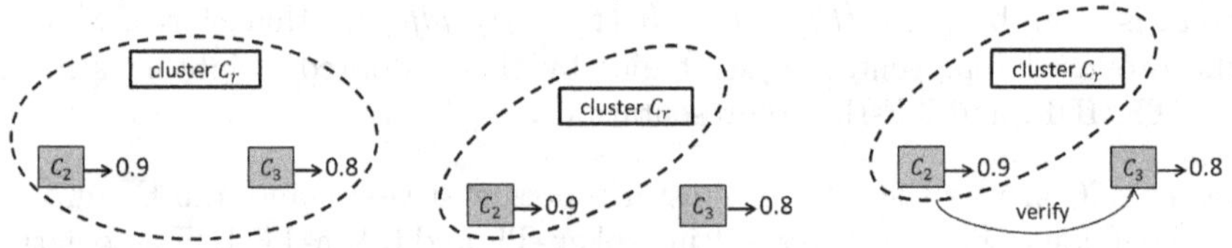

(a) Closure strategy   (b) Top-k strategy.   (c) Iterative strategy.

Fig. 3. Cluster merging strategies.

(2) S contains a single cluster: this single cluster is merged into C_r.
(3) S contains more than one cluster: we apply a merging strategy, considering that the elements in S were not identified as similar to one another in previous *SjClust* iterations.

The new cluster C_r is also sent to the Output Manager in cases (2) and (3), and in case (1) if singleton clusters are allowed to appear in the result.

Now, we present three strategies for case (3) as depicted in Fig. 3.

- *Closure:* the simplest strategy is to merge all clusters in S into C_r (Fig. 3(a)). This strategy corresponds to calculating the *transitive closure* of the similarity graph induced by input sets. The main problem of this strategy is that it tends to produce bigger clusters with several sets representing non-duplicates, thereby leading to poor precision in the results.
- *Top-K:* in this strategy, we first sort the elements in S according to their similarity to the probe set. Then, we take the K closest clusters and merge them into C_r (Fig. 3(b)). An issue with this strategy is choosing the value of K: we can have the same issue of poor precision as Closure if K is too large; conversely, we can face the opposite problem if K is too small, i.e., smaller clusters are formed with duplicates in different clusters, thereby leading to poor recall.

– *Iterative:* this strategy is a specialization of Top-K, which aims at allowing the use of a small K value to maintain precision, while avoiding a drop in recall. First, the K closest clusters are merged into C_r; afterward the algorithm proceeds iteratively, evaluating the similarity between C_r and the following $K+1, K+2, \ldots, |S|$ clusters, in decreasing order of similarity to the original probe set. If the similarity between the current cluster C_{K+i} and C_r is greater than the original threshold τ, then C_{K+i} is merged into C_r and the algorithm proceeds to the next representative; otherwise it stops. This strategy is similar in spirit to the merge-and-refine strategy to duplicate identification [6], which exploits the insight that a merging operation can lead to new matches.

A cluster C is called an invalid cluster after having been merged into another cluster. Invalid clusters have to be ignored in the subsequent processing. Since there are several references to clusters in the inverted lists and the Output Manager, we need some *garbage collection* mechanism to remove references to invalid clusters. We use a simple attribute in the cluster object to indicate whether it is valid or not. This attribute is checked every time a reference to a cluster is found in the candidate evaluation phase (see line 5 in Algorithm 1) and references to invalid clusters are promptly discarded.

5.3   The Output Manager

At each *SjClust* iteration, a probe set is converted into a new cluster and indexed. Afterward, this cluster may progressively become part of bigger clusters, up to a point when no new element can be added to the current cluster; we say then that this cluster is closed. A cluster is trivially closed when the input is exhausted or when the weight of the current probe set is too large to be similar to this cluster. In the latter situation, we know that no following probe set can be similar either, because the input is sorted in increasing order of set weights. We now define the concept of closed cluster, before presenting the details of the Output Manager component.

Definition 5 (Closed Cluster). *Let* $\mathcal{R} = (r_i)_{i=1}^{n+1}$ *be a set collection, where* $w(r_1) > 0$, $w(r_i) \leq w(r_{i+1})$, *and* $w(r_{n+1}) = \infty$. *Let* C *be a cluster and* CR_C *its representative; let* $r_i \in \mathcal{R}$ *be the current probe set.* C *is a closed cluster if* $w(CR_C) < min(r_i)$.

In the above definition, note that we have conceptually extended $\mathcal{R}$ with set r_{n+1} to ensure that all sets r_i, $i \leq n$, can belong to a closed cluster.

The Output Manager is the *SjClust* component in charge of sending closed clusters to the output. The Output Manager is illustrated in Fig. 4. It contains two data structures: a temporary repository and an output buffer. Clusters generated in the merging phase are first stored in the temporary repository. It is a kind of priority queue, which maintains clusters sorted in increasing order of their representative weights. We use a simple but highly efficient implementation based on linked lists. The weight of incoming clusters is usually larger than the

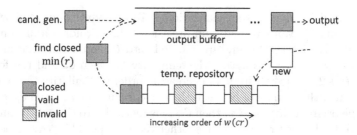

Fig. 4. The Output Manager.

weight of most of the stored ones, and, thus, we typically only need to scan a few positions from the tail to the head of the list to find the point of insertion – the worst case, when a full scan has to be performed, is quite rare for long lists.

We search the temporary repository for closed clusters at the end of each *SjClust* iteration using the $min\,(r)$ value of the current probe cluster. The search is performed from the head to the tail of the list. Closed clusters are sent to the output buffer as they are found and the search is stopped when the first non-closed cluster is met. Note that the temporary repository may also contain invalid clusters, e.g, clusters that were merged into other clusters. Entries to invalid clusters are removed both during insertion and search time and, thus, the size of the temporary repository is kept to a minimum.

The output buffer is a queue, which can be used to deliver clusters in a pipelined execution either in pull- or push-model. Besides from the temporary repository, the output buffer can also receive closed clusters from candidate evaluation phase. This occurs when references to closed clusters are found in the inverted lists (see line 6 in Algorithm 1; in this part, the algorithm is extended with a call to the Output Manager to send the closed cluster to the output buffer). References to closed clusters also need to be garbage collected. They are set as invalid after being sent to the output buffer, so their references can be removed afterwards from inverted lists or the temporary repository.

6   Experimental Assessment and Analysis

We now present an experimental study of our *SjClust* framework. The goal of the empirical experiments is to evaluate and compare quality and performance of the algorithms proposed.

6.1   Datasets

We evaluated our algorithms on publicly available datasets from the Stringer Project[3], which have already been used to evaluate clustering algorithms for duplicate identification [15,16]. These datasets were generated using the UIS

---

[3] http://dblab.cs.toronto.edu/project/stringer/clustering/.

database generator[4]. Starting with a clean dataset as source, UIS generates duplicates by performing controlled textual transformations, such as character-level modifications (insertions, deletions, and substitutions), word swapping, and domain specific abbreviations, such replacing "Incorporated" with"Inc.". Two datasets were used as source: *DBLP* containing information about titles of computer science publications (dblp.uni-trier.de/xml) and *Company*, containing company names.

Table 2. Information about duplicate datasets.

Group	Name	Percentage of	
		Erroneous duplicates	Errors in duplicates
High error	H1	90	30
	H2	50	30
Average error	M1	30	30
	M2	10	30
	M3	90	10
	M4	50	10
Low error	L1	30	10
	L2	10	10

We used all 58 datasets made available by the Stringer Project in our evaluation. In the rest, we concentrate on a representative subset of 16 datasets, 8 datasets for each source. Results for the other datasets followed similar trends. The parameters used in the generation processes are reproduced in Table 2. The "dirtiness level" of a generated dataset is determined by the percentage of duplicates to which transformations are applied (*erroneous duplicates*) and the extent of transformations applied to each erroneous duplicate (*errors in duplicates*). The percentage of token swap and abbreviations for all datasets were 20% and 50%, respectively. The datasets are grouped according to their "dirtiness level", i.e., high, medium, and low error. The number of clusters in each dataset, as provided by the Stringer Project, is 500. Samples of the datasets are also publicly available[5].

We converted strings to upper-case letters, eliminated repeated white spaces, and generated the corresponding token sets using q-grams of size 3; for weighted sets, we used the IDF weighting scheme. No further data pre-processing were performed, such as removal of stop words. We then sorted the tokens in each set using $\mathcal{O}_{idf}$ and the set collections in ascending size order. Some important statistics about the resulting medium-error datasets are listed in Table 3; the statistics of the other datasets are similar. Average set size of DBLP is about

---

[4] http://www.cs.utexas.edu/users/ml/riddle/data/dbgen.tar.gz.
[5] http://dblab.cs.toronto.edu/project/stringer/datasets/sample.htm.

Table 3. Dataset statistics: average values over medium-error datasets.

Dataset	# sets	Set size	Set weight	# unique tokens	% rare tokens	% frequent tokens	% stop tokens
DBLP	5050	61.3	223.4	11519	58	2.1	0.12
Company	4980	25.7	95.5	6565	61.6	1	0.25

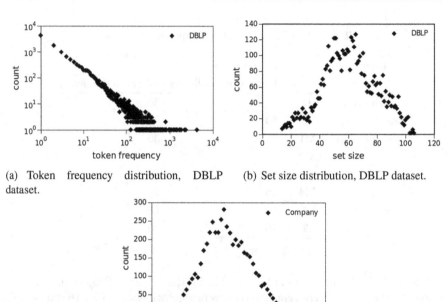

(a) Token frequency distribution, DBLP dataset.

(b) Set size distribution, DBLP dataset.

(c) Set size distribution, Company dataset.

Fig. 5. Token frequency and set size distributions.

2.3x greater than of Company, which is reflected in the corresponding average set weight accordingly. DBLP contains more unique tokens than Company. The percentage of rare tokens (i.e., tokens appearing in 0.1% or less of the set collection) is greater in Company, whereas DBLP has a greater percentage of frequent tokens (i.e., tokens appearing in 5% or more of the set collection). On the other hand, Company has proportionally more extremely frequent tokens, which we call stop tokens (i.e., tokens appearing in 25% or more of the set collection). Distributions of token frequency and set size are plotted in Fig. 5. Only the token frequency distribution of a single medium-error DBLP dataset is shown because the distributions of all the other datasets follow approximately a similar Zipf distribution. We also observe that the set size distributions of DBLP and Company have similar shapes.

6.2   Evaluation Metrics

We evaluate the quality of the results using two metrics: the pairwise F1 measure, denoted by *pF1*, and the closest cluster F1 measure, denoted by *ccF1*. The first metric is based on counting the number of pairs of duplicates correctly identified and is defined as follows [27]. Let G be set of ground truth clusters, i.e., the clusters whose duplicates have been all correctly identified, and D be the set of clusters returned by some cluster algorithm. Further, given a set of clusters P, let *pairs* (P) be a function that returns the set of distinct pairs of elements that are in the same cluster. For example, if $P = \{\langle a, b\rangle, \langle d, e, f\rangle\}$, then *pairs* $(P) = \{(a, b), (d, e), (d, f), (e, f)\}$. Thus, the pairwise precision and recall are defined as

$$pPr\,(G, D) = \frac{|pairs\,(G) \cap pairs\,(D)|}{pairs\,(D)}, \text{ and } pRe\,(G, D) = \frac{|pairs\,(G) \cap pairs\,(D)|}{pairs\,(G)}.$$

Therefore:
$$pF1\,(G, D) = \frac{2 \cdot pPr\,(G, D) \cdot pRe\,(G, D)}{pPr\,(G, D) + pRe\,(G, D)}.$$

The *pPr* measure is the fraction of duplicate pairs within the result, whereas the *pRe* measure is the fraction of identified duplicate pairs over the total amount of duplicate pairs. The *pF1* measure is the weighted harmonic mean of *pPr* and *pRe*.

The closest cluster F1 measure is based on summing up the pairwise Jaccard similarity of (unweighted) clusters. The corresponding precision and recall are defined as follows [6].

$$ccPr\,(G, D) = \frac{\sum_{d \in D} max_{g \in G}\ J\,(d, g)}{|D|}, \text{ and } ccRe\,(G, D) = \frac{\sum_{g \in G} max_{d \in D}\ J\,(g, d)}{|G|}.$$

Therefore:
$$ccF1\,(G, D) = \frac{2 \cdot ccPr\,(G, D) \cdot ccRe\,(G, D)}{ccPr\,(G, D) + ccRe\,(G, D)}.$$

The closest cluster measures take into account similarity between the clusters returned in the result and the ground truth clusters. The *ccPr* measure is the sum of the maximum Jaccard similarity for all r's divided by $|D|$, whereas the *ccRe* measure is the sum of the maximum Jaccard similarity for all g's divided by $|G|$. The *ccF1* measure is the weighted harmonic mean of *ccPr* and *ccRe*.

Regarding the performance experiments, the processing cost of the algorithms is measured in average wall-clock time over repeated runs.

6.3   Experimental Environment and Setup Details

We ran our experiments on an Intel Xeon E5-26200 six-core, 2 GHz, 15 MB CPU cache, and 16 GB of main memory. All algorithms were implemented using Java JDK 8 (Oracle). We implemented the set similarity join described in [30]; this implementation provided the basis for the own *SjClust* implementation as well as was used directly in the performance experiments. *SjClust* was set to not produce singletons. We used Jaccard as similarity function in all evaluations, which is arguably the most popular set similarity function. While other set similarity functions such as Dice and Cosine could lead to different accuracy results, comparison of similarity functions for duplicate detection is beyond the scope of this article. Nevertheless, it is well-known that no single similarity function is the best for all scenarios (e.g., see [12]).

6.4   Accuracy Results

We now report and analyze accuracy results. In the experimental charts, the representation strategy TF-IDF is abbreviated to TI and the merging strategies Closure, Top-K, and Iterative are abbreviated to C, T, and I, respectively. The combination of representation and merging strategies is represented by their abbreviated form connected by a hyphen, i.e., TI-T represents the combination of TF-IDF and Top-K.

First, we show the average of the best accuracy values for each group of datasets, i.e., high-, medium-, and low-error datasets. We evaluated each algorithm with threshold value varying from 0.2 to 0.8; for methods employing the merging strategies Top-K and Iterative, we further varied the K value from 1 to 5. The best result value obtained for each metric is reported.

Figure 6 shows the results on unweighted datasets. Our first observation is that all algorithms achieved high accuracy on low-error DBLP datasets, with values above 0.85 for both pF1 and ccF1 metrics (Fig. 6(a)). In particular, strategies based on TF and TF-IDF representations obtained nearly perfect accuracy. Results degrade as the error level increases in the DBLP datasets (Figs. 6(b) and (c)). Nevertheless, such degradation is moderate for TF and TF-IDF, which show good robustness to quality decrease of the underlying datasets: pF1 (ccF1) values are above 0.95 (0.9) and 0.77 (0.65) on medium and high-error datasets, respectively. Strategies based on TF representation is clearly the best on high-error datasets.

IDF-based strategies achieved the worst results in general due to low recall values. The IDF-based ordering on the complete representation shifts low-frequency tokens to the cluster representative (recall to the discussion in Sect. 5.1). In this context, representatives contain tokens that appear in a few set elements in the corresponding cluster. As a result, objects representing duplicates, i.e., probe sets and representatives, cannot be easily identified because they have fewer tokens in common and, thus, lower similarity.

Figures 6(d)–(f) show the results on Company datasets. Results are worse as compared to those obtained on DBLP datasets. The explanation is that the

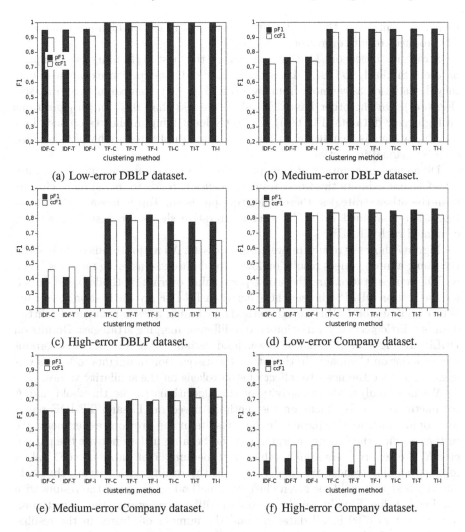

(a) Low-error DBLP dataset.

(b) Medium-error DBLP dataset.

(c) High-error DBLP dataset.

(d) Low-error Company dataset.

(e) Medium-error Company dataset.

(f) High-error Company dataset.

Fig. 6. Best accuracy results for all clustering methods on unweighted datasets.

Company dataset is characterized by the presence of extremely high-frequency words. For example, the word "Corporation" appears in more than 20% of the company names, whereas "Inc." appears in more than 50%. As a result, the separation between duplicates and non-duplicates is much more challenging because there are many similar string representing distinct company names. In the same vein, the results of TF are worse than those of TF-IDF. Such high-frequency words lead to stop tokens, which are then shifted to the cluster representative in the TF strategy. As a result, clusters representing distinct strings can be evaluated as similar and erroneously merged due to the presence of stop tokens in their representatives, thereby hurting precision. In fact, on high-error datasets, TF produces results even worse than IDF.

Strategies based on TF-IDF are clearly the best-performing on Company datasets. Similarly to DBLP datasets, TF-IDF did not experience dramatic accuracy degradation as we move from low-error (Fig. 6(d)) to medium-error datasets (Fig. 6(e)). On the other hand, F1 values are less than 0.45 for all algorithms on high error datasets (Fig. 6(f)). Correctly identifying duplicates on such low-quality datasets is a challenge as some generated duplicates are hardly identified even by manual inspection.

Differences in accuracy are less pronounced when comparing merging strategies. Closure exhibits the worst results because it tends to merge more clusters than the other strategies, thereby hurting precision. Top-K has a slight advantage when combined with TF, whereas Iterative shows the best results when combined with TF-IDF.

Figure 7 show the results on weighted datasets. All major trends remain about the same: almost perfect results on low-error datasets; clustering methods based on IDF representation are the worst-performing overall; methods based on TF are the best on DBLP, whereas those based on TF-IDF are the best on Company; better accuracy on DBLP for all methods, including greater resilience to dirtier datasets; little accuracy variation across different merging strategies. Results on DBLP are slight better for the unweighted variant, while the weighted variant was superior on Company. In the latter, the association of weights to tokens was useful to reduce the negative effect of stop tokens on the similarity values.

We now analyze the sensitivity of the algorithms to the threshold and K parameter values. We focus on the methods based on TF and TF-IDF representation, which were achieved the best results in the previous experiment. We further exclude the Closure merging method because it does not use the parameter K. We report average pF1 values over medium-error datasets; ccF1 values followed similar trends. We used $K = 1$ in the results with varying threshold and the best threshold for given clustering method was used in the results with varying K value. Finally, we also report the difference between the correct number of clusters (500 in all datasets) and the number of cluster in the results: negative and positive values indicate that the method created fewer and greater cluster than the ground truth, respectively.

Figure 8 show the results for unweighted datasets. On DBLP, the best threshold value for all methods is 0.3 and accuracy steadily drops for greater values (Fig. 8(a)). Despite the increase in precision, the drastic drop in recall leads to smaller pF1 values.

Looking at Fig. 8(b), we see that the TF representation produces fewer clusters than TF-IDF in almost all cases. As already mentioned, TF tends to produce representatives containing tokens with higher frequency, which leads to greater similarity between those representatives and input sets. As a result, more clusters are consolidated in the merging phase. We also observe that the number of cluster produced by all algorithms increases with the threshold value up to 0.5 and then decreases afterwards. At first, higher thresholds cause cluster splits

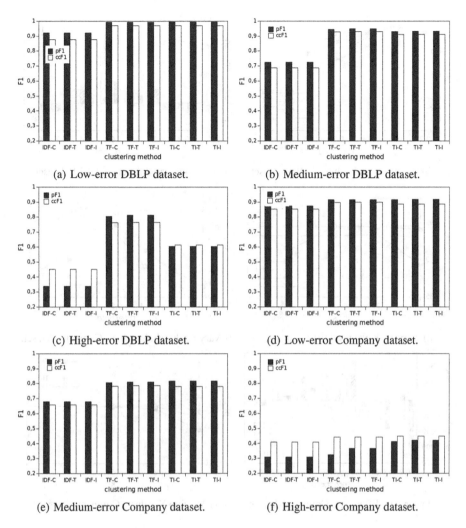

Fig. 7. Best accuracy results for all clustering methods on weighted datasets.

without substantially changing the total number of set elements appearing in the result. For threshold values greater than 0.5, an increasing number of splits results in singleton clusters, which are not sent to the output in the *SjClust* setting used in the experiments (recall Sect. 6.3).

Regarding the results with varying K values (Fig. 8(c)), the accuracy of TI-T substantially increases with $K = 2$. Further increments in K values do not lead to better results for any algorithm; actually, there is even an accuracy drop for TF-T with $K = 4$.

Figure 8(d) shows the results with varying threshold on the Company dataset. Methods based on the TF-IDF representation exhibit similar behavior as com-

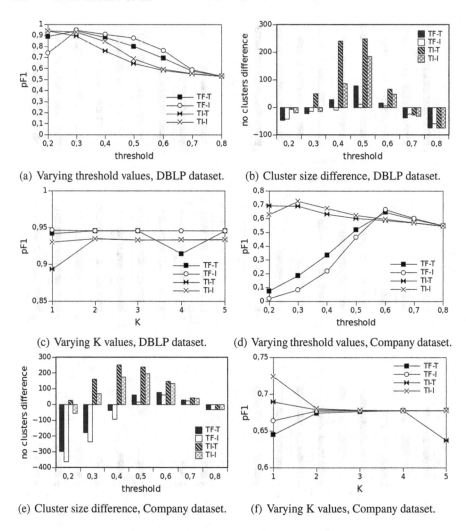

(a) Varying threshold values, DBLP dataset.

(b) Cluster size difference, DBLP dataset.

(c) Varying K values, DBLP dataset.

(d) Varying threshold values, Company dataset.

(e) Cluster size difference, Company dataset.

(f) Varying K values, Company dataset.

Fig. 8. Average accuracy with varying parameter values on unweighted, medium-error datasets.

pared to the results on DBLP: the best accuracy is obtained at threshold 0.3 followed by a steady drop at greater values. On the other hand, methods based on TF peak only at threshold 0.6. As already mentioned, Company contains more stop tokens, which may be placed at cluster representatives by the TF strategy. As a result, clusters of non-duplicates can be erroneously merged at low threshold values. Figure 8(e) illustrates this behavior: for lower threshold values, TF-based methods produce much fewer clusters than the ground truth. The results with varying K values are shown in Fig. 8(f). The best K values are 1 and 2 for methods based on TF-IDF and TF, respectively; no further accuracy increase is obtained for greater values.

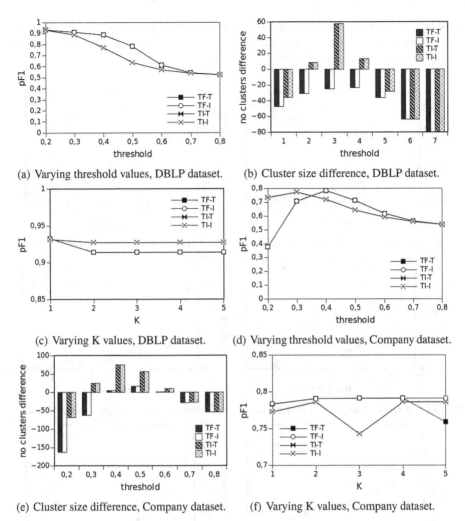

(a) Varying threshold values, DBLP dataset.

(b) Cluster size difference, DBLP dataset.

(c) Varying K values, DBLP dataset.

(d) Varying threshold values, Company dataset.

(e) Cluster size difference, Company dataset.

(f) Varying K values, Company dataset.

Fig. 9. Average accuracy with varying parameter values on weighted, medium-error datasets.

Finally, Fig. 9 show the results with varying threshold and K values on weighted datasets. The trends are very similar to those observed on unweighted sets. The main difference is that best accuracy is typically achieved at threshold values: the best threshold value for all methods is 0.2 on DBLP, and methods based on TF peak at threshold 0.4.

6.5   Performance Results

We now report and analyze performance results. For this experiment, we generated a dataset from DBLP containing 20k groups of 5 duplicates (totaling

100k strings). Besides using a larger dataset, we also appended the corresponding author names to each publication title. As a result, the average set size and weight are increased accordingly.

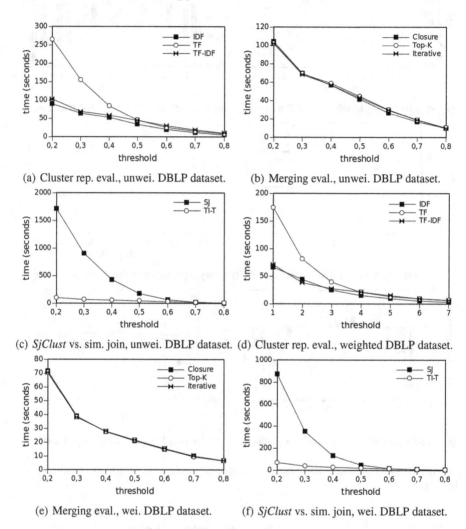

(a) Cluster rep. eval., unwei. DBLP dataset.

(b) Merging eval., unwei. DBLP dataset.

(c) *SjClust* vs. sim. join, unwei. DBLP dataset.

(d) Cluster rep. eval., weighted DBLP dataset.

(e) Merging eval., wei. DBLP dataset.

(f) *SjClust* vs. sim. join, wei. DBLP dataset.

Fig. 10. Performance results.

The results are show in Fig. 10. We first compare the three proposed representation strategies using Top-K as merging strategy. Figure 10(a) shows the results on unweighted sets. While there is relatively little difference between IDF and TF-IDF, TF is about 2.5x slower than them in average at low threshold values. Because TF uses more frequent tokens in the cluster representatives, the corresponding prefixes have more incidences of such tokens even with the posterior IDF-based ordering. As a result, token collisions in the prefixes of dissimilar objects (i.e., sets and representatives) are more frequent, reducing pruning power because those objects need to be verified. The results are similar for weighted sets (Fig. 10(d)). TF-based methods are now about 2.9x slower in average at low threshold values. All algorithms run faster on weighted sets because prefixes based on unweighted sets normally exhibit worse filtering effectiveness as compared to weighted ones [30].

We now compare the performance of the merging strategies; we fixed the cluster representation to TF-IDF. There is no noticeable performance difference among them, as shown in Figs. 10(b) and (e) for unweighted and weighted datasets, respectively. Even with the tendency to performing more merging, Closure exhibits nearly the same performance as compared to Top-K and Iterative. The underlying algorithm exploits token ordering to optimize the merging process and, therefore, the negative impact on performance is reduced. Also, most merging operations involve no more than 2 clusters.

Our next experiment compared *SjClust* with similarity join. Recall that for duplicate identification, similarity join is followed by clustering algorithm, which only starts after the similarity join has completed. Hence, the results showed here for similarity join are only a (loose) lower bound for the scenario of sequential composition of similarity join and clustering. For *SjClust*, we used TF-IDF and Top-K as representation and merging strategies, respectively. Figures 10(c) and (f) show the results for unweighted and weighted datasets, respectively. Remarkably, *SjClust* is dramatically faster than similarity join. For the threshold value of 0.2, *SjClust* is 17x and 12x times faster on unweighted and weighted sets, respectively. The reason is that prefix filtering is ineffective for low threshold values, which causes an explosion in the number of candidates and, consequently, in the number of similarity calculations. This limitation may prevent the use of similarity joins in duplicate identification in large datasets, because low threshold values are often required to obtain accurate results. In contrast, *SjClust* drastically reduces the number of similarity calculations by restricting them to cluster representatives, which are much fewer than the original sets.

Table 4. Percentage of the input consumed before starting producing results.

Threshold	0.2	0.3	0.4	0.5	0.6	0.7	0.8
Unweighted DBLP	88.5%	33.8%	14.5%	7.1%	5.8%	5.3%	8.1%
Weighted DBLP	97.2%	68.8%	29.5%	12.5%	7.9%	6.9%	11.2%

Finally, we illustrate the non-blocking behavior of *SjClust*. Table 4 shows the number of input sets processed before *SjClust* starts producing cluster results. For threshold of 0.8, the first cluster is produced before processing less than 8.1% of the input on unweighted datasets and 11.2% on weighted datasets. Even at threshold 0.2, the first result is produced before consuming the whole input on both unweighted and weighted datasets.

7   Conclusions and Future Work

In this article, we presented *SjClust*, a framework to integrate clustering into set similarity join algorithms. We demonstrated the flexibility of *SjClust* in incorporating different clustering methods by proposing several cluster representation and merging strategies. *SjClust* is an order of magnitude faster than the original set similarity join algorithm for lower thresholds, which are often needed in practice to obtain accurate results in duplicate identification. Furthermore, our proposal produces results earlier, thereby avoiding blocking behavior. We described *SjClust* and its main components in detail and experimentally evaluated its accuracy and efficiency using different datasets. Future work is mainly oriented towards enriching our framework with advanced features such as *uncertain data management* (e.g., [22]), *adaptiveness* (e.g., [8]), and *execution time prediction* (e.g, [33]).

Acknowledgments. This research was partially supported by the Brazilian agencies CNPq and CAPES.

References

1. Altwaijry, H., Kalashnikov, D.V., Mehrotra, S.: Query-driven approach to entity resolution. PVLDB **6**(14), 1846–1857 (2013)
2. Altwaijry, H., Mehrotra, S., Kalashnikov, D.V.: Query: a framework for integrating entity resolution with query processing. PVLDB **9**(3), 120–131 (2015)
3. Andritsos, P., Fuxman, A., Miller, R.J.: Clean answers over dirty databases: a probabilistic approach. In: Proceedings of the ICDE Conference, p. 30 (2006)
4. Baeza-Yates, R.A., Ribeiro-Neto, B.A.: Modern Information Retrieval - The Concepts and Technology Behind Search, 2 edn. Pearson Education Limited, Harlow, England (2011)
5. Bayardo, R.J., Ma, Y., Srikant, R.: Scaling up all pairs similarity search. In: Proceedings of the WWW Conference, pp. 131–140 (2007)
6. Benjelloun, O., Garcia-Molina, H., Menestrina, D., Su, Q., Whang, S.E., Widom, J.: Swoosh: a generic approach to entity resolution. The VLDB J. **18**(1), 255–276 (2009)
7. Beskales, G., Soliman, M.A., Ilyas, I.F., Ben-David, S.: Modeling and querying possible repairs in duplicate detection. PVLDB **2**(1), 598–609 (2009)
8. Cannataro, M., Cuzzocrea, A., Mastroianni, C., Ortale, R., Pugliese, A.: Modeling adaptive hypermedia with an object-oriented approach and XML. In: WebDyn 2002 (2002)
9. Chaudhuri, S., Ganjam, K., Ganti, V., Motwani, R.: Robust and efficient fuzzy match for online data cleaning. In: Proceedings of the SIGMOD Conference, pp. 313–324 (2003)
10. Chaudhuri, S., Ganti, V., Kaushik, R.: A primitive operator for similarity joins in data cleaning. In: Proceedings of the 22nd International Conference on Data Engineering, p. 5 (2006)
11. Christen, P.: Data Matching - Concepts and Techniques for Record Linkage, Entity Resolution, and Duplicate Detection. Springer, Heidelberg (2012). https://doi.org/10.1007/978-3-642-31164-2

12. Cohen, W.W., Ravikumar, P.D., Fienberg, S.E.: A comparison of string distance metrics for name-matching tasks. In: Proceedings of IJCAI 2003 Workshop on Information Integration on the Web, pp. 73–78 (2003)
13. Doan, A.H., Halevy, A.Y., Ives, Z.G.: Principles of Data Integration. Morgan Kaufmann, Waltham (2012)
14. Elmagarmid, A.K., Ipeirotis, P.G., Verykios, V.S.: Duplicate record detection: a survey. TKDE **19**(1), 1–16 (2007)
15. Hassanzadeh, O., Chiang, F., Miller, R.J., Lee, H.C.: Framework for evaluating clustering algorithms in duplicate detection. PVLDB **2**(1), 1282–1293 (2009)
16. Hassanzadeh, O., Miller, R.J.: Creating probabilistic databases from duplicated data. VLDB J. **18**(5), 1141–1166 (2009)
17. Hernández, M.A., Stolfo, S.J.: The merge/purge problem for large databases. In: Proceedings of the SIGMOD Conference, pp. 127–138 (1995)
18. Idreos, S., Papaemmanouil, O., Chaudhuri, S.: Overview of data exploration techniques. In: Proceedings of the SIGMOD Conference, pp. 277–281 (2015)
19. Kazimianec, M., Augsten, N.: PG-Skip: proximity graph based clustering of long strings. In: Yu, J.X., Kim, M.H., Unland, R. (eds.) DASFAA 2011. LNCS, vol. 6588, pp. 31–46. Springer, Heidelberg (2011). https://doi.org/10.1007/978-3-642-20152-3_3
20. Köpcke, H., Thor, A., Rahm, E.: Evaluation of entity resolution approaches on real-world match problems. PVLDB **3**(1), 484–493 (2010)
21. Koudas, N., Sarawagi, S., Srivastava, D.: Record linkage: similarity measures and algorithms. In: Proceedings of the SIGMOD Conference, pp. 802–803 (2006)
22. Leung, C.K.-S., Cuzzocrea, A., Jiang, F.: Discovering frequent patterns from uncertain data streams with time-fading and landmark models. In: Hameurlain, A., Küng, J., Wagner, R., Cuzzocrea, A., Dayal, U. (eds.) Transactions on Large-Scale Data- and Knowledge-Centered Systems VIII. LNCS, vol. 7790, pp. 174–196. Springer, Heidelberg (2013). https://doi.org/10.1007/978-3-642-37574-3_8
23. Liu, H., Ashwin Kumar, T.K, Thomas, J.P.: Cleaning framework for big data - object identification and linkage. In: Proceedings of the Big Data Congress, pp. 215–221 (2015)
24. Mann, W., Augsten, N., Bouros, P.: An empirical evaluation of set similarity join techniques. PVLDB **9**(9), 636–647 (2016)
25. Mazeika, A., Böhlen, M.H.: Cleansing databases of misspelled proper nouns. In: Proceedings of the VLDB Workshop on Clean Databases (2006)
26. McCallum, A., Nigam, K., Ungar, L.H.: Efficient clustering of high-dimensional data sets with application to reference matching. In: Proceedings of the SIGKDD Conference, pp. 169–178 (2000)
27. Menestrina, D., Whang, S., Garcia-Molina, H.: Evaluating entity resolution results. PVLDB **3**(1), 208–219 (2010)
28. Ribeiro, L.A., Cuzzocrea, A., Bezerra, K.A.A., do Nascimento, B.H.B.: *SjClust*: towards a framework for integrating similarity join algorithms and clustering. In: Proceedings of the ICEIS Conference (2016)
29. Ribeiro, L.A., Cuzzocrea, A., Bezerra, K.A.A., do Nascimento, B.H.B.: Incorporating clustering into set similarity join algorithms: the *SjClust* framework. In: Hartmann, S., Ma, H. (eds.) DEXA 2016. LNCS, vol. 9827, pp. 185–204. Springer, Cham (2016). https://doi.org/10.1007/978-3-319-44403-1_12
30. Ribeiro, L.A., Härder, T.: Generalizing prefix filtering to improve set similarity joins. Inf. Syst. **36**(1), 62–78 (2011)
31. Sarawagi, S., Kirpal, A.: Efficient set joins on similarity predicates. In: Proceedings of the SIGMOD Conference, pp. 743–754 (2004)

32. Schneider, N.C., Ribeiro, L.A., de Souza Inácio, A., Wagner, H.M., von Wangenheim, A.: SimDataMapper: an architectural pattern to integrate declarative similarity matching into database applications. In: Proceedings of the SBBD Conference, pp. 967–972 (2015)
33. Sidney, C.F., Mendes, D.S., Ribeiro, L.A., Härder, T.: Performance prediction for set similarity joins. In: Proceedings of the SAC Conference, pp. 967–972 (2015)
34. Tang, N.: Big RDF data cleaning. In: Proceedings of the ICDE Conference Workshops, pp. 77–79 (2015)
35. Wang, J., Kraska, T., Franklin, M.J., Feng, J.: CrowdER: crowdsourcing entity resolution. PVLDB 5(11), 1483–1494 (2012)
36. Xiao, C., Wang, W., Lin, X., Yu, J.X., Wang, G.: Efficient similarity joins for near-duplicate detection. TODS 36(3), 15 (2011)
37. Zhang, F., Xue, H.-F., Xu, D.-S., Zhang, Y.-H., You, F.: Big data cleaning algorithms in cloud computing. iJOE 9(3), 77–81 (2013)

A Query Processing Framework
for Large-Scale Scientific Data Analysis

Leonidas Fegaras[(✉)]

University of Texas at Arlington, Arlington, TX 76019-0015, USA
`fegaras@cse.uta.edu`

Abstract. Current scientific applications must analyze enormous amounts of array data using complex mathematical data processing methods. This paper describes a distributed query processing framework for large-scale scientific data analysis that captures array-based computations using SQL-like queries and optimizes and evaluates these computations using state-of-the-art parallel processing algorithms. Instead of providing a library of concrete distributed algorithms that implement certain matrix operations efficiently, we generalize these algorithms by making them parametric in such a way that the same efficient implementations that apply to the concrete algorithms can also apply to their generic counterparts. By specifying matrix operations as generic algebraic operators, we are able to perform inter-operator optimizations, such as fusing matrix transpose with matrix multiplication, resulting to new instantiations of the generic algebraic operators, without having to introduce new efficient algorithms on the fly. We report on a prototype implementation of our framework on three Big Data platforms: Hadoop Map-Reduce, Apache Spark, and Apache Flink, using Apache MRQL, which is a query processing and optimization system for large-scale, distributed data analysis. Finally, we evaluate the effectiveness of our framework through experiments on three queries: a matrix multiplication query, a simple query that combines matrix multiplication with matrix transpose, and a complex iterative query for matrix factorization.

Keywords: Big data · Scientific data analysis · Query processing

1 Introduction

In recent years, it has become easier and cheaper than ever to collect data but harder to turn these data into value. In computational science, the explosion in scientific data generated by experiments and simulations has created a major challenge for many scientific projects. For data scientists who need to analyze vast volumes of data, data-intensive processing is fast becoming a necessity. They need algorithms capable of scaling to petabytes and faster tools that are more sophisticated, more reliable, and easier to use.

© Springer-Verlag GmbH Germany, part of Springer Nature 2018
A. Hameurlain et al. (Eds.): TLDKS XXXVIII, LNCS 11250, pp. 119–145, 2018.
https://doi.org/10.1007/978-3-662-58384-5_5

As datasets grow larger, new frameworks in distributed Big Data analytics have become essential tools to large-scale machine learning and scientific discoveries. Among these frameworks, the Map-Reduce programming model [14] has emerged as a generic, scalable, and cost effective solution for Big Data processing on clusters of commodity hardware. The Map-Reduce paradigm is a scale-out solution that brings computations to the data, rather than data to the computations. This is a drastic departure from high-performance computing models, which make a clear distinction between processing and storage nodes. Very soon, though, it became apparent that the Map-Reduce model has many limitations. To address these limitations, new alternative frameworks have been introduced recently that perform better than Map-Reduce for a wider spectrum of workloads, such as Google's Pregel [33], Apache Spark [9], and Apache Flink [2], which are in-memory distributed computing systems.

Currently, many programmers prefer to use a higher-level declarative language to code their data-centric applications, such as Apache Hive [5] and PigLatin [36], instead of coding them directly in an algorithmic language, such as Java. For instance, Hive is used for over 90% of Facebook Map-Reduce jobs. Most Map-Reduce query languages though provide a limited syntax for operating on data collections, in the form of simple relational joins and group-bys. They cannot express complex data analysis tasks, such as PageRank, data clustering, and matrix factorization, using SQL-like syntax exclusively. Because of these limitations, these languages enable users to plug-in custom scripts into their queries for those jobs that cannot be declaratively coded in their query language. This nullifies the benefits of using a declarative query language and may result in platform-dependent, suboptimal, error-prone, and hard-to-maintain code. Furthermore, some of these languages are inappropriate for complex scientific and graph analysis applications, because they do not directly support iteration in declarative form and are not able to handle complex scientific data. But there are some recent query systems, such as Apache MRQL [8], which are powerful enough to express complex data analysis tasks.

In the past, large-scale data processing was mainly done in the realm of scientific computing. In recent years, the volume of data generated by scientists through experiments and simulations has been steadily increasing at an unprecedented rate. For example, the Large Hadron Collider at CERN and astronomy's Pan-STARRS5 array of celestial telescopes are capable of generating several petabytes of data per day, which need to be made available and analyzed by scientists on worldwide grids of computers. Data-intensive scientific computing shares some of the key ingredients of cloud computing. Just like in cloud computing, scientific computing is driven to use the most efficient computing techniques available, including high-performance computing and low-level data management. Many scientific data generated by scientific experiments and simulations come in the form of arrays, such as the results from high-energy physics, cosmology, and climate modeling. In addition, many algorithms for scientific data analysis and simulation are frequently expressed in terms of array operations. Furthermore, most scientific file formats used by scientists to store data, such as HDF5 [22] and NetCDF [35], are based on array structures. Since most of the data generated by scientists are in array form, current scientific applications must analyze enormous amounts of array data using complex mathematical data processing methods. Scientists are typically comfortable with numerical analysis tools, such as MatLab, but are not familiar with the intricacies of Big Data analysis and distributed computing. A declarative distributive query language capable of expressing complex mathematical operations on arrays could help them develop their data analysis applications without any prior knowledge of distributed computing.

The goal of this paper is to support large-scale scientific data analysis by (1) extending an existing distributed query language, namely Apache MRQL [8], with array operations that can capture most array-based computations in declarative form and (2) by developing a query processing framework that can optimize and evaluate these computations using state-of-the-art parallel processing algorithms. Other proposed systems [11,27,38,41] focus on storage structures and indexing techniques for arrays, such as chunking and tiling, to achieve better performance on certain parallel array computations. Although such storage layouts may speed up the processing of individual array operations, they produce results in a certain layout that may need to be restructured before they are used by the subsequent matrix operations. Furthermore, such schemes do not address inter-operation optimization, which is the focus of our work. Our approach is to accept any kind of array representation and storage but at the same time be able to recognize certain array operations in a query and translate them into efficient parallel array processing algorithms. For example, matrix multiplication $X \times Y$ between two sparse matrices X and Y can be implemented efficiently in a distributed environment using a 2D mesh of processors [24,44] by distributing the data to worker nodes in the form of a grid of partitions, where each partition contains only those rows from X and those columns from Y needed to compute a single grid partition of the resulting matrix. If a query language were to adopt a certain matrix representation and provide a fixed number of matrix operations in the form of predefined operators or library functions, then the task of recognizing these operations and mapping them to efficient algorithms would have become easy. Such an approach though does not leave many opportunities of inter-operator optimization, such as fusing matrix transpose with matrix multiplication, because the resulting fused operation would have to be a new operation that requires the introduction of a new efficient algorithm on the fly. Instead of looking at concrete algorithms that implement specific mathematical operations, our objective is to generalize these algorithms by making them parametric in such a way that the same efficient implementations that apply to the concrete algorithms can also apply to their generic counterparts.

The most effective method of making an algorithm parametric is to make it higher-order by abstracting parts of its computations into its functional parameters. Such a higher-order operation must capture the essence of the concrete algorithm it generalizes by facilitating an equivalent data distribution and by supporting a similar parallel processing method. To generate such a higher-order operation from a query, a query evaluator must be able to recognize certain syntactic patterns in the query, in their most generic form, that can be mapped to this operation. This task can become more feasible if it is done at the algebraic operation level, rather than at the syntactic level. That is, instead of introducing source-to-source transformations to match parts of a query with certain generic syntactic patterns that correspond to a generic operation, our approach is to translate queries to algebraic forms and then normalize and rewrite these forms into these algorithms using algebraic rewrite rules. We believe that this approach is very effective when applied, not only to matrix operations, but also to a wide spectrum of queries whose functionality is in essence equivalent to these matrix operations.

The contribution of this work can be summarized as follows:

- We define a higher-order operator, called *GroupByJoin*, that generalizes many algorithms that correlate two data sources using an equi-join followed by a group-by with aggregation.
- We provide an efficient implementation of GroupByJoin based on an algorithm that generalizes the SUMMA parallel algorithm for matrix multiplication on two Big Data frameworks: Map-Reduce and Spark.
- We provide an extension to the query optimization framework for MRQL to generate physical plans that use the GroupByJoin operator. This is accomplished with algebraic rewrite rules that recognize certain patterns in the algebraic terms derived from MRQL queries that are equivalent to a GroupByJoin operation. We show how these rewrite rules can be used, in conjunction with the existing algebraic optimization rules in MRQL, to minimize the amount of data shuffling in queries that contain consecutive matrix operations.
- We report on a prototype implementation of our framework using Apache MRQL running on top of three different Big Data platforms: Hadoop Map-Reduce, Apache Spark, and Apache Flink. We show the effectiveness of our methods through experiments on three queries, a matrix multiplication query, a simple query that combines matrix multiplication with matrix transpose, and a very complex query for matrix factorization, which not only is iterative but it also contains many matrix operations at every iteration step.

The rest of this paper is organized as follows. We compare our approach with related work in Sect. 2. We summarize our earlier work on query optimization for MRQL in Sect. 3. We highlight the basic ideas behind our approach in Sect. 4. We introduce the higher-order operator GroupByJoin in Sect. 5). We provide an efficient implementation of GroupByJoin based on the SUMMA algorithm on two Big Data frameworks: Map-Reduce (Sect. 6) and Spark (Sect. 7). We present our framework for translating and optimizing MRQL queries to GroupByJoin operations in Sect. 8. Finally, we evaluate our framework through experiments on three MRQL queries in Sect. 9.

2   Related Work

One of the major drawbacks of the Map-Reduce model is that, to simplify reliability and fault tolerance, it does not preserve data in memory between the map and reduce tasks of a Map-Reduce job or across consecutive jobs, which imposes a high overhead to complex workflows and graph algorithms, such as PageRank and matrix factorization, that require repetitive Map-Reduce jobs. To achieve better performance for such complex workflows, it is crucial to minimize the required number of Map-Reduce jobs, mostly because of the high overhead of dumping the intermediate results between consecutive Map-Reduce jobs to the HDFS. As an alternative solution, some recent systems for cloud computing go beyond Map-Reduce by maintaining dataset partitions in the memory of the compute nodes. These systems include the main memory Map-Reduce M3R [40], Apache Spark [9], Apache Flink [2], and distributed GraphLab [32].

There are also a number of higher-level languages that make Map-Reduce programming easier, such as HiveQL [42], PigLatin [36], SCOPE [12], and Dryad/Linq [28]. Apache Hive [42,43] provides a logical RDBMS environment on top of the Map-Reduce engine, well-suited for data warehousing. Using its high-level query language, HiveQL, users can write declarative queries, which are optimized and translated into Map-Reduce jobs that are executed using Hadoop. HiveQL does not handle nested collections uniformly: it uses SQL-like syntax for querying data sets but uses vector indexing for nested collections. Unlike MRQL, HiveQL has many limitations. It does not allow query nesting in predicates and select expressions, but allows a table reference in the from-part of a query to be the result of a select-query. Apache Pig [23] resembles Hive as it provides a user-friendly scripting language, called PigLatin [36], on top of Map-Reduce, which allows explicit filtering, map, join, and group-by operations. Like Hive, PigLatin performs very few optimizations based on simple rule transformations. PACT/Nephele [10] is a Map-Reduce programming framework based on workflows, which consist of high-order operators, such as map and reduce. These workflows are converted to logical execution plans for Nephele, a general distributed program execution engine. Even though PACT/Nephele workflow programs are very flexible and are not limited to rigid Map-Reduce pairs, they are hard to program, since programmers have to construct low-level workflows. SCOPE [12], an SQL-like scripting language for large-scale analysis, does not support sub-queries but provides syntax to simulate sub-queries using outer-joins. Like Hive, because of its limitations, SCOPE provides syntax for user-defined process/reduce/combine operations to capture explicit Map-Reduce computations. DryadLINQ [46] is a programming model for large scale data-parallel computing that translates programs expressed in the LINQ programming model to Dryad, which is a distributed execution engine for data-parallel applications. Unlike MRQL, the LINQ query syntax is very limited and has limited support for query nesting.

Vertex-centric graph-parallel programming is a new popular framework for large-scale graph processing. It was introduced by Google's Pregel [33] but is now available by many open-source projects, such as Apache Giraph [6], Apache Hama [4], and Spark's GraphX [7]. Most of these frameworks are based on the

Bulk Synchronous Parallelism (BSP) programming model [44]. VERTEXICA [26] and Grail [15] provide the same vertex-centric interface as Pregel but, instead of a distributed file system, they use a relational database to store the graph and the exchanged messages across the BSP supersteps. Unlike Grail, which can run on a single server only, VERTEXICA can run on multiple parallel machines connected to the same database server. Such configuration may not scale out very well because the centralized database may become the bottleneck of all the data traffic across the machines. Although MRQL is a general-purpose Big Data query system, graph queries in MRQL are expressed using SQL-like syntax since graphs are captured as regular distributed collections. These queries are translated to distributed self-joins over the graph data.

Many scientific data generated by scientific experiments and simulations come in the form of arrays, such as the results from high-energy physics, cosmology, and climate modeling. Many of these arrays are stored in scientific file formats that are based on array structures, such as, CDF (Common Data Format), FITS (Flexible Image Transport System), GRIB (GRid In Binary), NetCDF (Network Common Data Format), and various extensions to HDF (Hierarchical Data Format), such as HDF5 and HDF-EOS (Earth Observing System). HDF5 [22] is a data model and file format that enables the data to be organized into hierarchical structures, called groups and datasets. NetCDF [35] is a self-describing data format that supports the creation, access, and sharing of scientific data. It is commonly used in climatology, meteorology, and GIS applications. Many array-processing systems use special storage techniques, such as regular tiling, to achieve better performance on certain array computations. TileDB [37] is an array data storage management system that performs complex analytics on scientific data. It organizes array elements into ordered collections called fragments, where each fragment is dense or sparse, and groups contiguous array elements into data tiles of fixed capacity. Unlike our work, the focus of TileDB is the I/O optimization of array operations by using small block updates to update the array stores. SciDB [39,41] is a large-scale data management system for scientific analysis based on an array data model with implicit ordering. The SciDB storage manager decomposes arrays into a number of equal sized and potentially overlapping chunks, in a way that allows parallel and pipeline processing of array data. Like SciDB, ArrayStore [38] stores arrays into chunks, which are typically the size of a storage block. One of their most effective storage method is a two-level chunking strategy with regular chunks and regular tiles. SystemML [27] is an array-based declarative language to express large-scale machine learning algorithms, implemented on top of Hadoop. It supports many array operations, such as matrix multiplication, and provides alternative implementations to each of them. SciHadoop [11] is a Hadoop plugin that allows scientists to specify logical queries over arrays stored in the NetCDF file format [35]. Their chunking strategy, which is called the Baseline partitioning strategy, subdivides the logical input into a set of partitions (sub-arrays), one for each physical block of the input file. SciHive [25] is a scalable array-based query system that enables scientists to process raw array datasets in parallel with a SQL-like query language.

SciHive maps array datasets in NetCDF files to Hive tables and executes queries via MapReduce. Based on the mapping of array variables to Hive tables, SQL-like queries on arrays are translated to HiveQL queries on tables and then optimized by the Hive query optimizer. Unlike MRQL, SciHive implements matrix multiplication operations using relational joins, instead of group-by-joins. SciMATE [45] extends the Map-Reduce API to support the processing of the NetCDF and HDF5 scientific formats, in addition to flat-files. SciMATE supports various optimizations specific to scientific applications by selecting a small number of attributes used by an application and perform data partition based on these attributes. Finally, MLlib [34], which is part of MLbase [30], is a machine learning library built on top of Spark and includes algorithms for fast matrix manipulation based on native (C++ based) linear algebra libraries. Unlike MRQL, which supports ad-hoc data analysis based on arbitrary vector and matrix representations, MLlib provides a uniform rigid set of high-level APIs that consists of several statistical, optimization, and linear algebra primitives that can be used as building blocks for data analysis applications. Like all API-based frameworks, MLlib does not support inter-operation optimizations, which is the focus of our approach.

The monoid algebra described in Sect. 8.1 has been introduced in our previous work on algebras for distributed big data analysis [17,18], which in turn was based on our early work on monoid algebras and calculi for object-oriented databases [20,21]. The work reported in this paper extends our previous work on array-based computations for Map-Reduce [16] by providing an evaluation framework for Spark and implementations and performance results for both the Spark and Flink platforms.

3   Background: The MRQL Query Language

Apache MRQL [8] is a query processing and optimization system for large-scale, distributed data analysis. MRQL was originally developed by the author [18, 19], but is now an Apache incubating project with many developers and users worldwide. MRQL (the Map-Reduce Query Language) is an SQL-like query language for large-scale data analysis on computer clusters. The MRQL query processing system can evaluate MRQL queries in four modes: in Map-Reduce mode using Apache Hadoop [3], in BSP mode (Bulk Synchronous Parallel model) using Apache Hama [4], in Spark mode using Apache Spark [9], and in Flink mode using Apache Flink (previously known as Stratosphere) [2]. The MRQL query language is powerful enough to express most common data analysis tasks over many forms of raw in-situ data, such as XML and JSON documents, binary files, and CSV documents. MRQL is more powerful than other current high-level Map-Reduce languages, such as Hive [5] and PigLatin [36], since it can operate on more complex data and supports more powerful query constructs, thus eliminating the need for using explicit procedural code. With MRQL, users are able to express complex data analysis tasks, such as PageRank, k-means clustering, matrix factorization, etc, using SQL-like queries exclusively, while the MRQL query processing system is able to compile these queries to efficient Java code.

For example, the following MRQL query that calculates the k-means clustering algorithm (Lloyd's algorithm), by deriving k new centroids from the old (the stopping condition has been omitted):

```
1  repeat centroids = ...
2  step select < X: avg(s.X), Y: avg(s.Y) >
3        from s in  Points
4        group by k: ( select  c from c in  centroids
5                          order by distance(c,s ))[0]
```

Query 1. k-Means Clustering

where Points is a dataset of points on the X-Y plane, centroids is the current set of centroids (k cluster centers), and distance is a function that calculates the Euclidean distance between two points. The repeat query syntax '**repeat** $R = i$ **step** s' defines the dataset R as the fixpoint of the step s by starting with $R = i$ and reassigning R to s at each iteration step, where s is a query that depends on R. (For brevity, the stopping condition of the repeat query has been omitted.) Here, the initial value of centroids (the ... value) is a bag of k random points. The inner select-query in the group-by assigns the closest centroid to a point s (where [0] returns the first tuple of an ordered list). The outer select-query in the repeat step clusters the data points by their closest centroid, and, for each cluster, a new centroid is calculated from the average values of its points.

4   Our Framework

One of the objectives of our work is to accept any kind of array representation but at the same time be able to recognize certain array operations in a query and translate them into efficient parallel array processing algorithms. Sparse vectors and matrices can be captured as regular collections in MRQL. For example, a sparse matrix M can be represented as a collection of triples, (v, i, j), for $v = M_{ij}$. Then, the matrix multiplication between two sparse matrices X and Y can be expressed as follows in MRQL:

```
1  select ( sum(z), i, j )
2    from (x,i,k) in X, (y,k,j) in Y, z = x*y
3  group by i, j
```

Query 2. Matrix multiplication query

that is, we retrieve the values $X_{ik} \in X$ and $Y_{kj} \in Y$ for all i, j, k, and we set $z = X_{ik} * Y_{kj}$. The group-by operation in MRQL lifts each non-group-by variable defined in the from-part of the query from some type T to a bag of T, indicating that each such variable must now contain multiple values, one for each group. Consequently, after we group by the indexes i and j, the variable z will be lifted to a bag of numerical values $X_{ik} * Y_{kj}$, for all k. Hence, **sum(z)** in the query header will sum up all these values, deriving $\sum_k X_{ik} * Y_{kj}$ for the ij element of the resulting matrix.

Matrix multiplication is an important operation, used frequently in scientific computations and machine learning. Suppose that X is an $N * K$ matrix and Y is an $K * M$

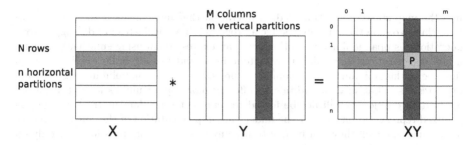

Fig. 1. Matrix multiplication: each partition P requires N/n rows from X and M/m columns from Y

matrix. If the previous matrix multiplication query for $X \times Y$ is evaluated naively using an equi-join followed by a group-by, the intermediate result of the join would have been of size $N * K * M$, which would have to be shuffled to the compute nodes of the cluster for the group-by operation. Instead, one may use the SUMMA algorithm for matrix multiplication [24], which has been adapted for the BSP distributed model [44] and later for Map-Reduce [13]. This algorithm distributes the data as a grid of $m * n$ partitions, so that each partition contains N/n full rows from X and M/m full columns from Y (Fig. 1). That is, the X elements are replicated m times and the Y elements are replicated n times. Then, each partition is assigned to a single node in a cluster, which must have enough free memory to multiply the associated submatrices of size $N/n * K$ and $K * M/m$. The goal of this method is to minimize replication (m and n) so that the memory of each worker node in the cluster is fully utilized by performing the submatrix multiplication in memory. When implemented using Map-Reduce, this algorithm requires only one Map-Reduce job: the map task replicates and distributes the data to reducers, while each reducer multiplies its submatrices in memory using a hash join.

How can such algorithm be incorporated into the evaluation engine of a query language? One solution is to provide a library of predefined functions for various matrix operations, using their most efficient implementation. But such an approach does not leave any opportunities for inter-operation optimization. Consider, for example, Matrix Factorization using Gradient Descent [29], used in machine learning applications, such as for recommender systems. The goal of this computation is to split a matrix R of dimension $n \times m$ into two low-rank matrices P and Q of dimensions $n \times k$ and $k \times m$, for small k, such that the error between the predicted and the original rating matrix $R - P \times Q^T$ is below some threshold, where $P \times Q^T$ is the matrix multiplication of P with the transpose of Q and '$-$' is cell-wise matrix subtraction. Matrix factorization can be implemented using an iterative algorithm that repeatedly applies the following rules to minimize the error matrix E:

$$E \leftarrow R - P \times Q^T \tag{1}$$
$$P \leftarrow P + \gamma(2E \times Q^T - \lambda P) \tag{2}$$
$$Q \leftarrow Q + \gamma(2E \times P^T - \lambda Q) \tag{3}$$

where γ is the learning rate and λ is the normalization factor used in avoiding overfitting. But matrix transpose and cell-wise operations can be fused with matrix multiplication, because they both correspond to a map operation, which can be incorporated into the map stage of the Map-Reduce operation that implements matrix multiplication, thus avoiding the extra map stage all together. That is, instead of defining matrix operations as opaque library functions, we can express them using sufficiently generic algebraic operations (i.e., higher-order functions) and use algebraic rewrite rules to fuse them, thus minimizing the number of processing stages and eliminating intermediate results. That way, in addition to offering more opportunities for optimization, application developers will not be forced to represent their data matrices in the single fixed representation used by the underlying implementation of the concrete matrix algorithms. Instead, they will be free to use any representation, thus focusing only on the computation logic.

In addition to array operations, by generalizing these algorithms, one can optimize a wider spectrum of queries that resemble matrix multiplication, such as calculating the shortest path distances of all node pairs in a graph. If we represent a graph G as a dataset of edges (i, j, d), where d is the distance between the graph nodes i and j, then this dataset is equivalent to a matrix G such that the distance d is the matrix value G_{ij}. Then, the shortest distance D_{ij} between i and j can be calculated by initially setting $D_{ij} = G_{ij}$ and $D_{ii} = 0$ and by repeatedly improving D_{ij} as follows:

$$D_{ij} \leftarrow \min(D_{ij}, \min_k(D_{ik} + G_{kj}))$$

which indicates that the shortest distance between a pair of nodes i and j in a graph G is the minimum $D_{ik} + G_{kj}$ among all graph nodes k, where D_{ik} is the shortest distance between i and k and G_{kj} is the distance between k and j. The operation $\min_k(D_{ik} + G_{kj})$ is similar to the matrix multiplication $D \times G$, but with addition instead of multiplication and minimum instead of addition. The MRQL query that expresses the shortest path distance algorithm is as follows:

```
1   repeat D = G union ( select (i,i,0)
2                           from (i,j,d) in G
3                           group by i )
4       step select (i,j,min(d))
5               from (i,k,d1) in D, (k,j,d2) in G, d = d1+d2
6               group by i, j
```

Query 3. Shortest distance query

As explained in Sect. 3, the repeat query syntax 'repeat $D = i$ step s' starts with $D = i$ and reassigns D with the result of s at each iteration step. The initial value of D (lines 1 through 3) contains, in addition to the edges in G, the edges $(i, i, 0)$ (that is, $D_{ii} = 0$) so that the minimum calculation in line 4 includes the case for k = i, giving d $= G_{ij}$. The select query in the repeat step (lines 4–6) looks very similar to the matrix multiplication query (Query 2).

5   The GroupByJoin Operation

In this section, we generalize matrix multiplication using an algebraic operation, called a *Group-By Join*. Given two arbitrary bags X and Y, the following generic MRQL query:

```
1   select h( k, reduce(acc,zero,z) )
```

```
2 │   from x in X, y in Y, z = (x,y)
3 │   where jx(x) = jy(y)
4 │   group by k: ( gx(x), gy(y) )
```

Query 4. Generic GroupByJoin Query

generalizes matrix multiplication, where

- the function jx is the left join key function,
- the function jy is the right join key function,
- the function gx is the left group-by function,
- the function gy is the right group-by function,
- the function h is the result function, and
- reduce(acc,zero,s) reduces the elements of a bag s using an accumulator acc, such that $\text{reduce}(\text{acc}, \text{zero}, \{z_1, z_2, \ldots, z_n\}) = \text{acc}(z_1, \text{acc}(z_2, \ldots, \text{acc}(z_n, \text{zero})))$ and $\text{reduce}(\text{acc}, \text{zero}, \{\}) = \text{zero}$.

This query joins the bags X and Y using the join keys jx and jy, then groups the join result by the group-by keys gx and gy, then aggregates the pairs z=(x,y) in each group using the reduce function, and finally transforms each result tuple using the function h. Note that, although the zero value in reduce(acc,zero,s) is not needed for a group-by aggregation since it is not possible for a group to be empty, it is needed for total aggregations on datasets that may be empty. To preserve bag semantics, function acc in reduce(acc,zero,s) must satisfy $\text{acc}(x, \text{acc}(y, z)) = \text{acc}(y, \text{acc}(x, z))$ and $\text{acc}(x, \text{zero}) = x$, for all x, y, and z.

The previous generic MRQL query is captured by the higher-order operation:

$$\text{GroupByJoin}(\text{ jx, jy, gx, gy, acc, zero, h, X, Y })$$

which generalizes the SUMMA algorithm by distributing X and Y into a grid of $n * m$ partitions based on their group-by and join key functions.

For example, the matrix multiplication in Query 2 is captured by the operation:

```
GroupByJoin( λ(x,i,k). k,          // the join key jx
             λ(y,k,j). k,          // the join key jy
             λ(x,i,k). i,          // the group-by key gx
             λ(y,k,j). j,          // the group-by key gy
             λ((x,y),c). c+x*y,    // the accumulator acc
             0,                    // the zero element
             λ((i,j),c). (c,i,j),  // the header h
             X, Y )                // the input datasets
```

where $\lambda p.\, e$ is an anonymous function such that, if $f = \lambda p.\, e$, then $f(p) = e$. For example, for $f = \lambda((i,j),c).\,(c,i,j)$, we have $f((i,j),c) = (c,i,j)$.

Another example, is the select query in the repeat step of Query 3:

```
select (i,j,min(d))
from (i,k,d1) in D, (k,j,d2) in G, d = d1+d2
group by i, j
```

which is captured by the operation:

```
GroupByJoin( λ(i,k,d1). k,              // the join key jx
             λ(k,j,d2). k,              // the join key jy
             λ(i,k,d1). i,              // the group-by key gx
             λ(k,j,d2). j,              // the group-by key gy
             λ((d1,d2),d). min(d,d1+d2), // the accumulator acc
             0,                         // the zero element
             λ((i,j),d). (i,j,d),       // the header h
             D, G )                     // the input datasets
```

6   The Implementation of GroupByJoin in Map-Reduce

A straightforward implementation of the GroupByJoin operation is a join followed by a group-by with aggregation. In this section, we implement the GroupByJoin operation in the Map-Reduce framework using the SUMMA algorithm for matrix multiplication [24], which is, as we will see, more efficient than the straightforward implementation. Our implementation is based on the reduce-side join algorithm for Map-Reduce (described below) but it uses special partition, grouping, and sorting functions to capture and optimize the SUMMA algorithm. Before we describe the GroupByJoin implementation, let's see how the following join query between two datasets R and S:

```
select r.C, s.D
from r in R, s in S
where r.A = s.B
```

can be implemented in Map-Reduce. If one of the two datasets, such as R, is small enough to fit in the memory of every worker node in the cluster, then we can broadcast R to all worker nodes. This algorithm, called the map-backed join, is a Map-Reduce job that consists of a map stage only, without a reduce stage. Before the Map-Reduce job, the dataset R is broadcast to all worker nodes and each worker node creates a built hash table from R. Then the map stage of each worker node joins its input split of S with the hash table by R by probing the hash table. This join is very efficient but it requires that one of the datasets can fit in memory. If neither R nor S can fit in the memory of a worker node, then the join can be implemented using the reduce-side join algorithm [31], shown in Fig. 2.

The Map-Reduce job shown in Fig. 2 has two mappers, one for each dataset:

- mapLeft: a mapper for the dataset R that generates key-value pairs where the key is the join key R.A
- mapRight: a mapper for the dataset S that generates key-value pairs where the key is the join key S.B

The two mappers send the R and S values associated with the same keys R.A=S.B to the same reducer, where they are reduced together. The mapLeft mapper tags the R tuples with 1 and the mapRight mapper tags the S tuples with 2 so that the reducer can tell them apart. Since the reduce method is evaluated for each different key, the values are all the tuples from R and S that correspond to the same key, which is equal to R.A and S.B. The nested loop in the reduce method separates the R from the S tuples by looking at the tag of the value: a value with tag 1 is an R tuple and a value with tag 2 is an S tuple. Finally, the R tuples are combined with the S tuples using a

```
1    mapLeft ( r ):
2       emit(r.A,(1,r))
3
4    mapRight ( s ):
5       emit(s.B,(2,s))
6
7    reduce ( key, values ):
8       for each (1,r) in values
9          for each (2,s) in values
10             emit(key,(r.C,s.D))
```

Fig. 2. Map-Reduce pseudo-code for the reduce-side join between the datasets R and S

```
1    mapLeft ( x ):
2       for each i in 0..m−1
3          emit ( ((hashCode(gx(x)) % n)*m+i, jx(x), 1), (1,x) )
4
5    mapRight ( y ):
6       for each i in 0..n−1
7          emit ( ((hashCode(gy(y)) % m)+m*i, jy(y), 2), (2,y) )
8
9    reduce ( ( partition ,joinkey,tag), values ):
10      if ( partition != current_partition )
11         flush (H)
12         current_partition ← partition
13      xs ←∅
14      // (1,x) tuples arrive before (2,y) tuples in values
15      for each leading (1,x) tuple in values
16         insert x into xs
17      for each (2,y) tuple in the rest of values
18         for each x in xs
19            key ← (gx(x),gy(y))
20            if (H[key] is null)
21               H[key] ← zero
22            H[key] ← acc( (x,y), H[key] )
23
24   cleanup ( ):
25      flush (H)
```

Fig. 3. Map-Reduce pseudo-code for GroupByJoin(jx, jy, gx, gy, acc, zero, h, X, Y)

nested loop, since these are the tuples that correspond to the same join key and must be joined together.

The GroupByJoin operation is based on the reduce-side join but it uses special replication and partitioning techniques, as required by the SUMMA algorithm. It distributes the data to the worker nodes in the form of a $n * m$ grid of partitions, where each partition contains only those rows from X and those columns from Y needed to compute a single partition of the resulting matrix.

Figure 3 shows the pseudo-code for the implementation of GroupByJoin in Map-Reduce. The rest of this section explains the code in detail. Each of the $n*m$ partitions is ideally assigned to a single worker node (a reducer), but in general each reducer may receive multiple partitions, and each partition may contain multiple groupings. Each grouping is handled separately by the reduce method. Similar to a regular reduce-side join on Map-Reduce, our GroupByJoin uses two mappers, mapLeft and mapRight, one for each input dataset, X and Y. Unlike a regular reduce-side join though, the mapLeft replicates each tuple m times while the mapRight mapper replicates each tuple n times, all under different join keys (lines 1–3 and 5–7 in Fig. 3). Both mappers emit (key,value) pairs. A mapper value takes the form (tag,data), where data is the input data and tag is the source number 1 or 2, to specify the input source (X or Y). A mapper key on the other hand is a triple (partition,joinkey,tag), where partition is one of the $n*m$ partitions, and joinkey is the join key value, jx(x) for the left mapper and jy(y) for the right mapper. More specifically, the partition number of a partition (i, j) in the grid of $n*m$ partitions is equal to $i * m + j$ (based on row-major numbering in the partition grid). The two mappers replicate the X and Y values under different partition numbers. A value x ∈ X is sent to all the row partitions (gx(x) mod n, *) (n partitions) while a value y ∈ Y is sent to all the column partitions (*, gy(y) mod m) (m partitions). Hadoop Map-Reduce supports custom partitioning, grouping, and sorting functions that control the shuffling of the map results to the reducers. These custom functions are adjusted in such a way that this Map-Reduce job implements the SUMMA algorithm efficiently. They are directly derived from the partition, joinkey, and tag components of the mapper key. In our Hadoop Map-Reduce implementation,

- the partition function returns the partition value of the mapper key,
- the grouping function returns the pair (partition,joinkey), and
- the sorting is based on partition (major order), joinkey (minor order), and tag (sub-minor order).

Each call to the reduce method is associated with a certain partition number and a certain joinkey, by means of the grouping function. Consequently, the values parameter of the reduce method contains all tuples from both X and Y whose join key is equal to joinkey. For matrix multiplication, when X is an $N*K$ matrix and Y is an $K*M$ matrix, the size of values will be $N/n + M/m$, one column from the X horizontal partition and one row from the Y vertical partition (Fig. 4).

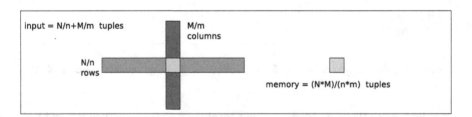

Fig. 4. Each reducer receives $N/n + M/m$ tuples per call and stores $(N * M)/(n * m)$ tuples

In Map-Reduce, the values argument of the reduce method can only be accessed once in a stream-like fashion, because these values are directly read from the merged runs stored on the reducer's local disk. But if we sort the values so that the X tuples appear before the Y tuples, then it would not be necessary to store the values in a vector to do the nested-loop join between the matched X and Y tuples. The reduce method in Fig. 3 stores the X tuples in a vector xs (lines 13–16) and then does a cross product between xs and the Y tuples (lines 17–22), followed by a group-by with aggregation. This is possible because the X tuples come before the Y tuples, by means of the sorting function, and all results in a group are guaranteed to occur within the same partition. The reduce method uses a key-value map H (implemented as a hash table) that holds the partial results of the aggregation after the join and group-by. Each reducer must have its own copy of H (a static variable in Java). It has to be maintained across multiple calls to the reduce method within the same partition. The body of the nested-loop join (lines 19–22) makes partial contributions to the group-by with aggregation by using the group-by key $(gx(x),gy(y))$ to accumulate the new pair (x,y) to the existing value associated with this key using the accumulator acc.

The code in lines 10–12 in Fig. 3 checks whether the reducer has seen the end of a partition. Function flush(H) applies the function h to each key-value pair in H and emits the results to the output file:

```
flush ( H ):
   for each (key, value) in H
      emit h(key, value)
   clear H
```

Given that a reducer may be assigned multiple partitions, the results of processing each partition are emitted by flush(H) at the end of each partition (when the partition number changes). This is possible because the input pairs arrive to a reducer sorted by a partition number (major order). The hash table H needs to be maintained across a partition only since each partition contains all the required data to complete the join. Thus, when the current partition is finished, the hash table H is flushed and the next partition is ready to be processed with an empty H. Thus, H should be large enough to fit the largest resulting partition. Ideally, if there is no data skew, the size of H should be the total size of the resulting dataset divided by $n*m$. In our matrix multiplication case, when X is an $N*K$ matrix and Y is an $K*M$ matrix, the size of the hash table H should be $(N*M)/(n*m)$ (see Fig. 4). Larger n and m requires more data replication and thus more network traffic, while smaller n and m may require a hash table that is too large to fit in memory. Thus, we must select the smallest n and m so that H can fit in memory. If there is available memory at each reducer to fit T tuples, then $(N*M)/(n*m) = T$. Our goal is to minimize data replication, which is equal to $N*K*m + K*M*n$, which is equivalent to minimizing $N/n + M/m$ (if we divide by the constant $K*n*m$). Given that $(N/n)*(M/m) = T$, the minimum $N/n + M/m$ is derived when $N/n = M/m = \sqrt{T}$. That is, given the amount of available memory at each reducer (T tuples), the optimal grid size that minimizes the amount of shuffling is $n = N/\sqrt{T}$ and $m = M/\sqrt{T}$.

7   The Implementation of GroupByJoin in Spark and Flink

In addition to Map-Reduce, the GroupByJoin operation has been implemented on Apache Spark [9] and Apache Flink [2] since these frameworks too are supported by the MRQL evaluation engine. These frameworks provide a similar API, although they have different performance characteristics. Hence, we describe the GroupByJoin implementation in Spark only but we evaluate GroupByJoin on both Spark and Flink.

The central Spark data abstraction is the Resilient Distributed Dataset (RDD), which is an immutable collection of values partitioned across multiple machines in a cluster. These RDD partitions are typically stored in the memory of the compute nodes. An RDD is resilient to failures; a lost RDD partition can be reconstructed from its input RDD partitions (from the RDDs that were used to compute this RDD). The evaluation of RDD transformations in Spark is deferred until an action is encountered that brings data to the master node or stores the data into a file. Spark collects the deferred transformations into a DAG and divides them into subsequences, called stages. Data shuffling occurs between stages, while transformations within a stage are combined into a single RDD transformation. Despite this inter-stage optimization, Spark cannot perform non-trivial optimizations, such as moving a filter operation before a join, because the functional arguments of the RDD operations are written in the host language and cannot be analyzed for code patterns at run-time. Spark has addressed this shortcoming by providing two additional APIs, called DataFrames and Datasets [1]. A Dataset combines the benefits of RDD (strong typing and powerful higher-order operations) with Spark SQL's optimized execution engine. A DataFrame is a Dataset organized into named columns as in a relational table. SQL queries in DataFrames are translated and optimized to RDD workflows at run-time using the Catalyst architecture.

```
1   def groupByJoin ( jx, jy, gx, gy, acc, zero, h, X, Y )
2     = { val XS = X.flatMap{ x => (0 until m).map{
3                               i => ( (gx(x).hashCode() % n)∗m+i, x ) } }
4       val YS = Y.flatMap{ y => (0 until n).map{
5                               i => ( (gy(y).hashCode() % m)+m∗i, y ) } }
6       XS.cogroup(YS,n∗m)
7         .flatMap{ case (p,(xs,ys))
8                   => val H = new HashMap
9                      val hx = new MultiMap
10                     xs.foreach{ x => hx.addBinding(jx(x),x) }
11                     ys.foreach{
12                       y => hx(jy(y)).foreach{
13                         x => val key = (gx(x),gy(y))
14                             if (!H.contains(key))
15                                H += (( key, zero ))
16                             H += (( key, acc( (x,y), H(key) ) ))
17                       }
18                     }
19                     H.map{ case (k,v) => h(k,v) }
20                 }
21     }
```

Fig. 5. Spark scala code for GroupByJoin

Figure 5 shows the code of the GroupByJoin method. The Scala types have been omitted for brevity. As it was done in the mapLeft and mapRight methods in Fig. 3, the code in lines 2–5 in Fig. 5 creates the RDDs XS and YS that replicate the elements of X m times and the elements of Y n times into a grid of $n*m$ partitions. (In Scala, X.flatmap(f) applies the function f to every element of the sequence X and concatenates the resulting lists into one list; while (0 until m) creates a new list $[0, \ldots, m-1]$.) Unlike mapLeft and mapRight though, Spark does not need to use a tag to separate the X from the Y values because it provides a special operation for reduce-side join, called cogroup. The n*m argument of cogroup indicates the number of reducers, which is also the number of the output partitions. Furthermore, the keys in XS and YS do not depend on the join keys jx and jy. This means that the join performed by cogroup is over the partition number only. But, as in Map-Reduce, each partition is self-sufficient to create its join result. That is, after the cogroup, there will be $n*m$ pairs (p,(xs,ys)), for each different partition p, ideally one pair for each reducer. This is not problematic because Spark keeps each RDD partition in memory in most cases. The flatMap in lines 7–20 performs a hash join between xs and ys. The partial results of the group-by aggregation are maintained in the hash table H, in the same way it was done in the reducer in Fig. 3. The flatMap functional constructs the built hash table hx for the input xs using a MultiMap (line 9), which is a hash table that maps a key to a set of values. Then, the foreach expression in lines 11–18 performs a loop over ys and probes the hash table hx using the join key jy(y), and in general returns a set of x values. Finally, the probed x is used along with y to add a new entry to the aggregation table with key (gx(x),gy(y)) (lines 14–16). After all values are aggregated, the result of the groupByJoin is calculated by applying the header function h to every value in the hash table H (line 19).

```
1   val XS = X.flatMap{ case x@(v,i,j)
2                            => (0 until m).map{ k => ( (i % n)*m+k, x ) } }
3   val YS = Y.flatMap{ case y@(v,i,j)
4                            => (0 until n).map{ k => ( (j % m)+m*k, y ) } }
5   XS.cogroup(YS,n*m)
6     .flatMap{ case (k,(xs,ys))
7                    => val H = new HashMap
8                       val hx = new MultiMap
9                       xs.foreach{ case x@(_,_,k)
10                                   => hx.addBinding(k,x) }
11                      ys.foreach{ case (y,k,j)
12                                  => hx(k).foreach{ case (x,i,_)
13                                                    => val key = (i,j)
14                                                       if (!H.contains(key))
15                                                          H += (( key, 0.0 ))
16                                                       H += (( key, x*y+H(key) ))
17                                  }
18                      }
19                      H.map{ case ((i,j),v) => (v,i,j) }
20            }
```

Fig. 6. Spark scala code for the SUMMA algorithm for $X \times Y$

To illustrate the GroupByJoin functionality better, the Spark code in Fig. 6 computes the matrix multiplication $X \times Y$ using the SUMMA algorithm. It is an instance of the GroupByJoin algorithm in Fig. 3. Every tuple (v,i,j) in X is replicated m times across all columns k in the row i of the $n * m$ grid, which corresponds to the partition (i % n)*m+k (lines 1–2). On the other hand, every tuple (v,i,j) in Y is replicated n times across all rows k in the column j of the grid, which corresponds to the partition (j % m)+m*k (lines 3–4). The XS.cogroup(YS,n*m) operation in line 5 performs a distributed join over $n * m$ partitions using the join keys (partition numbers) computed in lines 1–4. That is, the number of pairs returned by this join is $n * m$, one for each partition. Given that an RDD is in the distributed memory across the worker notes, each pair (k,(xs,ys)) corresponds to a different reducer, which ideally is a different worker node. The xs and ys collections have all the required data to derive the join result that corresponds to this partition. This computation is done in the hash join with group-by and aggregation in lines 7–19. The hash table H contains a partition of the resulting matrix and is populated during the final aggregation. The hash table hx is the built table from xs and is populated before the join (lines 9–10) using the key k for a tuple (x,i,k) in xs. The actual hash join is done in lines 11–18 by scanning ys (line 11) and probing the built hash table hx (line 12) using the hash key k from the tuple (y,k,j). The code in lines 13–16 updates the result table H by adding the product x*y to the exiting value. Finally, the code in line 19 converts the entries in the result table H into matrix values for the resulting matrix.

8   Translating Queries to GroupByJoin Operations

Based on the discussion in the Introduction, it would be hard to use source-to-source transformations to translate queries, such as matrix multiplication and shortest distance, to an algebraic form that contains GroupByJoin operations, because query syntax may take many different equivalent forms, which have to be recognized by these source-to-source transformations. Instead, our approach is to translate queries to their default algebraic forms and then normalize and rewrite these forms using algebraic rules.

8.1   The MRQL Algebra

The MRQL algebra used in this section has already been described in our previous work [17,18]. The most important algebraic operation in the MRQL algebra is cMap (also known as concat-map or flatten-map in functional programming languages), which generalizes the select, project, join, and unnest operators of the nested relational algebra. Given two arbitrary types α and β, the operation cMap(f, X) maps a bag X of type $\{\alpha\}$ to a bag of type $\{\beta\}$ by applying the function f of type $\alpha \rightarrow \{\beta\}$ to each element of X, yielding one bag for each element, and then by merging these bags to form a single bag of type $\{\beta\}$. Using a set former notation on bags, it is expressed as follows:

$$\text{cMap}(f, X) = \{ z \mid x \in X, z \in f(x) \} \tag{4}$$

Given an arbitrary type κ that supports value equality ($=$), an arbitrary type α, and a bag X of type $\{(\kappa, \alpha)\}$, the operation groupBy(X) groups the elements of the bag X by their first component and returns a bag of type $\{(\kappa, \{\alpha\})\}$, where the first component of each tuple is a unique group-by key and the second is the group (a bag) that contains all values that correspond to this key. For example, groupBy($\{(1,\text{"A"}), (2, \text{"B"}), (1,\text{"C"})\}$) returns $\{(1,\{\text{"A"},\text{"C"}\}), (2,\{\text{"B"}\})\}$. Although any join $X \bowtie_{j_x(x)=j_y(y)} Y$

can be expressed as a nested cMap, to facilitate the creation of physical plans for joins, the MRQL algebra provides a special join operator:

$$\begin{aligned} &\text{join}(j_x, j_y, h, X, Y) \\ &= \{\, h(x,y) \mid x \in X,\, y \in Y,\, j_x(x) = j_y(y) \,\} \\ &= \text{cMap}(\lambda x.\, \text{cMap}(\lambda y.\, \text{if } j_x(x) = j_y(y) \text{ then } \{h(x,y)\} \text{ else } \{\,\}, Y), X) \end{aligned}$$

where an anonymous function $\lambda x.\, e$ specifies a unary function (a lambda abstraction) f such that $f(x) = e$. This operation joins two bags, X of type $\{\alpha\}$ and Y of type $\{\beta\}$, using the join functions, j_x of type $\alpha \to \kappa$ and j_y of type $\beta \to \kappa$, and combines the joining values using the function h of type $(\alpha, \beta) \to \gamma$, deriving a bag of type $\{\gamma\}$. Finally, aggregations are captured by the operation reduce$(acc, zero, X)$, which reduces the elements of a bag X of type $\{\alpha\}$ into a value of type β, using an accumulator acc of type $(\alpha, \beta) \to \beta$ and a zero value $zero$ of type β. For example, reduce$(\lambda(x, s).\, x + s,\, 0,\, \{1, 2, 3\}) = 6$.

The algebraic terms derived from MRQL queries can be normalized using rewrite rules, such as:

$$\text{cMap}(f, \text{cMap}(g, S)) \to \text{cMap}(\lambda x.\, \text{cMap}(f, g(x)), S) \tag{5}$$

which fuses two cascaded cMaps into a nested cMap, thus avoiding the construction of the intermediate bag. This rule can be proven directly from the cMap definition in Eq. (4):

$$\begin{aligned} \text{cMap}(f, \text{cMap}(g, S)) &= \{\, z \mid w \in \{\, y \mid x \in S,\, y \in g(x) \,\},\, z \in f(w) \,\} \\ &= \{\, z \mid x \in S,\, y \in g(x),\, z \in f(y) \,\} \\ &= \{\, z \mid x \in S,\, z \in \{\, w \mid y \in g(x),\, w \in f(y) \,\} \,\} \\ &= \text{cMap}(\lambda x.\, \text{cMap}(f, g(x)), S) \end{aligned}$$

In addition, a cMap can be fused with a join resulting to a new join:

$$\begin{aligned} &\text{join}(\, j_x,\, j_y,\, h,\, X,\, \text{cMap}(\lambda y.\, \{f(y)\}, Y)\,) \\ &\qquad \to\ \text{join}(\, j_x,\, \lambda y.\, j_y(f(y)),\, \lambda(x,y).\, h(x, f(y)),\, X,\, Y\,) \end{aligned} \tag{6}$$

$$\begin{aligned} &\text{cMap}(\lambda v.\, \{f(v)\},\, \text{join}(\, j_x,\, j_y,\, h,\, X,\, Y\,)) \\ &\qquad \to\ \text{join}(\, j_x,\, j_y,\, \lambda(x,y).\, f(h(x,y)),\, X,\, Y\,)) \end{aligned} \tag{7}$$

8.2 Translating Algebraic Terms to GroupByJoin Operations

In an earlier work [18], we have presented a general framework for translating MRQL queries to algebraic terms. This framework uses novel optimization techniques to map these algebraic forms to efficient workflows of physical plan operations that are specific to the underlying distributed platform.

The framework described in this paper extends our earlier work [18] by introducing a new algebraic operation, GroupByJoin, and by providing rules for deriving Group-ByJoin operations from algebraic forms. By default, the generic MRQL query, Query 4:

```
select h( k, reduce(acc, zero, z) )
   from x in X, y in Y, z = (x,y)
   where jx(x) = jy(y)
   group by k: ( gx(x), gy(y) )
```

is translated to the following algebraic form:

cMap(λ(k,s). { h(k,reduce(acc,zero,s)) },
      groupBy(join(jx, jy,
                      λ(x,y). ((gx(x),gy(y)), (x,y)),
                      X, Y)))

which joins X and Y via the join keys jx and jy (i.e., a value x in X is joined with a value y in Y if jx(x)=jy(y)), and produces pairs (key, (x,y)), where key is the group-by key (gx(x),gy(y)). The group-by operation collects all (x,y) pairs that are associated with the same key into a group and the outer operation, cMap, accumulates each group s to a single value by reducing this group using reduce(acc,zero,s) and then applying the result function h. These algebraic forms can be derived from queries that may look very different from the previous query, since algebraic forms are normalized to a canonical form and, thus, queries that correspond to a GroupByJoin will always be translated to the same canonical algebraic form. The GroupByJoin operation is derived with the help of the following rule:

cMap(λ(k,s). { h(k,reduce(acc,zero,s)) },
      groupBy(join(jx, jy,
                      λ(x,y). ((gx(x),gy(y)), (x,y)),
                      X, Y)))
    $\rightarrow$ GroupByJoin(jx, jy, gx, gy, acc, zero, h, X, Y)

which rewrites the previously derived equi-join/group-by algebraic form to a Group-ByJoin. Note that the variables in this rule, such as x, can be matched with any term, while term functions, such as gx(x), are terms that contain their arguments as subterms. For example, the term function gx(x) matches any term that depends on the variable x. The pattern that represents a join followed by the groupBy in the previous rule matches most terms with a groupBy after join. The cMap functional argument that evaluates the aggregation reduce(acc,zero,s) though is more restrictive as it requires that each group s formed after groupBy be reduced by an aggregation that matches reduce(acc,zero,s), for some acc and zero.

For example, consider the MRQL query, Query 2, that captures matrix multiplication $X \times Y$:

    select (**sum**(z), i, j)
      from (x,i,k) **in** X, (y,k,j) **in** Y, z = x*y
    group by i, j

This query is translated into the following algebraic form:

cMap(λ((i,j),s). {(reduce(λ(v,c). c+v, 0, s), i, j)},
      groupBy(join(λ(x,i,k). k, λ(y,k,j). k,
                  λ((x,i,k),(y,l,j)). ((i,j), x*y),
                  X, Y)))

which joins the matrices X and Y so that a matrix element (x,i,k) in X is joined with a matrix element (y,k',j) if k=k'. These joined values contribute the key-value pair ((i,j), x*y) to the join result, where the key (i,j) is used as the group-by key by the groupBy operation. Then, all x*y values that correspond to the same group key (i,j) form a group s, which is reduced by the outer cMap by calculating the sum of all these values using reduce(λ(v,c). c+v, 0, s) (i.e., it reduces s using the accumulator + and an initial value 0). This algebraic form matches the left-hand side of our translation rule, which rewrites the algebraic form to the term:

GroupByJoin(λ(x,i,k). k, λ(y,k,j). k, λ(x,i,k). i, λ(y,l,j). j, λ(v,c). c+v, 0, λ((i,j),c). {(c,i,j)}, X, Y)

which is equivalent to the term derived in Sect. 5.

8.3   Optimization of GroupByJoin Operations

Optimization of matrix operations in our framework is done before algebraic terms are transformed to GroupByJoin operations using the existing MRQL optimizer. That is, join, groupBy, and cMap operations are fused together using the rewrite rules presented in Sect. 8.1, and then the resulting terms are transformed to GroupByJoin operations using the rewrite rule presented in Sect. 8.2.

For example, consider the composition of matrix multiplication with matrix transpose $X \times Y^T$, where matrix transpose Y^T is expressed as follows in MRQL:

select (y, j, i) **from** (y, i, j) **in** Y

which flips the two indexes, thus transposing the matrix Y. This query is translated to the following algebraic form:

cMap(λ(y,i,j). { (y,j,i) }, Y)

Therefore, from Sect. 8.2, the composition $X \times Y^T$ is:

    cMap(λ((i,j),s). {(reduce(λ(v,c). c+v, 0, s), i, j)},
          groupBy(join(λ(x,i,k). k, λ(y,k,j). k,
                         λ((x,i,k),(y,l,j)). ((i,j), x*y),
                         X,
                         cMap(λ(y,i,j). {(y,j,i)}, Y))))

(The only difference from the matrix multiplication algebraic form in Sect. 8.2 is the last line that transposes the matrix Y.) Using Eq. 6, the join is fused with the inner cMap giving:

cMap(λ((i,j),s). {(reduce(λ(v,c). c+v, 0, s), i, j)},
      groupBy(join(λ(x,i,k). k,
                     λ(y,j,k). k,
                     λ((x,i,k),(y,j,l)). ((i,j), x*y),
                     X, Y)))

This term is translated to the following algebraic operation:

GroupByJoin(λ(x,i,k). k, λ(y,j,k). k, λ(x,i,k). i, λ(y,j,l). j, λ((x,y),c). c+x*y, 0,
             λ((i,j),c). (c,i,j), X, Y)

which combines matrix multiplication with matrix transpose into a single GroupByJoin operation.

9   Performance Evaluation

The platform used for our evaluations is a small cluster of 9 nodes, built on the Chameleon cloud computing infrastructure, www.chameleoncloud.org. This cluster consists of nine m1.medium instances running Linux, each one with 4 GB RAM and

```
1   macro transpose ( X ) {          /* matrix transpose */
2     select (x,j,i)
3       from (x,i,j) in X
4   };
5   macro multiply ( X, Y ) {        /* matrix multiplication */
6     select (sum(z),i,j)
7       from (x,i,k) in X, (y,k,j) in Y, z = x*y
8       group by (i,j)
9   };
10  macro mult ( a, X ) {            /* multiplication by a constant */
11    select ( a*x, i, j )
12      from (x,i,j) in X
13  };
14  macro Cadd ( X, Y ) {            /* cell-wise addition */
15    select ( x+y, i, j )
16      from (x,i,j) in X, (y,i,j) in Y
17  };
18  macro Csub ( X, Y ) {            /* cell-wise subtraction */
19    select ( x-y, i, j )
20      from (x,i,j) in X, (y,i,j) in Y
21  };
22  macro factorize ( R, Pinit, Qinit ) {   /* matrix factorization */
23    repeat (E,P,Q) = (R,Pinit,Qinit)
24      step ( Csub(R,multiply(P,transpose(Q))),
25             Cadd(P,mult(a,Csub(mult(2,multiply(E,transpose(Q))),mult(b,P)))),
26             Cadd(Q,mult(a,Csub(mult(2,multiply(E,transpose(P))),mult(b,Q)))) )
27      limit 10
28  };
```

Fig. 7. Matrix factorization using gradient descent in MRQL

two VCPUs at 2.3 GHz. For our experiments, we used Hadoop 2.6.0 (Yarn), Spark 2.1.0, Flink 1.0.3, and MRQL 0.9.8. The cluster frontend was used exclusively as a Name-Node and ResourceManager, while the remaining 8 compute nodes were used as DataNodes and NodeManagers. There was a total of 16 VCPUs and a total of 28.5 GB of RAM available for compute tasks. The HDFS file system was formatted with the block size set to 128 MB and the replication factor set to 3. Each dataset used in our experiments was stored in a single HDFS file. Our experiments were run using MRQL on three evaluation modes: Hadoop Map-Reduce mode, Spark mode, and Flink mode. Each experiment was evaluated 5 times under the same data and configuration parameters. Each data point in the plots in Figs. 8, 9 and 10 represents the mean value of 5 experiments while the vertical error bar at each line point represents the minimum and maximum values among these 5 experiments.

We have experimentally validated the effectiveness of our methods for three MRQL queries, based on operations that are defined in Fig. 7: (1) a matrix multiplication query, multiply(X,Y), (2) a simple query multiply-transpose, multiply(X,transpose(Y)), and (3) a matrix factorization query using gradient descent, factorize(R,P,Q).

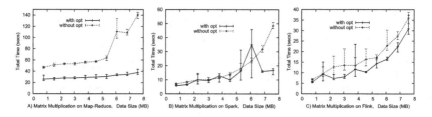

Fig. 8. Evaluation of matrix multiplication on (A) Map-Reduce, (B) Spark, and (C) Flink

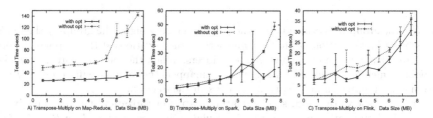

Fig. 9. Evaluation of multiply-transpose on (A) Map-Reduce, (B) Spark, and (C) Flink

The matrices X and Y used in the evaluation of the first two queries (matrix multiplication and multiply-transpose) were square matrices with dimensions $(i*40)*(i*40)$ and size $i*0.38$ MB, for $i \in [1,0]$. Consequently, the largest matrix used has dimensions 400 * 400 while the maximum total input size is 3.8 * 2 = 7.2 MB. The type of the matrix elements is (float, int, int), where the two integers are the row and column indexes, and the float is the value. Each matrix used in our experiments was dense (i.e, all matrix elements were provided) and filled with random values between 0.0 and 10.0, and the matrix elements were placed in random order. Figure 8 shows the results of evaluating the matrix multiplication query on Map-Reduce, Spark, and Flink, with and without using our optimization framework. That is, the "with opt" line is from evaluating the matrix multiplication query using a GroupByJoin operation and the "without opt" line is from the straightforward evaluation plan that consists of a join followed by a group-by with aggregation. In the latter case, the join is a simple reduce-side join. We can see that the performance improvement for Map-Reduce is more pronounced than that for Spark and Flink, especially for matrices larger than 280 * 280 (which corresponds to a total size of 5.32 MB). We get similar performance results for the multiply-transpose query in Fig. 9. The results for multiply-transpose are very similar to those for matrix multiplication because, the optimized version of the former is exactly the same as the optimized version of the latter query, while the non-optimized versions differ only in the extra map needed for the transpose operation, which can be performed efficiently by all three frameworks since it does not require any data shuffling. We also believe that, in the case Map-Reduce, the reason for the peak at MB is that the size of the intermediate data between the reduce-side join and the group-by with aggregation has reached a critical point where sorting and merging must be external (on the mappers local disk), rather than in-memory. More specifically, since the intermediate data produced by the join between two matrices of size N^2 is of

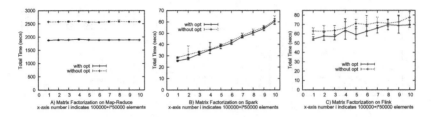

Fig. 10. Evaluation of matrix factorization on (A) Map-Reduce, (B) Spark, and (C) Flink

size N^3, the group-by workload after the join will be very high. The group-by though is implemented by partitioning the data and sorting the partitions at the mappers, before the data are shuffled and merged at the reducers. When the data are larger than the amount of memory allocated for sorting at a mapper, the mapper will necessarily use external sorting, which may explain the peak in the diagram.

Figure 10 shows the results of evaluating matrix factorization. Given a matrix R, our matrix factorization query in Fig. 7 calculates the error matrix $E = R - P \times Q^T$ and the factor matrices P and Q, so that R is approximately equal to $P \times Q^T$. For our experiments, we set this query to iterate 10 times and used the learning rate $a = 0.002$ and the normalization factor $b = 0.02$. The matrix to be factorized, R, was an $n \times m$ sparse matrix with random integer values between 1 and 5 in which only the 10% of the elements were provided (the rest were implicitly zero). The size of m was always kept equal to $10 * n$, while $n * m$ was set to $100000 + i * 50000$ elements, for $i \in [0, 9]$. That is, $n * m$ took the following values: 100 * 1000, 122 * 1220, 141 * 1410, 158 * 1580, 173 * 1730, 187 * 1870, 200* 2000, 212 * 2120, 223 * 2230, 234 * 2340. The initial factor matrices, Pinit and Qinit, had sizes $n * k$ and $m * k$, respectively, where $k = 10$ for all experiments (which is a low rank), and all their elements were initialized to 2.5. Figure 10 shows the results of evaluating the matrix factorization query on Map-Reduce, Spark, and Flink, with and without optimization. We can see that the improvement for the Map-Reduce evaluation is substantial (the optimized query is about 27% faster than the non-optimized one) mostly because the benefits of all the optimizations used in MRQL are accumulated and repeated at each iteration step. The results from the Map-Reduce evaluation look very similar for different data sizes (100 K through 550 K tuples) because all matrices (including the intermediate results) are split into 16 partitions in the HDFS (one for each compute node) and each partition can fit into one HDFS block (128 MBs) regardless of its size.

10   Conclusion and Future Work

We have presented a general framework for optimizing SQL-like queries that capture array-based computations on sparse arrays. In contrast to related work, we do not provide a library of predefined array operations. Instead, we are letting programmers express their array operations using normal SQL-like syntax, but, at the same time, we provide an optimization framework that translates these queries into efficient distributed array operations. That way, we are able to achieve inter-operation optimization that would be infeasible if these operations were expressed as black boxes. Our framework has been tested on three popular Big Data platforms that exhibit different functionality and performance characteristics. As a future work, we will apply our framework to more Big Data platforms, such as Apache Storm. In addition, we are planning to capture more data-parallel algorithms that have already been used in high-performance computing to implement matrix operations or other general linear algebra parallel algorithms. Furthermore, we are planning to experiment with a generalization of the group-by-join algorithm to capture n-way matrix multiplications. That is, instead of using chains of binary matrix operations, complex terms that involve multiple matrix operations would be translated into a single n-way group-by-join operation thus avoiding creating the intermediate matrices between the binary matrix operations. To accomplish this, the grid of partitions will have to be multi-dimensional, where each dimension corresponds to a different matrix. Then, the replication of the elements of a matrix will be done across the rest of the $n-1$ grid dimensions. That way, any complex term that consists of multiple matrix multiplications and other operations (such as, cell-wise operations and transpose), such as the body of matrix factorization, will be fused to a single n-ary group-by-join, thus achieving optimal performance.

Acknowledgments. Our performance evaluations were performed at the Chameleon cloud computing infrastructure, www.chameleoncloud.org, supported by NSF.

References

1. Armbrust, M., et al.: Spark SQL: relational data processing in spark. In: SIGMOD 2015 (2015)
2. Apache Flink (2018). http://flink.apache.org/
3. Apache Hadoop (2018). http://hadoop.apache.org/
4. Apache Hama (2018). http://hama.apache.org/
5. Apache Hive (2018). http://hive.apache.org/
6. Apache Giraph (2018). http://giraph.apache.org/
7. GraphX: Apache Spark's API for Graphs and Graph-Parallel Computation (2018). https://spark.apache.org/graphx/
8. Apache MRQL (incubating) (2018). http://mrql.incubator.apache.org/
9. Apache Spark (2018). http://spark.apache.org/
10. Battre, D., Ewen, S., Hueske, F., Kao, O., Markl, V., Warneke, D.: Nephele/PACTs: a programming model and execution framework for web-scale analytical processing. In: 1st ACM Symposium on Cloud computing (SOCC 2010), pp. 119–130 (2010)
11. Buck, J., et al.: SciHadoop: array-based query processing in hadoop. In: International Conference for High Performance Computing, Networking, Storage and Analysis (SC) (2011)
12. Chaiken, R., et al.: SCOPE: easy and efficient parallel processing of massive data sets. Proc. VLDB Endow. (PVLDB) **1**(2), 1265–1276 (2008)
13. A. Das, F.N. Afrati, S. Salihoglu, and J.D. Ullman. Upper and lower bounds on the cost of a map-reduce computation. In VLDB 2013 (2013)
14. Dean, J., Ghemawat, S.: MapReduce: Simplified data processing on large clusters. In: OSDI 2004 (2004)
15. Fan, J., et al.: The case against specialized graph analytics engines. In: CIDR (2015)

16. Fegaras, L.: A query processing framework for array-based computations. In: Hartmann, S., Ma, H. (eds.) DEXA 2016, Part I. LNCS, vol. 9827, pp. 240–254. Springer, Cham (2016). https://doi.org/10.1007/978-3-319-44403-1_15

17. Fegaras, L.: An Algebra for Distributed Big Data Analytics. Journal of Functional Programming, Special issue on Programming Languages for Big Data, Volume 27 (2017)

18. Fegaras, L., Li, C., Gupta, U.: An optimization framework for map-reduce queries. In: EDBT 2012 (2012)

19. Fegaras, L., Li, C., Gupta, U., Philip, J.J.: XML query optimization in map-reduce. In: International Workshop on the Web and Databases (WebDB) (2011)

20. Fegaras, L., Maier, D.: Towards an effective calculus for object query languages. In: International Conference on Management of Data (SIGMOD), pp. 47–58 (1995)

21. Fegaras, L., Maier, D.: Optimizing object queries using an effective calculus. ACM Trans. Database Syst. (TODS) **25**(4), 457–516 (2000)

22. Folk, M., Heber, G., Koziol, Q., Pourmal, E., Robinson, D.: An overview of the HDF5 technology suite and its applications. In: EDBT/ICDT Workshop on Array Databases (2011)

23. Gates, A.F., et al.: Building a high-level dataflow system on top of map-reduce: the pig experience. Proc. VLDB Endow. (PVLDB) **2**(2), 1414–1425 (2009)

24. Geijn, R.A., Watts, J.: SUMMA: scalable universal matrix multiplication algorithm. Concurr. Pract. Exp. **9**(4), 255–274 (1997)

25. Geng, Y., Huang, X., Zhu, M., Ruan, H., Yang, G.: SciHive: array-based query processing with HiveQL. In: IEEE International Conference on Trust, Security and Privacy in Computing and Communications (Trustcom) (2013)

26. Jindal, A., et al.: Vertexica: your relational friend for graph analytics!. PVLDB **7**(13), 1669–1672 (2014)

27. Ghoting, A., et al.: SystemML: declarative machine learning on mapreduce. In: IEEE International Conference on Data Engineering (ICDE) (2011)

28. Isard, M., Yu, Y.: Distributed data-parallel computing using a high-level programming language. In: ACM SIGMOD International Conference on Management of Data, pp. 987–994 (2009)

29. Koren, Y., Bell, R., Volinsky, C.: Matrix factorization techniques for recommender systems. In: IEEE Computer, August 2009

30. Kraska, T., Talwalkar, A., Duchi, J., Griffith, R., Franklin, M., Jordan, M.I.: MLbase: a distributed machine learning system. In: Conference on Innovative Data Systems Research (2013)

31. Lin, J., Dyer, C.: Data-Intensive Text Processing with MapReduce. Morgan & Claypool Publishers, San Rafael (2010)

32. Low, Y., Gonzalez, J., Kyrola, A., Bickson, D., Guestrin, C., Hellerstein, J.M.: Distributed GraphLab: a framework for machine learning and data mining in the cloud. In: VLDB 2012 (2012)

33. Malewicz, G., et al.: Pregel: a system for large-scale graph processing. In: ACM SIGMOD International Conference on Management of Data, pp. 135–146 (2010)

34. Meng, X., Bradley, J., Yavuz, B., et al.: MLlib: machine learning in apache spark. J. Mach. Learn. Res. **17**, 1–7 (2016)

35. NetCDF: Network Common Data Form. https://www.unidata.ucar.edu/software/netcdf/

36. Olston, C., Reed, B., Srivastava, U., Kumar, R., Tomkins, A.: Pig Latin: a not-so-Foreign language for data processing. In: ACM SIGMOD International Conference on Management of Data (2008)

37. Papadopoulos, S., Datta, K., Madden, S., Mattson, T.: The TileDB array data storage manager. PVLDB **10**(4), 349–360 (2016)
38. Soroush, E., Balazinska, M., Wang, D.: ArrayStore: a storage manager for complex parallel array processing. In: ACM SIGMOD International Conference on Management of Data (2011)
39. Soroush, E., Balazinska, M., Krughoff, S., Connolly, A.: Efficient iterative processing in the SciDB parallel array engine. In: 27th International Conference on Scientific and Statistical Database Management (SSDBM) (2015)
40. Shinnar, A., Cunningham, D., Herta, B., Saraswat, B.: M3R: Increased performance for in-memory Hadoop jobs. In: VLDB 2012 (2012)
41. The SciDB Development Team. Overview of SciDB: large scale array storage, processing and analysis. In: ACM SIGMOD International Conference on Management of Data (2010)
42. Thusoo, A., et al.: Hive: a warehousing solution over a map-reduce framework. Proc. VLDB Endow. (PVLDB) **2**(2), 1626–1629 (2009)
43. Thusoo, A., et al.: Hive: a petabyte scale data warehouse using hadoop. In: IEEE International Conference on Data Engineering (ICDE), pp. 996–1005 (2010)
44. Valiant, L.G.: A bridging model for parallel computation. CACM **33**(8), 103–111 (1990)
45. Wang, Y., Jiang, W., Agrawal, G.: SciMATE: a novel MapReduce-like framework for multiple scientific data formats. In: IEEE/ACM International Symposium on Cluster, Cloud and Grid Computing (CCGrid) (2012)
46. Yu, Y., et al.: DryadLINQ: a system for general-purpose distributed data-parallel computing using a high-level language. In: Symposium on Operating Systems Design and Implementation (OSDI) (2008)

Discovering Periodic-Correlated Patterns in Temporal Databases

J. N. Venkatesh[1(✉)], R. Uday Kiran[2,3], P. Krishna Reddy[1],
and Masaru Kitsuregawa[2,4]

[1] Kohli Center on Intelligent Systems (KCIS), International Institute of Information
Technology Hyderabad, Hyderabad, India
jn.venkatesh@research.iiit.ac.in,pkreddy@iiit.ac.in
[2] Institute of Industrial Science, The University of Tokyo, Tokyo, Japan
{uday_rage,kitsure}@tkl.iis.u-tokyo.ac.jp
[3] National Institute of Information and Communication Technologies, Tokyo, Japan
[4] National Institute of Informatics, Tokyo, Japan

Abstract. The *support* and *periodicity* are two important dimensions
to determine the interestingness of a pattern in a dataset. Periodic-
frequent patterns are an important class of regularities that exist in a
dataset with respect to these two dimensions. Most previous models on
periodic-frequent pattern mining have focused on finding all patterns in
a transactional database that satisfy the user-specified minimum support
($minSup$) and maximum periodicity ($maxPer$) constraints. These models suffer from the following two obstacles: (i) Current periodic-frequent
pattern models cannot handle datasets in which multiple transactions
can share a common time stamp and/or transactions occur at irregular time intervals (ii) The usage of single $minSup$ and $maxPer$ for
finding the patterns leads to the *rare item problem*. This paper tries
to address these two obstacles by proposing a novel model to discover
periodic-correlated patterns in a temporal database. Considering the
input data as a temporal database addresses the first obstacle, while
finding periodic-correlated patterns address the second obstacle. The
proposed model employs *all-confidence* measure to prune the uninteresting patterns in support dimension. A new measure, called *periodic-
all-confidence*, is being proposed to filter out uninteresting patterns in
periodicity dimension. A pattern-growth algorithm has also been discussed to find periodic-correlated patterns. Experimental results show
that the proposed model is efficient.

Keywords: Data mining · Pattern mining · Periodic patterns
Rare item problem · Pattern-growth technique

1 Introduction

Periodic-frequent pattern[1] mining is an important model in data mining. It
involves discovering all patterns in a transactional database that satisfy the

---

[1] A set of items represents a pattern (or an itemset).

© Springer-Verlag GmbH Germany, part of Springer Nature 2018
A. Hameurlain et al. (Eds.): TLDKS XXXVIII, LNCS 11250, pp. 146–172, 2018.
https://doi.org/10.1007/978-3-662-58384-5_6

user-specified minimum support ($minSup$) and maximum periodicity ($maxPer$) constraints [35]. The $minSup$ controls the minimum number of transactions that a pattern must cover, and the $maxPer$ controls the maximum interval within which a pattern must reoccur in the entire database. Finding periodic-frequent patterns is a significant task with many business applications. A classic application is market-basket analytics. It analyzes how regularly the itemsets are being purchased by the customers. An example of a periodic-frequent pattern is as follows:

$$\{Bat, Ball\} \quad [support = 5\%, \quad periodicity = 1 \text{ h}].$$

The above pattern says that 5% of the customers have purchased the items 'Bat' and '$Ball$,' and the maximum duration between any two consecutive purchases containing both of these items is no more than an hour. This predictive behavior of the customers' purchases may facilitate the users in product recommendation and inventory management.

Fournier-Viger et al. [11] extended the periodic-frequent pattern model to find periodic-utility patterns in a transactional database. Amphawan et al. [2] extended the model to find top-k periodic-frequent patterns in a transactional database. Uday et al. [24] extended the periodic-frequent pattern model to find partial periodic-frequent patterns in a transactional database. Nofong [27] extended the periodic-frequent pattern model to find productive periodic-frequent patterns. In this model, a periodic-frequent pattern is considered productive if its support is greater than the product of its subsets. The popular adoption and successful industrial application of this model suffers from the following obstacles: (i) Since the model accepts the transactional database as an input, the model implicitly assumes that all transactions in a database occur at a fixed time-interval. This assumption limits the applicability of the model as transactions in a database may occur at irregular time intervals. (ii) The $minSup$ and $maxPer$ play a key role in periodic-frequent pattern mining. They are used to prune the search space and limit the number of patterns being generated. Since only a single $minSup$ and $maxPer$ are used for the whole data, the model implicitly assumes that all items in the data have uniform $support$ and $periodicity$. However, this is seldom the case in many real-world applications. In many applications, some items appear very frequently in the data, while others rarely[2] appear. Moreover, rare items typically have high $periodicity$ (i.e., inter-arrival times) as compared against the frequent items. If the $support$ and $periodicity$ of items vary a great deal, we will encounter the following two problems:

- If the $maxPer$ is set too low and/or the $minSup$ is set too high, we will miss the periodic patterns involving rare items.
- To find the periodic patterns involving both frequent and rare items, we have to set a high $maxPer$ and a low $minSup$. However, this may result

---

[2] Classifying the items into either frequent or rare is a subjective issue that depends upon the user and/or application requirements.

in combinatorial explosion, producing too many patterns, because frequent items can combine with one another in all possible ways and many of them may be meaningless.

This dilemma is known as the *"rare item problem."* This paper tries to address both of these problems.

Prior to our study, researchers have tried to address the *rare item problem* using the concept of multiple *minSup* and *maxPer* constraints [20,33]. In this concept, each item in the database is specified with a *minimum item support* (*minIS*) and *maximum item periodicity* (*maxIP*). Next, the *minSup* and *maxPer* of a pattern are specified depending on its items *minIS* and *maxIP* values, respectively. Although this concept facilitates every pattern to satisfy a different *minSup* and *maxPer* values, it still suffers from an open problem of determining the items' *minIS* and *maxIP* values.

In this paper, we propose a model to discover periodic-correlated patterns in a temporal database. A temporal database is a collection of transactions ordered by their timestamps. A temporal database facilitates multiple transactions to share a common timestamp and time gaps in-between consecutive transactions. Thus, considering the input data as a temporal database addresses the first obstacle in periodic-frequent pattern model. In the literature, correlated pattern model was discussed to address the *rare item problem* in frequent pattern mining [28]. We extend this model to find periodic-correlated patterns in a temporal database. Thus, addressing the second obstacle of periodic-frequent pattern model. The proposed model considers a pattern as interesting if it satisfies the following two conditions: (*i*) if the *support* of a pattern is close to the *support* of its individual items, and (*ii*) if the *periodicity* of a pattern is close to the *periodicity* of its individual items. The renowned *all-confidence* [28] measure is used to determine how close is the *support* of a pattern with respect to the *support* of its individual items. To the best of our knowledge, there exists no measure to determine how close is the *periodicity* of a pattern with respect to the *periodicity* of its items. So forth, we introduce a new measure, called *periodic-all-confidence*, to determine the interestingness of a pattern. The *periodic-all-confidence* measure is used to determine how close is the *periodicity* of a pattern with respect to the *periodicity* of its individual items. These two measures facilitate us to achieve the objective of generating periodic-correlated patterns containing both frequent and rare items yet without causing frequent items to generate too many uninteresting patterns. A pattern-growth algorithm, called Extended Periodic-Correlated pattern-growth (EPCP-growth), has also been described to find all periodic-correlated patterns. Experimental results demonstrate that the proposed model can discover useful information and EPCP-growth is runtime efficient and highly scalable as well.

In [38], we have studied the problem of finding periodic-correlated patterns in transactional databases. In this paper, we first extend this study to temporal databases and provide theoretical correctness for EPCP-growth algorithm. We also evaluate the performance of EPCP-growth by conducting extensive experiments on both synthetic and real-world databases.

The rest of the paper is organized as follows. Section 2 describes related work on frequent pattern mining, periodic pattern mining and periodic-frequent pattern mining. Section 3 extends the (full) periodic-frequent pattern model to handle the temporal databases. Section 4 introduces the proposed model of finding periodic-correlated patterns in a temporal database. Section 5 describes EPCP-growth algorithm. Section 6 reports on experimental results. Finally, Sect. 7 concludes the paper with future research directions.

2   Related Work

2.1   Frequent Pattern Mining

Agrawal et al. [1] introduced the problem of finding frequent patterns in a transactional database. Since then, the problem of finding these patterns has received a great deal of attention [9,10,12,13,30,36,42]. The basic model used in most of these studies remained the same. It involves discovering all frequent patterns in a transactional database that satisfy the user-specified minimum support (*minSup*) constraint. The usage of single *minSup* for the entire database leads to the *rare item problem* (discussed in previous section). When confronted with this problem in real-world applications, researchers have tried to address it using the concept of multiple *minSups* [16,21,26]. In this concept, each item in the database is specified with a *support*-constraint known as *minimum item support* (*minIS*). Next, the *minSup* of a pattern is represented with the lowest *minIS* value of its items. Thus, every pattern can satisfy a different *minSup* depending upon its items. A major limitation of this concept is that it suffers from an open problem of determining the items' *minIS* values.

Brin et al. [6] introduced correlated pattern mining to address the *rare item problem*. The statistical measure, χ^2, was used to discover correlated patterns. Since then, several interestingness measures have been discussed based on the theories in probability, statistics, or information theory. Examples include *all-confidence, any-confidence, bond* [28] and *kulc* [5]. Each measure has its own selection bias that justifies the rationale for preferring one pattern over another. As a result, there exists no universally acceptable best measure to discover correlated patterns in any given database. Researchers are making efforts to suggest an appropriate measure based on user and/or application requirements [28,32,34,37,39].

Recently, *all-confidence* is emerging as a popular measure to discover correlated patterns [17,18,25,40,44,45]. It is because this measure satisfies both the *anti-monotonic* (see Definition 1) and *null-invariance* (see Definition 2) properties. The former property says that all non-empty subsets of a correlated pattern must also be correlated. This property plays a key role in reducing the search space, which in turn decreases the computational cost of mining the patterns. In other words, this property makes the correlated pattern mining practicable in real-world applications. The latter property discloses genuine correlation relationships without being influenced by the object co-absence in a database. In other words, this property facilitates the user to discover interesting patterns involving both frequent and rare items without generating a huge number of uninteresting patterns. In this paper, we use this measure to address the *rare item problem* in *support* dimension.

Definition 1. *(**Anti-monotonic property** [1]). A measure C is anti-monotone if and only if whenever a pattern (or an itemset) X violates C, so does any superset of X.*

Definition 2. *(**Null-invariance property** [34]). Let us consider a 2 x 2 contingency table (shown in Table 1) as a contingency matrix, $M = [f_{11}\ f_{10}; f_{01}\ f_{00}]$. Let an interestingness measure be a matrix operator, O, that maps the matrix M into a scalar value, k, i.e., $OM = k$. A binary measure of association is null-invariant if $O(M + C) = O(M)$, where $C = [00; 0k]$ and k is a positive constant.*

Table 1. A 2×2 contingency table for variables A and B

	B	$\overline{B}$	
A	f_{11}	f_{10}	f_{1+}
$\overline{A}$	f_{01}	f_{00}	f_{0+}
	f_{+1}	f_{+0}	N

Table 1 is an example of a contingency table for rule $A => B$, where A and B are the frequent itemsets and N denotes the total number of records. The number of records in which A and B occurs together is denoted by f_{11}. Similarly, f_{10} denotes the number of records in which A doesn't occur with B, f_{01} denotes the number of records in which B doesn't occurs with A and f_{00} denotes the number of records in which neither A nor B occurs.

2.2   Periodic Pattern Mining

Han et al. [14] introduced (partial) periodic pattern[3] model to find temporal regularities in time series data. The model involves the following two steps: (i) segment the given time series into multiple period-segments such that the length of each period-segment is equal to the user-specified *period* (*per*), and (ii) discover all patterns that satisfy the user-specified *minSup*.

Example 1. Let $I = \{abcde\}$ be the set of items and $S = a\{bc\}baebacea\{ed\}d$ be a time series data generated from I. If the user-defined *period* is 3, S is segmented into four period-segments such that each period-segment contains only 3 events (or itemsets). That is, $PS_1 = a\{bc\}b$, $PS_2 = aeb$, $PS_3 = ace$ and $PS_4 = a\{ed\}d$. Let $a * b$ be a pattern, where '$*$' denotes a wild (or do not care) character that can represent any itemset. This pattern appears in the period-segments of PS_1

---
[3] The term 'pattern' in a time series represents a set of itemsets (or sets of items).

and PS_2. Therefore, its *support* is 2. If the user-specified *minSup* is 2, then $a \star b$ represents a periodic pattern as its *support* is no less than *minSup*. In this example, braces for singleton itemsets have been eliminated for brevity.

Han et al. [13] have discussed Max-sub-pattern hitset algorithm to find periodic patterns. Chen et al. [8] developed a pattern-growth algorithm, and showed that it outperforms the Max-sub-pattern hitset algorithm. Aref et al. [4] extended Han's model for the incremental mining of partial periodic patterns. Yang et al. [41] studied the change in periodic behavior of a pattern due to noise, and enhanced the basic model to discover a class of periodic patterns known as asynchronous periodic patterns. Zhang et al. [43] enhanced the basic model of partial periodic patterns to discover periodic patterns in character sequences like protein data. Cao et al. [7] discussed a methodology to determine the *period* using auto-correlation. The popular adoption and successful industrial application of partial periodic pattern model suffers from the following two issues:

- **Rare item problem:** The usage of single *minSup* for the entire time series leads to the *rare item problem*.
- **Inability to consider temporal occurrence information of the items within a series:** The basic model of periodic patterns implicitly considers the data as an evenly spaced time series (i.e., all events within a series occur at a fixed time interval). This assumption limits the applicability of the model as events in many real-world time series datasets occur at irregular time intervals.

Yang et al. [41] used *"information gain"* as an alternative interestingness measure to address the problem. Chen et al. [8] extended Liu's model [26] to find periodic patterns in time series using multiple *minSups*. It has to be noted that these studies have focused on finding periodically occurring sets of itemsets in time series data, while the proposed study focuses on finding periodically occurring correlated itemsets in temporal databases.

2.3 Periodic-Frequent Pattern Mining

Ozden et al. [29] enhanced the transactional database by a time attribute that describes the time when a transaction has appeared, investigated the periodic behavior of the patterns to discover cyclic association rules. In this study, a database is fragmented into non-overlapping subsets with respect to time. The association rules that are appearing in at least a certain number of subsets are discovered as cyclic association rules. By fragmenting the data and counting the number of subsets in which a pattern occurs greatly simplifies the design of the mining algorithm. However, the drawback is that patterns (or association rules) that span multiple windows cannot be discovered.

Tanbeer et al. [35] discussed a model to find periodic-frequent patterns in a transactional database. This model eliminates the need of data fragmentation, and discovers all patterns in a transactional database that satisfy the user-specified *minSup* and *maxPer* constraints. A pattern-growth algorithm, called Periodic-Frequent Pattern-growth (PFP-growth), was also discussed to find these patterns. Uday et al. [19] have discussed a greedy search technique to efficiently compute the *periodicity* of a pattern. Anirudh et al. [3] have proposed an efficient pattern-growth algorithm based on the concept of period summary. In this concept, the *tid*-list of the patterns are compressed into partial periodic summaries, and later aggregated to find periodic-frequent patterns efficiently. The popular adoption and successful industrial application of periodic-frequent pattern model suffers from the following two issues: (*i*) cannot handle databases in which transactions are occurring at irregular time intervals and (*ii*) the rare item problem (both issues are discussed in Sect. 1). This paper tries to address both of these issues.

Uday et al. [20] extended Liu's model [26] to address the *rare item problem* in periodic-frequent pattern mining. In this model, every item $i_j \in I$ in the database is specified with $minIS$ and $maxIP$ values. The $minSup$ and $maxPer$ for a pattern $X \subseteq I$ are specified as follows:

$$minSup(X) = min(minIS(i_j)|\forall i_j \in X)$$
$$and \qquad\qquad\qquad\qquad\qquad\qquad (1)$$
$$maxPer(X) = max(maxIP(i_j)|\forall i_j \in X)$$

where, $minSup(X)$ represents the *minimum support* of X, $maxPer(X)$ represents the *maximum periodicity* of X, $minIS(i_j)$ denotes the *minimum item support* of an item $i_j \in X$ and $maxIP(i_j)$ denotes the *maximum item periodicity* of an item $i_j \in X$.

The usage of item-specific $minIS$ and $maxIP$ values facilitates every pattern to satisfy a different $minSup$ and $maxPer$ depending on its items. However, the major limitation of this model is the computational cost because the generated periodic-frequent patterns do not satisfy the *anti-monotonic property*. Akshat et al. [33] proposed an alternative periodic-frequent pattern model using the item-specific $minIS$ and $maxIP$ values. In this model, the $minSup$ and $maxPer$ for a pattern X are specified as follows:

$$minSup(X) = max(minIS(i_j)|\forall i_j \in X)$$
$$and \qquad\qquad\qquad\qquad\qquad\qquad (2)$$
$$maxPer(X) = min(maxIP(i_j)|\forall i_j \in X)$$

The periodic-frequent patterns discovered by this model satisfy the anti-monotonic property. Henceforth, this model is practicable in real-world applications.

An open problem that is common to above two studies [20,33] is the methodology to specify items' $minIS$ and $maxIP$ values. Uday et al. [20] have described the following methodology to address this problem:

$$minIS(i_j) = max(\gamma \times S(i_j),\ LS)$$
$$and \qquad\qquad\qquad\qquad\qquad\qquad (3)$$
$$maxIP(i_j) = max(\beta \times S(i_j) + Per_{max},\ Per_{min})$$

where $i \in I$ and $S(i)$ is the *support* of the item i. In Eq. 3, LS is the user-specified lowest *minimum item support* allowed and $\gamma \in [0,1]$ is a parameter that controls how the $minIS$ values for items should be related to their *supports*. In Eq. 3, Per_{max} and Per_{min} are the user-specified maximum and minimum *periodicities* such that $Per_{max} \geq Per_{min}$ and $\beta \in [-1,0]$ is a user-specified constant.

Although Eq. 3 facilitates every item to have different $minIS$ and $maxIP$ values, it suffers from the following limitations: (i) This methodology requires several input parameters from the user. (ii) Equation 3 determines the $maxIP$ of an item by taking into account only its *support*. As a result, this equation implicitly assumes that all items having the same *support* will also have similar *periodicities* in a temporal database. However, this is seldom the case as items with similar *support* can have different *periodicities*. We have observed that employing this methodology to specify items' $maxIP$ values in the temporal databases, where items can have similar *support* but different *periodicities* can still lead to the *rare item problem*.

Example 2. Consider a hypothetical transactional database containing 100 transactions. Let 'x' and 'y' be two items in the database having the same *support* (say, $sup(x) = sup(y) = 40$), but different *periodicities* (say, $per(x) = 11$ and $per(y) = 30$). Since Eq. 3 determines the $maxIP$ values by taking into account only the *support* of the items, both 'x' and 'y' will be assigned a common $maxIP$ value although their actual *periodicity* is different from one another. This can result either in missing interesting patterns or generating too many patterns. For instance, if we set $\beta = -0.5$, $Per_{min} = 10$ and $Per_{max} = 50$, then $maxIP(x) = maxIP(y) = 20$. In this case, we miss the periodic-frequent patterns containing 'y' because $per(y) \nleq maxIP(y)$. In order to find the periodic-frequent patterns containing both 'x' and 'y' items, we have to set a high β value. When β is set at -0.375, we derive $maxIP(x) = maxIP(y) = 35$. In this case, we find periodic-frequent patterns containing 'y' because $per(y) \leq maxIP(y)$. However, we may also witness too many patterns containing the item 'x' because its $maxIP$ value is three times higher than its *periodicity*.

Rashid et al. [31] introduced standard deviation as an alternative measure of $maxPrd$. Nofong [27] employed mean as an alternative measure to determine the periodic interestingness of a pattern. Unfortunately, these alternative interestingness measures are impracticable on very large databases because the discovered patterns do not satisfy the downward closure property.

Recently, Uday et al. [22,23] have studied the problem of finding (partial) periodic patterns in temporal databases. In this paper, we extended the (full) periodic-frequent pattern model to handle the temporal databases.

3   Periodic-Frequent Pattern Model

In this section, we redefine the periodic-frequent pattern model [35] by taking into account the temporal databases. Care has been taken such that the nomenclature of redefined model is consistent with the nomenclature of the basic model of periodic-frequent patterns.

Let I be the set of items. Let $X \subseteq I$ be a **pattern** (or an itemset). A pattern containing β number of items is called a β-**pattern**. A **transaction**, $t_k = (tid, ts, Y)$ is a tuple, where $tid \in \mathbb{R}$ represents transactional-identifier, $ts \in \mathbb{R}$ represents the timestamp at which the pattern Y has occurred. A **temporal database** TDB over I is a set of transactions, $TDB = \{t_1, \cdots, t_m\}$, $m = |TDB|$, where $|TDB|$ can be defined as the number of transactions in TDB. Let ts_{min} and ts_{max} denote the minimum and maximum timestamps in TDB, respectively. For a transaction $t_k = (tid, ts, Y)$, $k \geq 1$, such that $X \subseteq Y$, it is said that X occurs in t_k and such timestamp is denoted as ts^X. Let $TS^X = \{ts_j^X, \cdots, ts_k^X\}$, $j, k \in [1, m]$ and $j \leq k$, be an **ordered set of timestamps** where X has occurred in TDB. In this paper, we call this list of timestamps of X as **ts-list** of X. The number of transactions containing X in TDB is defined as the **support** of X and denoted as $sup(X)$. That is, $sup(X) = |TS^X|$. Let ts_j^X and ts_r^X, $j \leq q < r \leq k$, be the two consecutive timestamps in TS^X. The time difference (or an inter-arrival time) between ts_r^X and ts_q^X is defined as a **period** of X, say p_a^X. That is, $p_a^X = ts_r^X - ts_q^X$. Let $P^X = (p_1^X, p_2^X, \cdots, p_r^X)$ be the set of all *periods* for pattern X. The **periodicity** of X, denoted as $per(X) = max(p_1^X, p_2^X, \cdots, p_r^X)$. The pattern X is a **frequent pattern** if $sup(X) \geq minSup$, where $minSup$ refers to the user-specified *minimum support* constraint. The frequent pattern X is said to be **periodic-frequent** if $per(X) \leq maxPer$, where $maxPer$ refers to the user-specified *maximum periodicity* constraint. The redefined **problem definition** of periodic-frequent pattern mining involves discovering all patterns in TDB that satisfy the user-specified $minSup$ and $maxPer$ constraints. The *support* of a pattern can be expressed in percentage of $|TDB|$. Similarly, the *period* and *periodicity* of a pattern can be expressed in percentage of $(ts_{max} - ts_{min})$.

Example 3. Table 2 shows the temporal database with the set of items $I = \{a, b, c, d, e, f, g, h\}$. The set of items '$a$' and '$b$,' i.e., '$ab$' is a pattern. This pattern contains only two items. Therefore, this is a 2-pattern. In the first transaction, $t_1 = (101, 1, ab)$, 101 (from the left hand side) represents the transaction identifier of the transaction, 1 denotes the timestamp at which the transaction has occurred and 'ab' represents the itemset occurring in this transaction. In the entire database, this pattern appears at the timestamps of $1, 2, 5, 7$ and 10. Therefore, $TS^{ab} = \{1, 2, 5, 7, 10\}$. The *support* of '$ab$,' i.e., $sup(ab) = |TS^{ab}| = |1, 2, 5, 7, 10| = 5$. If the user-specified $minSup = 5$, then 'ab' is a frequent pattern because $sup(ab) \geq minSup$. The minimum and maximum timestamps of all transactions in this database are 1 and 12, respectively. Therefore, $ts_{min} = 1$ and $ts_{max} = 12$. All periods for this pattern are: $p_1^{ab} = 0 \ (= 1 - ts_{min})$, $p_2^{ab} = 1 \ (= 2 - 1)$, $p_3^{ab} = 3 \ (= 5 - 2)$, $p_4^{ab} = 2 \ (= 7 - 5)$, $p_5^{ab} = 3 \ (10 - 7)$ and $p_6^{ab} = 2 \ (= ts_{max} - 10)$. Therefore, $P^{ab} = (0, 1, 3, 2, 3, 2)$. The *periodicity* of '$ab$,' i.e., $per(ab) = max(0, 1, 3, 2, 3, 2) = 3$. If the user-defined $maxPer = 3$, then the frequent pattern 'ab' is a periodic-frequent pattern because $per(ab) \leq maxPer$.

The two key differences between the Tanbeer's model [35] and the above model of periodic-frequent patterns are as follows: (i) In the above model, the first period of a pattern is calculated using ts_{min}, where as the first period of a pattern in Tanbeer's model is calculated with reference to initial time, which is zero. (*ii*) Since the Tanbeer model considers input data as a transactional database with transactions occurring at a fixed time interval, the *periodicity* of a pattern is expressed in percentage of $|TDB|$, whereas in the above model the *periodicity* of a pattern is expressed in percentage of $(ts_{max} - ts_{min})$.

Table 2. Running example: A temporal database

tid	ts	Items	tid	ts	Items
101	1	a, b	107	7	a, b, c, e
102	3	a, b, d	108	8	c, d
103	3	c, d, g	109	9	c, d
104	4	c, e, f	110	10	a, b, e, f
105	5	a, b	111	11	c, d, g
106	7	h	112	12	a, e, f

The above redefined model of periodic-frequent patterns still suffers from the *rare item problem* (refer Example 4). In the next section, we describe periodic-correlated pattern model to address this problem.

Example 4. Consider the rare items '*e*' and '*f*' in Table 2. If we set a high *minSup* and a short *maxPer*, say *minSup* = 5 and *maxPer* = 3, we will miss the periodic-frequent patterns containing these rare items. In order to discover the periodic-frequent patterns containing these rare items, we have to set a low *minSup* and a long *maxPer*, say *minSup* = 2 and *maxPer* = 6. All periodic-frequent patterns discovered at these threshold values are shown in the column titled **I** in Table 3. It can be observed from this table that setting a low *minSup* and a long *maxPer* has not only resulted in finding '*ef*' as a periodic-frequent pattern, but also resulted in generating the uninteresting patterns '*ce*' and '*cd*' as periodic-frequent patterns. The pattern '*ce*' is uninteresting (with respect to *support* dimension), because the rare item '*e*' is randomly occurring with a frequent item '*c*' in very few transactions. The pattern '*cd*' is uninteresting (with respect to *periodicity* dimension), because it contains the frequent items '*c*' and '*d*' appearing together at very long inter-arrival times (or *periodicity*).

4   Periodic-Correlated Pattern Model

To address the *rare item problem* in periodic-frequent pattern mining, we need a model that extracts interesting patterns involving both frequent and rare items yet filtering out uninteresting patterns. After conducting the initial investigation on the nature of interesting patterns found in various databases, we have made a key observation that most of the interesting periodic patterns discovered in a database have their *support* and *periodicity* close to that of its individual items. The following example illustrates our observation.

Table 3. Periodic-frequent patterns discovered from Table 2. The terms *Pat, sup, allConf, per* and *perAllConf* refer to *pattern, support, all-confidence, periodicity* and *periodic-all-confidence*, respectively. The columns titled **I**, **II** and **III** represent the periodic-frequent patterns generated using basic model, extending *all-confidence* to the basic model and the proposed model, respectively.

Pat	sup	allConf	per	perAllConf	I	II	III
a	6	1	3	1	✓	✓	✓
b	5	1	3	1	✓	✓	✓
c	6	1	3	1	✓	✓	✓
d	5	1	5	1	✓	✓	✓
e	4	1	4	1	✓	✓	✓
f	3	1	6	1	✓	✓	✓
ab	5	0.833	3	1	✓	✓	✓
ef	3	0.75	6	1.5	✓	✓	✓
ce	2	0.4	5	1.67	✓	✗	✗
cd	4	0.8	5	1.67	✓	✓	✗

Example 5. In a supermarket, cheap and perishable goods (e.g., bread and butter) are purchased more frequently and periodically than the costly and durable goods (e.g., bed and pillow). Among all the possible combinations of the above four items, we normally consider {bread, butter} and {bed, pillow} as interesting patterns, because only these two patterns generally have *support* and *periodicity* close to the *support* and *periodicity* of its individual items. All other uninteresting patterns, {bread, bed}, {bread, pillow}, {butter, bed} and {butter, pillow}, generally have *support* and *periodicity* relatively far away from the *support* and *periodicity* of its individual items as compared against the above two patterns.

Henceforth, in this paper we consider a pattern as interesting if its *support* and *periodicity* are close to the *support* and *periodicity* of its individual items. In this context, we need two measures to determine the interestingness of a pattern with respect to both *support* and *periodicity* dimensions.

In the literature, researchers have discussed several measures to address the *rare item problem* in *support* dimension [34,39]. In this paper, we use *all-confidence* to address the *rare item problem* in *support* dimension. (The reason for choosing this measure for finding periodic-correlated patterns has been described in Sect. 2).

Continuing with the model of periodic-frequent patterns (discussed in the previous section), the proposed model of periodic-correlated patterns is as follows.

Definition 3. *(All-confidence of X)*. *The all-confidence of X, denoted as allConf(X), is the ratio of support of X to the maximal support of an item $i_j \in X$. That is, $allConf(X) = \frac{sup(X)}{max(sup(i_j)|\forall i_j \in X)}$.*

For a pattern X, $allConf(X) \in (0, 1]$. As per the *all-confidence* measure, a pattern is interesting in *support* dimension if its *support* is close to the *support* of all of its items. The parameter *minAllConf* indicates the user-specified minimum *all-confidence* threshold value. Based on *minSup* and *minAllConf* thresholds, all the interesting patterns involving rare items in *support* dimension are extracted.

Definition 4. (*Correlated pattern* X). *The pattern X is said to be correlated if $sup(X) \geq minSup$ and $allConf(X) \geq minAllConf$. The terms minSup and minAllConf, respectively represent the user-specified minimum support and minimum all-confidence.*

Example 6. In Table 2, the *support* of the patterns a, b and ab are 6, 5 and 5, respectively. Therefore, the *all-confidence* of ab, i.e., $allConf(ab) = \frac{sup(ab)}{max(sup(a), sup(b))} = \frac{5}{max(6,5)} = 0.833$. If the user-specified $minSup = 2$ and $minAllConf = 0.6$, then ab is a correlated pattern because $sup(ab) \geq minSup$ and $allConf(ab) \geq minAllConf$.

The usage of *all-confidence* alone is insufficient to completely address the *rare item problem*. The reason is that this measure does not take into account the *periodicity* dimension of a pattern.

Example 7. The column titled **II** in Table 3 shows the periodic-frequent patterns discovered when *all-confidence* is used along with *support* and *periodicity* measures. **The *minSup*, *minAllConf* and *maxPer* values used to find these patterns are 2, 0.6 and 6, respectively.** It can be observed from the discovered periodic-frequent patterns that though *all-confidence* is able to prune the uninteresting pattern '*ce*,' it has failed to prune another uninteresting pattern '*cd*' from the list of periodic-frequent patterns generated by the basic model. Henceforth, the *rare item problem* has to be addressed with respect to both *support* and *periodicity* dimensions.

As there exists no measure in the literature that determines the interestingness of a pattern with respect to the *periodicities* of all of its items, we propose a new measure, ***periodic-all-confidence***, to extract interesting patterns in *periodicity* dimension involving rare items, which is defined as follows.

Definition 5. (*Periodic-all-confidence of* X). *The periodic-all-confidence of X, denoted as $perAllConf(X)$, is the ratio of periodicity of X to the minimal periodicity of an item $i_j \in X$. That is, $perAllConf(X) = \frac{per(X)}{min(per(i_j)|\forall i_j \in X)}$.*

Example 8. In Table 2, the *periodicity* of the patterns a, b and ab are 3, 3 and 3, respectively. Therefore, the *periodic-all-confidence* of ab, i.e., $perAllConf(ab) = \frac{per(ab)}{min(per(a), per(b))} = \frac{3}{min(3,3)} = 1$.

For a pattern X, $perConf(X) \in [1, \infty)$. As per the *periodic-all-confidence* measure, a pattern is interesting in *periodicity* dimension, if the *periodicity* of a pattern is close to the *periodicity* of all of its items. The parameter *maxPerAllConf* indicates the maximum *periodic-all-confidence* threshold set by the user. Based on *maxPer* and *maxPerAllConf* thresholds, the interesting patterns involving rare items in *periodicity* dimension can be extracted.

Henceforth, the periodic-correlated pattern is defined as follows.

Definition 6. *(Periodic-correlated pattern X). The pattern X is said to be periodic-correlated if $sup(X) \geq minSup$, $allConf(X) \geq minAllConf$, $per(X) \leq maxPer$ and $perAllConf(X) \leq maxPerAllConf$. The terms minSup, minAllConf, maxPer and maxPerAllConf, respectively represent the user-specified minimum support, minimum all-confidence, maximum periodicity and maximum periodic-all-confidence.*

Example 9. *If the user-specified $minSup = 2$, $minAllConf = 0.6$, $maxPer = 6$ and $maxPerAllConf = 1.5$, then the pattern 'ab' is said to be a periodic-correlated pattern, because $sup(ab) \geq minSup$, $allConf(ab) \geq minAllConf$, $per(ab) \leq maxPer$ and $perAllConf(ab) \leq maxPerAllConf$.*

Example 10. *The column titled* **III** *in Table 3 shows the complete set of periodic-correlated patterns discovered from Table 2. It can be observed that the proposed model has not only discovered the periodic-correlated patterns containing rare items but also pruned the uninteresting patterns 'cd' and 'ce.' This clearly demonstrates that the proposed model discovers periodic-correlated patterns containing rare items without generating too many uninteresting patterns.*

The discovered periodic-correlated patterns satisfy the *anti-monotonic property* (see Lemma 1). The correctness is straightforward to prove from Properties 1 and 2.

Property 1. *If $X \subset Y$, then $TS^X \supseteq TS^Y$. Therefore, $sup(X) \geq sup(Y)$ and $allConf(X) \geq allConf(Y)$.*

Property 2. *If $X \subset Y$, then $per(X) \leq per(Y)$. Therefore, $perAllConf(X) \leq perAllConf(Y)$ as $\frac{per(X)}{min(per(i_j)\forall i_j \in X)} \leq \frac{per(Y)}{min(per(i_j)\forall i_j \in Y)}$.*

Lemma 1. *If $X \subset Y$, then $TS^X \supseteq TS^Y$. Therefore, $sup(X) \geq sup(Y)$, $allConf(X) \geq allConf(Y)$, $per(X) \leq per(Y)$ and $perAllConf(X) \leq perAllConf(Y)$.*

Definition 7. *Problem Definition: Given the temporal database (TDB) and the user-specified minimum support (minSup), minimum all-confidence (minAllConf), maximum periodicity (maxPer) and maximum periodic-all-confidence (maxPerAllConf), the problem of finding periodic-correlated patterns involves discovering all patterns that satisfy the minSup, minAllConf, maxPer and maxPerAllConf thresholds. The support of a pattern can be expressed in percentage of $|TDB|$. The periodicity of a pattern can be expressed in percentage of $(ts_{max} - ts_{min})$.*

5 Proposed Algorithm

Tanbeer et al. [35] have proposed Periodic-Frequent pattern-growth (PF-growth) to discover periodic-frequent patterns using *support* and *periodicity* measures. Unfortunately, this algorithm cannot be directly used for finding the periodic-correlated patterns with our model. The reason is that PF-growth does not determine the interestingness of a pattern using *all-confidence* and *periodic-all-confidence* measures. In this paper, we extend PF-growth to determine the interestingness of a pattern using these two measures. We call the proposed algorithm as Extended Periodic-Correlated pattern-growth (EPCP-growth). The proposed algorithm involves two steps: (*i*) construction of Extended Periodic-Correlated pattern-tree (EPCP-tree), (*ii*) recursively mining EPCP-tree to discover periodic-correlated patterns. Before we describe these two steps, we explain the structure of EPCP-tree.

5.1 Structure of EPCP-tree

The structure of EPCP-tree consists of a prefix-tree and a EPCP-list. The EPCP-list consists of three fields: item name (*i*), *support* (*s*) and *periodicity* (*p*). The structure of prefix-tree in EPCP-tree is similar to that of the prefix-tree in FP-tree [15]. However, to obtain both *support* and *periodicity* of the patterns, the nodes in EPCP-tree explicitly maintain the occurrence information for each transaction by maintaining an occurrence timestamp list, called *ts-list*, only at the tail node of every transaction. Complete details on prefix-tree are available in [35].

One can assume that the structure of the prefix-tree in an EPCP-tree may not be memory efficient since it explicitly maintains timestamps of each transaction. However, it has been argued that such a tree can achieve memory efficiency by keeping transaction information only at the tail nodes and avoiding the support count field at each node [35].

5.2 Construction of EPCP-tree

Since the periodic-correlated patterns generated by the proposed model satisfy the *anti-monotonic property*, periodic-correlated items (or 1-patterns) play a key role in efficient discovery of higher order periodic-correlated patterns. These items are discovered by populating the EPCP-list (lines 1 to 18 in Algorithm 1). Figures 1(a), (b), (c), (d) and (e) show the steps involved in finding periodic-correlated items from EPCP-list. The user-specified *minSup*, *minAllConf*, *maxPer* and *maxPerAllConf* values are 2, 0.6, 6 and 1.5, respectively.

After finding periodic-correlated items, prefix-tree is constructed by performing another scan on the database (lines 19 to 23 in Algorithm 1). A EPCP-tree is constructed as follows. First, create the root node of the tree and labeled it as "*null*." Scan the database a second time. The items in each transaction are processed in *EPCP* order (i.e., sorted according to descending support count), and a branch is created for each transaction such that only the tail-nodes record the timestamps of transactions. For example, the scan of the first transaction,

Algorithm 1. Construction of EPCP-tree (TDB: Temporal database, $minSup$: minimum support, $minAllConf$: minimum all-confidence, $maxPer$: maximum periodicity, $maxPerAllConf$: maximum periodic-all-confidence)

1: Let id_l be a temporary array that records the ts of the last appearance of each
    item in the TDB. Let $t = \{tid, ts_{cur}, X\}$ denote the current transaction with
    tid, ts_{cur} and X representing the transanction identifier, timestamp of the current
    transaction and pattern, respectively.
2: **for** each transaction $t \in TDB$ **do**
3:     **if** an item i occurs for the first time **then**
4:         Insert i into the EPCP-list with $sup^i = 1$, $per^i = ts_{min} - ts_{cur}$ and $id_l^i = 1$.
5:     **else**
6:         $sup^i = sup^i + 1$.
7:         **if** $(ts_{cur} - id_l^i) > per^i$ **then**
8:           $per^i = ts_{cur} - id_l^i$.
9:         **end if**
10:     **end if**
11: **end for**
12: **for** each item i in EPCP-list **do**
13:     **if** $(ts_{max} - id_l^i) > per^i$ **then**
14:         $per^i = ts_{max} - id_l^i$.
15:     **end if**
16: **end for**
17: Remove items from the EPCP-list that do not satisfy $minSup$ and $maxPer$.
18: Sort the remaining items in EPCP-list in descending order of their *support*. Let
    this sorted list of items be $EPCP$.
19: Create a root node in EPCP-tree, T, and label it *"null."*
20: **for** each transaction $t \in TDB$ **do**
21:     Sort the items in t in $EPCP$ order. Let this list of sorted periodic-frequent items
    in t be $[p|P]$, where p is the first item and P is the remaining list.
22:     Call $insert\_tree([p|P], ts_{cur}, T)$.
23: **end for**

"101 : 1 : *ab*," which contains two items (a, b in $EPCP$ order), leads to the construction of the first branch of the tree with two nodes, $\langle a \rangle$ and $\langle b : 1 \rangle$, where a is linked as a child of the root and $b : 1$ is linked to a. The EPCP-tree generated after scanning the first transaction is shown in Fig. 2(a). The scan on the second transaction, "102 : 3 : *abd*," containing the items a, b and d in CI order, would result in a branch where a is linked to the root, b is linked to a and $d : 3$ is linked to b. However, this branch would share a common prefix, ab, with the existing path for first transaction. Therefore, we create a single new node $\langle d : 3 \rangle$, and link $d : 3$ to b as shown in Fig. 2(b). A similar process is repeated for the remaining transactions and the tree is updated accordingly. Figure 2(c) shows the EPCP-tree constructed after scanning the entire database. In EPCP-tree, an item header table is built so that each item points to its occurrences in the tree via a chain of node-links, to facilitate tree traversal. For simplicity, we do not show these node-links in trees, however, they are maintained as in FP-tree.

i	s	p	id_l	i	s	p	id_l	i	s	p	id_l	i	s	p	i	s	p
a	1	1	1	a	2	2	3	a	6	3	12	a	6	3	a	6	3
b	1	1	1	b	2	2	3	b	5	3	10	b	5	3	c	6	3
				d	1	3	3	d	5	5	11	d	5	5	b	5	3
								c	6	3	11	c	6	3	d	5	5
								g	2	8	11	g	2	8	e	4	4
								e	4	4	12	e	4	4	f	3	6
								f	3	6	12	f	3	6			
								h	1	7	7	h	1	7			
(a)				**(b)**				**(c)**				**(d)**			**(e)**		

Fig. 1. Construction of EPCP-list for Table 2. (a) After scanning the first transaction (b) After scanning the second transaction (c) After scanning every transaction (d) Updated EPCP-list (e) Final EPCP-list with sorted list of periodic-correlated items

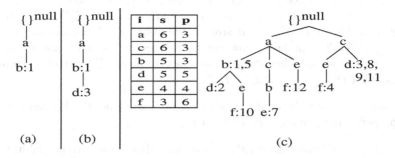

Fig. 2. Construction of EPCP-tree for Table 2. (a) After scanning first transaction (b) After scanning second transaction (c) After scanning every transaction

The EPCP-tree maintains the complete information of all periodic-correlated patterns in a database. The correctness is based on Property 3 and shown in Lemmas 2 and 3. For each transaction $t \in TDB$, EPCP(t) is the set of all candidate items in t, i.e., $EPCP(t) = item(t) \cap EPCP$, and is called the candidate item projection of t.

Property 3. An EPCP-tree maintains a complete set of candidate item projections for each transaction in a database only once.

Lemma 2. *Given a TDB and user-defined minSup, minAllConf, maxPer, and maxPerAllConf thresholds, the complete set of all periodic-correlated item projections of all transactions in the TDB can be derived from the EPCP-tree.*

Proof. Based on Property 3, each transaction $t \in TDB$ is mapped to only one path in the tree, and any path from the root up to a tail node maintains the complete projection for exactly n transactions (where n is the total number of entries in the ts-list of the tail node).

Algorithm 2. Insert_tree($[p|P]$, ts_{cur}, T)

1: **if** T does not have a child N satisfying $p.itemName = N.itemName$ **then**
2:     Create a new node N and set its parent as T. Let its node-link be linked to the nodes with the same item via the node-link structure.
3: **end if**
4: Remove p from P.
5: **if** P is non-empty **then**
6:     Call Insert_tree($[P]$, ts_{cur}, N)
7: **else**
8:     Add ts_{cur} to T (i.e., leaf node).
9: **end if**

Lemma 3. *The size of the EPCP-tree (without the root node) on a TDB for user-defined minSup, minAllConf, maxPer, and maxPerAllConf thresholds, is bounded by $\sum_{t \in TDB} |EPCP(t)|$.*

Proof. According to the EPCP-tree construction process and Lemma 2, each transaction t contributes at most one path of size $|EPCP(t)|$ to an EPCP-tree. Therefore, the total size contribution of all transactions can be $\sum_{t \in TDB} |EPCP(t)|$ at best. However, since there are usually many common prefix patterns among the transactions, the size of an EPCP-tree is normally much smaller than $\sum_{t \in TDB} |EPCP(t)|$.

Before we discuss the mining of EPCP-tree, we explore the following important property and lemma of an EPCP-tree.

Property 4. A tail node in an EPCP-tree maintains the occurrence information for all the nodes in the path (from the tail node to the root) at least in the transactions in its ts-list.

Lemma 4. *Let $Z = \{a_1, a_2, \cdots, a_n\}$ be a path in an EPCP-tree where node a_n is the tail node carrying the ts-list of the path. If the ts-list is pushed-up to node a_{n1}, then a_{n1} maintains the occurrence information of the path $Z' = \{a_1, a_2, \cdots, a_{n1}\}$ for the same set of transactions in the ts-list without any loss.*

Proof. Based on Property 4, a_n maintains the occurrence information of path Z' at least in the transactions in its ts-list. Therefore, the same ts-list at node a_{n1} maintains the same transaction information for Z' without any loss.

5.3 Mining EPCP-tree

Algorithm 3 describes the procedure for mining periodic-correlated patterns from EPCP-tree. The EPCP-tree is mined by calling EPCP-growth as (EPCP-tree, *null*). This algorithm resembles FP-growth. However, the key difference is that once the pattern-growth is achieved for a suffix 1-pattern (or item), it is completely pruned from the EPCP-tree by pushing its ts-list to respective parent nodes.

The working of this algorithm is as follows. We proceed to construct the prefix tree for each candidate item in the EPCP-list, starting from the bottom most item, say i. To construct the prefix-tree for i, the prefix sub-paths of node i are accumulated in a tree-structure, PT_i. Since i is the bottom-most item in the EPCP-list, each node labeled i in the EPCP-tree must be a tail node. While constructing PT_i, based on Property 4, we map the ts-list of every node of i to all items in the respective path explicitly in the temporary array (one for each item). This temporary array facilitates the calculation of sup, $allConf$, per, $perAllConf$ of each item in PT_i (line 2 in Algorithm 3). If an item j in PT_i has $sup \geq minSup$, $allConf \geq minAllConf$, $per \leq maxPer$ and $perAllConf \leq maxPerAllConf$, then we construct its conditional tree and mine it recursively to discover the recurring patterns (lines 3 to 9 in Algorithm 3). Moreover, to enable the construction of the prefix-tree for the next item in the EPCP-list, based on Lemma 4, the ts-lists are pushed-up to the respective parent nodes in the original EPCP-tree and in PT_i as well. All nodes of i in the original EPCP-tree and is entry in the EPCP-list are deleted thereafter (line 10 in Algorithm 3).

Using Properties 3 and 4, the conditional tree CT_i for PT_i is constructed by removing all those items from PT_i that have $sup \leq minSup$, or $allConf \leq minAllConf$, or $per \geq maxPer$ or $perAllConf \geq maxPerAllConf$. If the deleted node is a tail node, its ts-list is pushed-up to its parent node. The contents of the temporary array for the bottom item j in the EPCP-list of CT_i represent TS_{ij} (i.e., the set of all timestamps where items i and j have appeared together in the database). The same process of creating a prefix-tree and its corresponding conditional tree is repeated for further extensions of "ij". The whole process of mining for each item is repeated until EPCP-list $\neq \emptyset$.

Table 4 summarizes the working of this algorithm. First, we consider item 'f,' which is the bottom-most item in the EPCP-list, as a suffix pattern. This item appears in three branches of the EPCP-tree (refer Fig. 2(c)). The paths formed by these branches are $\{cef : 4\}$, $\{abef : 10\}$ and $\{aef : 12\}$ (format of these branches is $\{nodes : timestamps\}$). Therefore, considering 'f' as a suffix item, its corresponding three prefix paths are $\{ce : 4\}$, $\{abe : 10\}$ and $\{ae : 12\}$, which form its conditional pattern base (refer Fig. 3(a)). Its conditional EPCP-tree contains only a single path, $\langle e : 4, 10, 12 \rangle$; '$a$,' '$b$' and '$c$' are not included because their all-confidence and periodic-all-confidence do not satisfy the $minAllConf$ and $maxPerAllConf$ respectively. Figure 3(b) shows the conditional EPCP-tree of 'f.' The single path generates the pattern $\{ef : 3, 0.75, 6, 1.5\}$ (format is $\{pattern: support, all-confidence, periodicity, periodic-all-confidence\}$). The same process of creating prefix-tree and its corresponding conditional tree is repeated for further extensions of 'ef.' Next, 'f' is pruned from the original EPCP-tree and its ts-lists are pushed to its parent nodes, as shown in Fig. 3(c). All the above processes are once again repeated until EPCP-list $\neq \emptyset$.

Algorithm 3. EPCP-growth($Tree$, α)

1: **for** each a_i in the header of $Tree$ **do**
2:    Generate pattern $\beta = a_i \cup \alpha$. Construct an array TS^β, which represents the set of timestamps at which β has appeared in TDB. Next, compute from TS^β, $sup(\beta)$, $allConf(\beta)$, $per(\beta)$ and $perAllConf(\beta)$ and compare them with $minSup$, $minAllConf$, $maxPer$ and $maxPerAllConf$, respectively.
3:    **if** $sup(\beta) \geq minSup$, $allConf(\beta) \geq minAllConf$, $per(\beta) \leq maxPer$ and $perAllConf(\beta) \leq maxPerAllConf$ **then**
4:       Output β as a periodic-correlated pattern as $\{\beta: sup, allConf, per, perAllConf\}$.
5:       Traverse $Tree$ using the node-links of β, and construct β's conditional pattern base and β's conditional EPCP-tree $Tree_\beta$.
6:       **if** $Tree_\beta \neq \emptyset$ **then**
7:          call EPCP-growth($Tree_\beta$, β);
8:       **end if**
9:    **end if**
10:    Remove a_i from the $Tree$ and push a_i's ts-list to its parent nodes.
11: **end for**

Table 4. Mining EPCP-tree by creating conditional (sub -) pattern bases

Item	sup	per	Cond. Pattern Base	Cond. EPCP-tree	Per. Freq. Patterns
f	3	6	$\{ce:4\}, \{abe:10\},$ $\{ae:12\}$	$\langle e:4,10,12\rangle$	$\{ef: 3, 0.75, 6, 1.5\}$
e	4	4	$\{c:4\}, \{abc:7\},$ $\{ab:10\}, \{a:12\}$	$-$	$-$
d	5	5	$\{ab:3\}, \{c:3,8,9,11\}$	$-$	$-$
b	5	3	$\{a:1,2,5,10\}, \{ac:7\}$	$\langle a:1,2,5,7,10\rangle$	$\{ab:5,0.833,3,1\}$
c	6	3	$\{a:7\}$	$-$	$-$

6   Experimental Results

In this section, we show that the proposed model discovers interesting patterns pertaining to both frequent and rare items by pruning uninteresting patterns. We also evaluate the proposed model against the existing models of periodic-correlated patterns [20, 33, 35].

The algorithms, *PF-growth*, *MCPF-growth*, *MaxCPF-growth* and *EPCP-growth* are written in C++ and run with Fedora 22 on a 2.66 GHz machine with 8 GB of memory. We have conducted experiments using both synthetic (**T10I4D100K**) and real-world (**Retail** and **FAA-Accidents**) databases. The T10I4D100K data-base is generated using the IBM data generator [1]. This database contains 878 items with 100,000 transactions. The **Retail** database contains the market basket data from a Belgian retail store. This database contains 16,471 items with 88,162 transactions. The **FAA-Accidents** database is

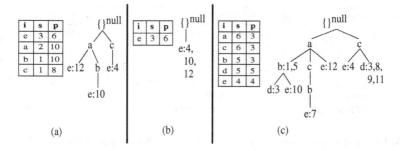

Fig. 3. Mining of EPCP-tree for Table 2. (a) Prefix-tree of suffix item 'f,' i.e., PT_f (b) Conditional tree of suffix item 'f,' i.e., CT_f (c) EPCP-tree after pruning item 'f.'

constructed from the accidents data recorded by FAA from 1-January-1978 to 31-December-2014. This database contains 9,290 items with 98,864 transactions.

6.1 Patterns Generated by the Proposed Model

Figure 4(a)–(c) shows the number of patterns generated at different *minAll-Conf* and *maxPerAllConf* values in T10I4D100K, Retail and FAA-Accidents databases. *The minSup and maxPer are set at 0.01% and 40%.* The following observations can be drawn: (i) The increase in *minAllConf* results in decrease of periodic-correlated patterns. The reason is that as *minAllConf* increases, the *support* threshold value of a pattern increases. (ii) The increase in *maxPerAllConf* results in increase of patterns. The reason is that as *max-PerAllConf* increases, the *periodicity* threshold value of a pattern increases.

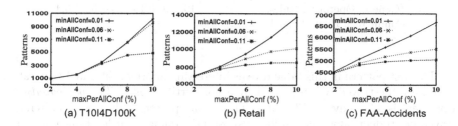

Fig. 4. Periodic-correlated patterns generated at different *maxAllConf* and *maxPer-AllConf* values

Figure 5 show the runtime requirements of EPCP-growth at different *max-PerAllConf* and *minAllConf* values in T10I4D100K, Retail and FAA-Accidents databases. The following observations can be drawn: (i) The increase in *minAllConf* decreases the runtime of EPCP-growth. The reason is that increase in *minAllConf* decreases the number of periodic-correlated patterns. (ii) The increase in *maxPerAllConf* results in increase of runtime of EPCP-growth.

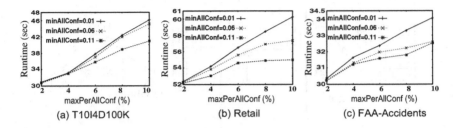

Fig. 5. Runtime requirements of EPCP-growth at different *maxAllConf* and *maxPerAllConf* values

Table 5 shows some of the interesting patterns discovered in FAA database. The *minSup*, *minAllConf*, *maxPer* and *maxPerAllConf* values used are 0.01%, 0.01, 40% and 9, respectively. *It can be observed from their support values that our model has discovered interesting patterns involving both frequent and rare items effectively.* Please note that the *periodicity (per)* is expressed in days.

Table 5. Some of the interesting patterns discovered in FAA-Accidents database

S. No.	Patterns	sup	allConf	per	perAllConf
1	{Pilot Not Certificated, Destroyed}	13	0.06	4756	7.77
2	{Student, Substantial}	136	0.02	893	29.77
3	{Boeing, Substantial}	214	0.02	214	26.35
4	{Private-Pilot, Cessna, CE-172, Minor}	1,661	0.03	117	23.4
5	{General Operating Rules, Commercial Pilot, Minor}	10,399	0.15	32	6.4

The first pattern in this table reveals interesting information that 13 aircrafts have been 'destroyed' when piloted by a non-certified pilot. The *periodicity* of this event is 4756 days (≈13 years). The second pattern indicates 136 aircrafts driven by student pilots have suffered substantial damages at least once in every ≈2.5 years. The third pattern indicates that Boeing aircrafts have suffered substantial damages at least once in every ≈7 months. The fourth pattern reveals the information that Cessna airlines CE-172 driven by private pilots have encountered minor damages at least once in every ≈4 months. The last pattern reveals the information that at least once in every 32 days, an aircraft driven by commercial pilots has witnessed minor damages during general operating rules. It can be observed that the first three patterns have low *support* and high *periodicity*. These patterns are often difficult to find with existing approaches due to combinatorial explosion. Thus, the proposed model can efficiently discover useful information pertaining to both frequent and rare items.

6.2 Comparison of Proposed Model Against the Existing Models

For *MCPF-growth* and *MaxCPF-growth*, we use Eq. 3 to specify items' *minIS* and *maxIP* values. Setting the α and β values in this equation has been a non-trivial task as the patterns discovered by these algorithms can be different from the patterns discovered by *EPCP-growth*. After conducting several experiments, we have empirically set the following values for *MCPF-growth* and *MaxCPF-growth* algorithms, such that both algorithms discover almost all periodic-frequent patterns discovered by *EPCP-growth*.

Figure 6 shows the number of periodic-frequent patterns generated at different *minSup* values (*Y-axis* is plotted on logscale). For *EPCP-growth*, we have fixed $minAllConf = 0.01$, $maxPer = 40\%$ and $maxPerAllConf = 9$ and vary *minSup* values. For *MCPF-growth* and *MaxCPF-growth*, we have set $\gamma = 0.01$, $LS = minSup$, $\beta = -0.4$, $Per_{max} = 40\%$ and $Per_{min} = 10\%$. For *PF-growth*, we have set $maxPer = 40\%$ and vary *minSup* values. It can be observed that the proposed model has generated less of number of patterns because *all-confidence* has pruned the uninteresting patterns having support much less than the support of individual items.

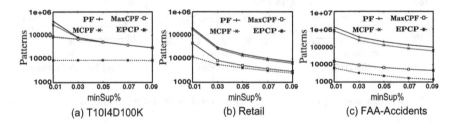

(a) T10I4D100K   (b) Retail   (c) FAA-Accidents

Fig. 6. Periodic-Correlated patterns generated at different minSup values

Figure 7 shows the number of periodic-frequent patterns generated at different *maxPer* values (*Y-axis* is plotted on logscale). For *EPCP-growth*, we have fixed $minSup = 0.01\%$, $minAllConf = 0.01$ and $maxPerAllConf = 9$ and vary *maxPer* values. For *MCPF-growth* and *MaxCPF-growth*, we have set $\gamma = 0.01$, $LS = 0.01\%$, $\beta = -0.4$, $Per_{max} = maxPer$ and $Per_{min} = 10\%$. For *PF-growth*, we have set $minSup = 0.01\%$ and vary *maxPer* values. It can be observed that the proposed model has generated less number of patterns at different *maxPer* values. It is because *periodic all-confidence* has pruned out those uninteresting patterns whose *periodicity* was much higher than the periodicity of its individual items.

From Figs. 6 and 7, it can be observed that the proposed model has generated lesser number of periodic-frequent patterns than the other models, because the existing models have suffered from the *rare item problem*.

Figures 8 show the runtime taken by various models at different *minSup* values (*Y-axis* is plotted on logscale). It can be observed that, in all the databases

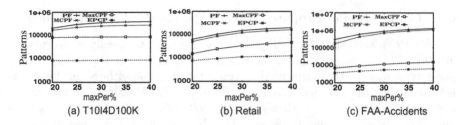

Fig. 7. Periodic-Correlated patterns generated at different maxPer values

the proposed model takes lesser runtime to find periodic-frequent patterns than *PF-growth* and *MCPF-growth*. But the proposed model takes slightly more runtime than *MaxCPF-growth*. So the proposed model is not adding any significant overhead in mining periodic-correlated patterns.

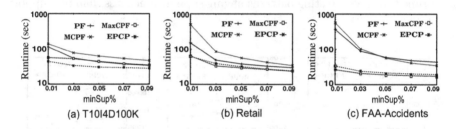

Fig. 8. Runtime requirements of various models at different minSup values

Figure 9 shows the runtime taken by various models at different *maxPer* values (*Y-axis* is plotted on logscale). Similar observations to that of varying *minSup* can be drawn.

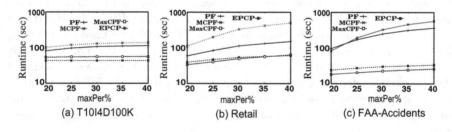

Fig. 9. Runtime requirements of various models at different maxPer values

6.3 Scalability

We studied the scalability of EPCP-growth on execution time by varying the number of transactions in a database. We used Kosarak, T10I4D1000K and T25I6D1000K datasets for this experiment. We divided the database into five equal parts, i.e., 20% transactions in each part. Then we investigated the performance of EPCP-growth by accumulating each part with previous parts and running EPCP-growth each time. Figure 10(a), (b) and (c) show the graph of runtime requirements of EPCP-growth in Kosarak, T10I4D1000K and T25I6D1000K databases, respectively. It is clear from the graphs that as the database size increases, overall tree construction and mining time increase. However, the figure shows stable performance of about linear increase in runtime with respect to the database size.

Figure 11(a), (b) and (c) show the graph of memory requirements of EPCP-growth in Kosarak, T10I4D1000K and T25I6D1000K databases, respectively. Similar observations to that of runtime requirements can be drawn. Therefore, it can be observed from the scalability test that EPCP-growth scales linearly with the increase in database size.

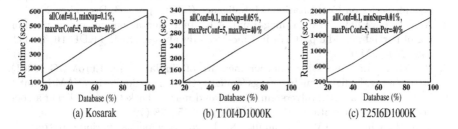

Fig. 10. Runtime requirements of *EPCP*-growth in various databases

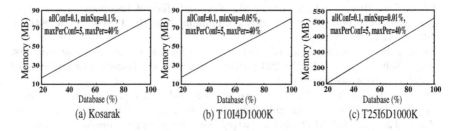

Fig. 11. Memory requirements of *EPCP*-growth in various databases

7 Conclusions and Future Work

This paper introduces a model to address the rare item problem in both *support* and *periodicity* dimensions. A new interestingness measure, *periodic-all-confidence*, is proposed to address the problem in *periodicity* dimension. An efficient pattern-growth algorithm has been proposed to discover all periodic-correlated patterns in a database. Experimental results demonstrate that the proposed model is efficient. As a part of future work, we would like to study the change in periodic behavior of rare items due to noise.

Acknowledgements. This research was partly supported by Real World Information Analytics project of National Institute of Information and Communications Technology, Japan.

References

1. Agrawal, R., Imieliński, T., Swami, A.: Mining association rules between sets of items in large databases. In: SIGMOD, pp. 207–216 (1993)
2. Amphawan, K., Lenca, P., Surarerks, A.: Mining Top-K periodic-frequent pattern from transactional databases without support threshold. In: Papasratorn, B., Chutimaskul, W., Porkaew, K., Vanijja, V. (eds.) IAIT 2009. CCIS, vol. 55, pp. 18–29. Springer, Heidelberg (2009). https://doi.org/10.1007/978-3-642-10392-6_3
3. Anirudh, A., Kirany, R.U., Reddy, P.K., Kitsuregaway, M.: Memory efficient mining of periodic-frequent patterns in transactional databases. In: 2016 IEEE Symposium Series on Computational Intelligence (SSCI), pp. 1–8, December 2016
4. Aref, W.G., Elfeky, M.G., Elmagarmid, A.K.: Incremental, online, and merge mining of partial periodic patterns in time-series databases. IEEE TKDE **16**(3), 332–342 (2004). Mar
5. Bradshaw, J.: Yams - yet another measure of similarity. In: EuroMUG (2001). http://www.daylight.com/meetings/emug01/Bradshaw/Similarity/YAMS.html
6. Brin, S., Motwani, R., Silverstein, C.: Beyond market baskets: generalizing association rules to correlations. In: SIGMOD, pp. 265–276 (1997)
7. Cao, H., Cheung, D.W., Mamoulis, N.: Discovering partial periodic patterns in discrete data sequences. In: Dai, H., Srikant, R., Zhang, C. (eds.) PAKDD 2004. LNCS (LNAI), vol. 3056, pp. 653–658. Springer, Heidelberg (2004). https://doi.org/10.1007/978-3-540-24775-3_77
8. Chen, S.S., Huang, T.C.K., Lin, Z.M.: New and efficient knowledge discovery of partial periodic patterns with multiple minimum supports. J. Syst. Softw. **84**(10), 1638–1651 (2011). Oct
9. Deng, Z.H.: Diffnodesets: an efficient structure for fast mining frequent itemsets. Appl. Soft Comput. **41**, 214–223 (2016). http://www.sciencedirect.com/science/article/pii/S156849461600017X
10. Deng, Z.H., Lv, S.L.: Prepost+: an efficient n-lists-based algorithm for mining frequent itemsets via childrenparent equivalence pruning. Expert Syst. Appl. **42**(13), 5424–5432 (2015). http://www.sciencedirect.com/science/article/pii/S0957417415001803
11. Fournier-Viger, P., Lin, J.C.-W., Duong, Q.-H., Dam, T.-L.: PHM: mining periodic high-utility itemsets. In: Perner, P. (ed.) ICDM 2016. LNCS (LNAI), vol. 9728, pp. 64–79. Springer, Cham (2016). https://doi.org/10.1007/978-3-319-41561-1_6
12. Han, J., Cheng, H., Xin, D., Yan, X.: Frequent pattern mining: Current status and future directions. DMKD **14**(1) (2007)
13. Han, J., Dong, G., Yin, Y.: Efficient mining of partial periodic patterns in time series database. In: ICDE, pp. 106–115 (1999)

14. Han, J., Gong, W., Yin, Y.: Mining segment-wise periodic patterns in time-related databases. In: KDD, pp. 214–218 (1998)
15. Han, J., Pei, J., Yin, Y., Mao, R.: Mining frequent patterns without candidate generation: a frequent-pattern tree approach. Data Min. Knowl. Discov. $8(1)$, 53–87 (2004). Jan
16. Hu, Y.H., Chen, Y.L.: Mining association rules with multiple minimum supports: a new mining algorithm and a support tuning mechanism. Decis. Support Syst. $42(1)$, 1–24 (2006)
17. Kim, S., Barsky, M., Han, J.: Efficient mining of top correlated patterns based on null-invariant measures. In: PKDD, pp. 177–192 (2011)
18. Kim, W.Y., Lee, Y.K., Han, J.: Ccmine: efficient mining of confidence-closed correlated patterns. In: Advances in Knowledge Discovery and Data Mining, pp. 569–579 (2004)
19. Kiran, R.U., Kitsuregawa, M.: Novel techniques to reduce search space in periodic-frequent pattern mining. In: Bhowmick, S.S., Dyreson, C.E., Jensen, C.S., Lee, M.L., Muliantara, A., Thalheim, B. (eds.) DASFAA 2014. LNCS, vol. 8422, pp. 377–391. Springer, Cham (2014). https://doi.org/10.1007/978-3-319-05813-9_25
20. Uday Kiran, R., Krishna Reddy, P.: Towards efficient mining of periodic-frequent patterns in transactional databases. In: Bringas, P.G., Hameurlain, A., Quirchmayr, G. (eds.) DEXA 2010. LNCS, vol. 6262, pp. 194–208. Springer, Heidelberg (2010). https://doi.org/10.1007/978-3-642-15251-1_16
21. Uday Kiran, R., Krishna Reddy, P.: Novel techniques to reduce search space in multiple minimum supports-based frequent pattern mining algorithms. In: EDBT, pp. 11–20 (2011)
22. Uday Kiran, R., Shang, H., Toyoda, M., Kitsuregawa, M.: Discovering partial periodic itemsets in temporal databases. In: Proceedings of the 29th International Conference on Scientific and Statistical Database Management, Chicago, IL, USA, 27–29 June 2017, pp. 30:1–30:6 (2017). http://doi.acm.org/10.1145/3085504.3085535
23. Uday Kiran, R., Venkatesh, J.N., Fournier-Viger, P., Toyoda, M., Reddy, P.K., Kitsuregawa, M.: Discovering periodic patterns in non-uniform temporal databases. In: Kim, J., Shim, K., Cao, L., Lee, J.-G., Lin, X., Moon, Y.-S. (eds.) PAKDD 2017. LNCS (LNAI), vol. 10235, pp. 604–617. Springer, Cham (2017). https://doi.org/10.1007/978-3-319-57529-2_47
24. Uday Kiran, R., Venkatesh, J., Toyoda, M., Kitsuregawa, M., Reddy, P.K.: Discovering partial periodic-frequent patterns in a transactional database. J. Syst. Softw. 125, 170–182 (2017). http://www.sciencedirect.com/science/article/pii/S0164121216302382
25. Lee, Y.K., Kim, W.Y., Cao, D., Han, J.: Comine: efficient mining of correlated patterns. In: ICDM, pp. 581–584 (2003)
26. Liu, B., Hsu, W., Ma, Y.: Mining association rules with multiple minimum supports. In: KDD, pp. 337–341 (1999)
27. Nofong, V.M.: Discovering productive periodic frequent patterns in transactional databases. Ann. Data Sci. $3(3)$, 235–249 (2016)
28. Omiecinski, E.R.: Alternative interest measures for mining associations in databases. IEEE Trans. Knowl. Data Eng. 15, 57–69 (2003)
29. Özden, B., Ramaswamy, S., Silberschatz, A.: Cyclic association rules. In: ICDE, pp. 412–421 (1998)
30. Pyun, G., Yun, U., Ryu, K.H.: Efficient frequent pattern mining based on linear prefix tree. Knowl. Based Syst. 55, 125–139 (2014). http://www.sciencedirect.com/science/article/pii/S0950705113003249

31. Rashid, M.M., Karim, M.R., Jeong, B.-S., Choi, H.-J.: Efficient mining regularly frequent patterns in transactional databases. In: Lee, S., Peng, Z., Zhou, X., Moon, Y.-S., Unland, R., Yoo, J. (eds.) DASFAA 2012. LNCS, vol. 7238, pp. 258–271. Springer, Heidelberg (2012). https://doi.org/10.1007/978-3-642-29038-1_20

32. Surana, A., Uday Kiran, R., Krishna Reddy, P.: Selecting a right interestingness measure for rare association rules. In: International Conference on Management of Data, pp. 105–115 (2010)

33. Surana, A., Uday Kiran, R., Krishna Reddy, P.: An efficient approach to mine periodic-frequent patterns in transactional databases. In: Cao, L., Huang, J.Z., Bailey, J., Koh, Y.S., Luo, J. (eds.) PAKDD 2011. LNCS (LNAI), vol. 7104, pp. 254–266. Springer, Heidelberg (2012). https://doi.org/10.1007/978-3-642-28320-8_22

34. Tan, P.N., Kumar, V., Srivastava, J.: Selecting the right interestingness measure for association patterns. In: Knowledge Discovery and Data Mining, pp. 32–41 (2002)

35. Tanbeer, S.K., Ahmed, C.F., Jeong, B.-S., Lee, Y.-K.: Discovering periodic-frequent patterns in transactional databases. In: Theeramunkong, T., Kijsirikul, B., Cercone, N., Ho, T.-B. (eds.) PAKDD 2009. LNCS (LNAI), vol. 5476, pp. 242–253. Springer, Heidelberg (2009). https://doi.org/10.1007/978-3-642-01307-2_24

36. Uno, T., Kiyomi, M., Arimura, H.: LCM ver.3: collaboration of array, bitmap and prefix tree for frequent itemset mining. In: Proceedings of the 1st International Workshop on Open Source Data Mining: Frequent Pattern Mining Implementations, OSDM 2005, pp. 77–86. ACM, New York (2005). http://doi.acm.org/10.1145/1133905.1133916

37. Vaillant, B., Lenca, P., Lallich, S.: A clustering of interestingness measures. In: Suzuki, E., Arikawa, S. (eds.) DS 2004. LNCS (LNAI), vol. 3245, pp. 290–297. Springer, Heidelberg (2004). https://doi.org/10.1007/978-3-540-30214-8_23

38. Venkatesh, J.N., Uday Kiran, R., Krishna Reddy, P., Kitsuregawa, M.: Discovering periodic-frequent patterns in transactional databases using all-confidence and periodic-all-confidence. In: Hartmann, S., Ma, H. (eds.) DEXA 2016. LNCS, vol. 9827, pp. 55–70. Springer, Cham (2016). https://doi.org/10.1007/978-3-319-44403-1_4

39. Wu, T., Chen, Y., Han, J.: Re-examination of interestingness measures in pattern mining: a unified framework. DMKD 21(3), 371–397 (2010)

40. Xiong, H., Tan, P.N., Kumar, V.: Hyperclique pattern discovery. Data Mining Knowl. Discov. 13(2), 219–242 (2006)

41. Yang, J., Wang, W., Yu, P.S.: Mining asynchronous periodic patterns in time series data. IEEE Trans. Knowl. Data Eng. 15, 613–628 (2003)

42. Zaki, M.J., Parthasarathy, S., Ogihara, M., Li, W.: New algorithms for fast discovery of association rules. Technical report, Rochester, NY, USA (1997)

43. Zhang, M., Kao, B., Cheung, D.W., Yip, K.Y.: Mining periodic patterns with gap requirement from sequences. ACM Trans. Knowl. Discov. Data 1(2), August 2007

44. Zhou, Z., Wu, Z., Wang, C., Feng, Y.: Efficiently Mining Mutually and Positively Correlated Patterns. In: Li, X., Zaïane, O.R., Li, Z. (eds.) ADMA 2006. LNCS (LNAI), vol. 4093, pp. 118–125. Springer, Heidelberg (2006). https://doi.org/10.1007/11811305_12

45. Zhou, Z., Wu, Z., Wang, C., Feng, Y.: Mining both associated and correlated patterns. In: Alexandrov, V.N., van Albada, G.D., Sloot, P.M.A., Dongarra, J. (eds.) ICCS 2006. LNCS, vol. 3994, pp. 468–475. Springer, Heidelberg (2006). https://doi.org/10.1007/11758549_66

Author Index

Printed in the United States
By Bookmasters